The Tarot

An Astrological Journey
Through the Major Arcana

Lani Sharp

Second Edition

Copyright © 2017

All rights reserved. This book or any portion thereof may not be reproduced or used in any manner whatsoever without the express written permission of the author except for the use of brief quotations in a book review.

Printed in Australia
First Edition printed: 2017
Second Edition printed: 2019
ISBN: 978-0-6485929-3-8

White Light Publishing
Melton, VIC, Australia 3337
whitelightpublishing.com.au

❦ DEDICATION ❧

This book is dedicated to The Star Tarot Card, as I am Aquarian who has a Divine affinity and resonance with this card, and she is in turn my Guiding Light. Her esoteric meanings and profound symbolism have proven to me time and again that dreams can and *do* come true. The future is indeed bright and hope ever abounds.

I *Know* & I *Believe*.

And to the infinitude of lessons inherent in the Tarot & in the Universe:

Thank You, Thank You, Thank You.

Afoot and light-hearted
I take to the open road,
Healthy, free, the world before me,
The long brown path …
Leading wherever I choose.

Walt Whitman

❧ ABOUT THE AUTHOR ❦

Lani Sharp is an author, mother, astrologer, Tarot reader, naturopath, witch, crystal gazer, believer, dreamer and free spirit at heart, whose foray into the Tarot began one day in 2009 in Australia's Far North, her spiritual home. As soon as she sat opposite the mystical card reader on that fateful afternoon, she knew there was no turning back - and from that day onwards, the Tarot has spoken to the depths of her soul. She loves to awaken others' interest in the topic too and hopes to provide some guidance for the amazing discoveries along the all-powerful Journey.

You can find Lani on Instagram at *lani_sharp_author*, and Facebook at *Astrology Magic* and *Lani Sharp Author*.

★ CONTENTS ★

INTRODUCTION	1
HOW TO USE THIS BOOK	3
TAROT CARDS ★ A MYSTICAL DIVINATION TOOL	4
MY OWN PERSONAL TAROT JOURNEY	6
WHY ARE TAROT CARDS CALLED MYSTERIES?	7
INTERPRETING / READING THE CARDS	8
THE RIDER-WAITE DECK	10
OTHER TAROT DECKS	12
ASTROLOGY & THE TAROT	13
THE 36 DECANS & THE TAROT	15
THE 36 DECANS & CORRESPONDING CARDS	17
THE ASTROLOGICAL ELEMENTS & THE TAROT	18
THE CHAKRAS & THE TAROT CONNECTION	22
THE ZODIAC SIGNS & THEIR CONNECTION WITH THE CHAKRAS	25
AT A GLANCE ★ SYMBOLISM & IMAGERY	32
A JOURNEY THROUGH THE LIFE EXPERIENCE	40
NUMBERS & THE TAROT DECK	41
THE 22 MAJOR ARCANA CARDS & THE HUMAN LIFE EXPERIENCE	48
0 ★ THE FOOL - Uranus & the Element of Air	48
1 ★ THE MAGICIAN – Mercury	57
2 ★ THE HIGH PRIESTESS - The Moon & Element of Water	66
3 ★ THE EMPRESS - Venus	74
4 ★ THE EMPEROR - Aries	82
5 ★ THE HIEROPHANT - Taurus	90
6 ★ THE LOVERS - Gemini	97
7 ★ THE CHARIOT - Cancer	105
8 ★ STRENGTH – Leo	112
9 ★ THE HERMIT - Virgo	119
10 ★ WHEEL OF FORTUNE - Jupiter	126
11 ★ JUSTICE - Libra	134
12 ★ THE HANGED MAN - Neptune	141
13 ★ DEATH – Scorpio	149
14 ★ TEMPERANCE - Sagittarius	158
15 ★ THE DEVIL - Capricorn	165
16 ★ THE TOWER - Mars	173
17 ★ THE STAR – Aquarius	180
18 ★ THE MOON - Pisces	188
19 ★ THE SUN - The Sun	196
20 ★ JUDGEMENT - Pluto & the Element of Fire	203
21 ★ THE WORLD - Saturn & the Element of Earth	210
GLOSSARY	218

INTRODUCTION

Along with astrology, the Tarot is one of the most important and powerful systems of self-empowerment in the Western tradition, and indeed – like astrology – it has passed beyond cultural limitation and become global and universal in acceptance and application. However, unlike astrology, the Tarot is powered by the imagination to enable the user to soar beyond Earth and the Solar System to all the dimensions of the Universe ... Active work with both astrology and the Tarot should be fundamental to all your empowerment work.

Carl Llewellyn Weshcke & Joe H. Slate

The Tarot represents a pictorial symbolic map of the inner world, and provides us with a particular opportunity to reflect upon whether there is a deeper spiritual dimension to our existence. The pictures on the 78 Tarot cards are worth more than a thousand words - they can actually paint a picture of you. The Tarot's symbolism encompasses everything from ancient cave paintings, to magical belief systems, to Jungian archetypes ^, and examining them can create a unique metaphor for the story of your life, where you're heading on your wondrous journey, and indeed at what stage you are at presently.

The precise origin of Tarot cards is obscure, but one popular theory is that the deck dates back to Ancient Egypt and that the god Thoth * was its creator. Tarot and playing cards may have had their beginning as long ago as Ancient Egypt (although the earliest complete sets of Tarot cards to have survived are all Italian and appear to date to some time between 1420 and 1450), since scholars have reportedly recognised the Major Arcana as Egyptian hieroglyphic books *. Other scholars, however, report uncanny similarities between playing cards and early Eastern games and deities. Further, it is not known with certainty whether the Major Arcana cards, with their emblematic designs, and the Minor Arcana cards in their familiar four suits, were devised separately and at a later date combined into one pack by an innovative genius, or if they were created as a 78-card deck from the beginning.

As well as no one really knowing where the Tarot originated, no one really knows how and why it works, but what we do know is that if we can 'tune in' to the images, archetypes and symbolism of the cards, we can gain access to a deeper understanding of ourselves and the people and events in our lives.

* Thoth, or Tehuti, is an ancient Egyptian god, depicted in some vignettes as the dog-headed baboon but mostly as an ibis-headed man. Thoth is the Greek Hermes, the god of medicine, healing, astrology, learning, truth, magic, libraries and books, keeper of the Akashic records, lord of karma, and time lord. Called 'The Lord of the Divine Books' and 'Scribe of the Company of Gods', Thoth usually is portrayed as an ibis-headed man with a pen and ink holder, or as a baboon-headed man holding a crescent Moon. He is a healer and magician, and because of his magical act of resorting the eye of Horus - the magical All-seeing eye that is a popular amulet - he became the patron god of occultists in ancient Egypt. Thoth is petitioned in many of the spells in the Egyptian *Book of the Dead*. The Greeks associated their god Hermes so closely with Thoth that the two blended together, and became identified with the mythical figure of Hermes Trismegistus, patron of magicians and alleged author of the Hermetic books of occult philosophy and wisdom. The *Book of Thoth*, or the 'Key to Immortality', kept in a secret location, is believed to reveal many secrets for the expansion and regeneration of collective consciousness, that will enable mortals to behold the gods. This

book is said to be contained within the Tarot. Thoth's symbols are the white feather and the caduceus, his colour is amethyst and the ibis is sacred to him.

^ **A NOTE ON ARCHETYPES** ★ Archetypes are cosmic stereotypes based on primal patterns of thought that serve as a framework for our understanding of the world. Carl Jung, the Swiss psychotherapist and psychological theorist, was the first person to popularise the concept of archetypes, theorising that they are inborn, instinctive and imprinted on every human's subconscious mind. Archetypes transcend the limits of time and place. Some well-known examples are the animus, the anima, the mother, the father, the shadow, the maiden, the wise old man, the wise old woman, the hero, and the heroine. Every card in the Major Arcana embodies various archetypal figures, from the Earth Mother (The Empress) and the Wizard (The Magician), to the Divine Child (The Sun).

HOW TO USE THIS BOOK

Chances are, if you have chosen this book, that you are one - or all four - of the following:

1. Curious about the Tarot and its meanings
2. Interested in deeper self-exploration, enhanced self-knowledge or overall self-development
3. At a crossroads in some area of your life
4. Needing some general or specific guidance on a pressing issue or area of life

If none of the above apply to you, you can skip reading this part. But if you do fall into one or more of these categories, you might like to simply close your eyes, open up or go to a random page, and read the message it reveals. It's as simple as that. Whichever page you 'choose', will undoubtedly contain a special message for you and your question, because every card and suit of the Tarot deck is rich in meaning about the entire individual and collective human life experience, regardless of your background, make-up, beliefs or circumstances. Open up or go to a random page right now and read the first word, line or paragraph that you are drawn to. What does its message reveal to you?

Alternatively, you could just read this book from beginning to end like you would an ordinary book. Or, if you are drawn to the astrological component of this book, you might choose to begin at your zodiac sign's first Tarot card to see what it reveals to you.

Whichever Path you choose, the end result will likely be the same - you will experience an elevated sense of personal enlightenment in some small, or hopefully profound, way. However, you are affected, I do hope that the messages contained in my words help to shift you or move you in some meaningful way. And isn't that what most of us are seeking on this wondrous journey? Happy travelling!

TAROT CARDS ★ A MYSTICAL DIVINATION TOOL

The Tarot deck is a set of cards used for divination and fortune telling. It has a long history and has assumed an air of mystery over the centuries. The deck consists of seventy-eight cards in total and is divided into two subsections: The Major Arcana (22 cards) and the Minor Arcana (56 cards). The Major Arcana comprises 22 trump, or key, cards; the Minor Arcana comprises the remaining 56 cards, which are often called pips. The Major Arcana contains the most familiar imagery of the Tarot, such as Death, the Hanged Man, The Star, and The Devil.

The Tarot deck most widely used today is known as the Rider-Waite, or Universal Waite, deck and was first published in 1910 by the Rider Company. The designs were drawn by the artist Pamela Colman Smith at the instigation of Arthur Edward Waite, a prominent member of the secret esoteric society the Hermetic Order of the Golden Dawn, a movement founded in England in 1886. Within the society, the Tarot was identified as giving access to the secrets of the Universe. Arthur Waite, born 2 October 1957 in New York, was an author, mystic, magician, alchemist and occultist who was active in both Rosicrucianism and Freemasonry. Waite had been influenced by a nineteenth century philosopher, Eliphas Levi, who had stated in a book written in the 1850s, that 'an imprisoned person with no other book than the Tarot, if he knew how to use it, could in a few years acquire Universal knowledge'. A grandiose statement perhaps, but probably not far from the truth.

The Major Arcana reflects major turning points in our lives: our commitments, milestones, rites of passage, triumphs and tragedies, while the Minor Arcana deals more with the day-to-day aspects and smaller intricacies of life. The Tarot, rather than telling the future outright, seems to help the seeker make choices and examine more closely what is going on in their life at the time of the reading; therefore, it helps to point to a route through difficult or trying circumstances. The Tarot is ambiguous, allowing much room for interpretation, yet can be surprisingly accurate. The best Tarot readers understand that no card has any one meaning, but rather is a metaphor for a variety of interpretations. Ultimately, Tarot cards are a tool to unlock your imagination, and how you read the cards is up to you. But as a tool for understanding ourselves and for plugging in to a great universal wisdom. The vivid imagery, archetypal impressions and other symbolism contained in the Tarot remind us that we should seek the answers to our questions not just through reason and external study, but through deeply felt inner experience. After all, we are who we are, and the very essence of ourselves invariably always offers us the answers to our own questions; the Tarot just provides a brighter light to illuminate our Path. Indeed, with practice, you can learn to become your very own fortune teller, your own diviner, your own Magician, your own wizard, your own *oracle*!

* Court de Gebelin's writing in Volume I of *Le Monde Primitif* in 1781, presents a strong argument in favour of the Egyptian origin of Tarot cards. According to Gebelin, the 22 Major Arcana cards are an ancient Egyptian book, *The Book of Thoth*, which was saved from the ruins of burning Egyptian temples. Thoth was the Egyptian Mercury said to be one of the early Kings and mythical inventor of speech and hieroglyphs or letters with their accompanying mysticism. Its basis was an alphabet in which all gods are letters, all letters ideas, all ideas numbers and all numbers perfect signs. Many studiers of the occult recognise the pages of

hieroglyphic books in the Tarot cards, in that they embody the principles of the esoteric philosophies of the Egyptians in a series of symbols and emblematic figures. Gebelin believed that the mystical Tarot symbols were subsequently spread throughout European by wandering gypsies.

MY OWN PERSONAL TAROT JOURNEY

My 'Tarot Journey' began in 2009, when I took a blind leap of faith to follow my dream by making a big bold move, Fool-style, on my own from Melbourne to Cairns, enjoying a scenic road trip up the east coast of Australia to get there. Tropical Cairns, in Australia's Far North, was always a part of my grand vision, but as with almost anything in life, had its challenges. Having just left a six-year relationship and all my friends and family behind, I was truly starting anew. A clean slate - or so I thought! Trouble is, no matter where we physically move to in life, our spirit, soul, essence and true character still remains with us, and can even plague us if past issues or restricting attitudes haven't been dealt with adequately - as I soon enough found out.

After a few months of being in my new home, I needed some guidance and reassurance that my new path was the right one for me, and if it wasn't, which one was? In other words, standing at a crossroads of so many options, which road should I be taking from here? Or should I just stay put and make this big dream of mine work? To answer these questions, I went and saw a Tarot reader. Walking past a New Age crystal shop one day, I was drawn to a sign out the front which read: "Tarot Readings Today: Please Enquire Inside." Always one to gravitate towards a little guidance, I didn't hesitate and walked straight in. Little did I know that that reading would change the course of my life! The man who read my cards typified a true textbook card reader to me: gypsy-like in appearance, older in age, clothed in purple velvet, exuding an air of eccentricity and cool but intriguing detachment, and possessing a deep-voiced heavy accent I could barely understand. But for some strange reason I heard the words I knew I most needed to understand; and they were the ones I took away with me.

A Tarot reading is potentially a deeply personal and intimate experience, particularly one that is face-to-face, so I won't go into any detail about what he told me, but let's just put it this way: his words were prophetic. Everything he said in that reading occurred (I wrote down the main points on some notepaper as he was speaking). Which led me to the thought that perhaps on a deep and unseen level, what we glean from a Tarot reading becomes a part of our psyche, our essence, a self-fulfilling prophecy if you like, and we may even subconsciously *will* it to come about. Anything we believe or expect, whether positive or negative in nature, usually manifests in our physical and material experience. I am also a deeply spiritual person and try to keep connected with my intuition - the astrology, crystal therapy and other healing work that I do ensures this, as it is a necessary and vital part of what I do. But above all, I believe deeply in symbolism and 'signs' and what they can tell us about ourselves.

The Tarot experience reflects this deep-held belief in me, and as a result I live my life based on the symbolic insights it, and the other esoteric arts such as astrology and crystallography, can offer, ever illuminating the journey ahead. After all, the more enlightened I am, the more I can shine that inner lamp upon the Path for others. And so, shortly after that fateful Tarot reading in Cairns back in 2009, I began to delve into the enormous Universe of the Tarot.

Being an Aquarian, my special card is The Star, and I think this sums the essence of my character and my life perfectly. Every day I wake up with a renewed sense of vigour, hope and the faith that something magical is always just around the very next corner.

I hope you get as much from this book as I did in writing it for you. I wish you all the best in your own journey and sincerely hope that the cards of the 22 Major Arcana, and particularly the cards which align with your particular zodiac sign, provide some insights and guidance for your own onward Path. Even if just one idea contained within these pages connects with your soul and helps to shift something in your life for the better, then I have done my job here well. All the very best on your adventures!

WHY ARE TAROT CARDS CALLED MYSTERIES?

The word 'arcana' is the plural for the word 'arcanum', which means: 'A deep secret; a mystery; specialised knowledge; a secret essence or remedy; an elixir.' To refine it down into simple terms, 'arcana' is the Latin for *mystery*. In the past, Tarot cards were called 'mysteries', as the cards were used to reveal both the secrets of the soul and unveil the future, something which had previously been a mystery. Many Tarot readers refer to the symbols associated with the cards as a mysterious language which can only be deciphered by experienced cartomancers (Tarot readers). It is therefore necessary to learn and to understand their symbolic language in order to discover the 'mysteries' contained in the cards. We call Tarot cards 'arcana' to highlight their secret and veiled nature, and the precautions one should take to interpret their meaning.

INTERPRETING / READING THE CARDS

The practical applications of the Tarot pack occur during the shuffling, spreading and interpretation of the cards. Some people seem naturally born with the gift of premonition and intuition, although we are all gifted with these; those to whom it seems to come instinctively are simply more in tune with their rich inner tapestries and inborn sixth sense than others may be. But reading and interpreting the Tarot is a skill that we can all learn and indeed master.

The allegorical cards of the Tarot deck stimulate the mind and reveal a story based upon the meaning of each card as interpreted by the responsiveness of the reader, diviner or interpreter. It has been said that cartomancy awakens the mind to the existence of future possibilities which may have been otherwise overlooked. A person proceeding in a given established pattern may significantly modify the final outcome through the realisation of newfound opportunities subsequently achieved through greater efforts and concentrated study. Therefore, we are in fact very qualified masters of our fate and capable of modifying our own destinies within certain limits.

There are numerous methods of spreading the Tarot cards and some of them are exceedingly complicated and cumbersome. So, it is advisable to start simple. When I was a beginner, I began with three-card readings; in essence, the three cards symbolised the past, present and future of the questioner. Once I became confident in these, I moved onto five, seven, and twelve-card spreads (the latter representing the twelve houses of the astrological horoscope, which symbolise different life areas, such as money, sex, marriage, secrets, career, the ego, spiritual matters, friendships and so on).

The shuffling must be done by the person who wishes to have the interpretation or prediction concerning herself or an answer to a pressing question, and not by the diviner, reader or interpreter. This is because the person who shuffles the card impregnates them with her own personal magnetism and thereby creates a rapport between the conscious and subconscious states of her mind and the cards. The sequence of the cards, consciously or subconsciously, is set by the manner of the shuffling as determined by the questioner without looking at the cards. This means that the questioner has an un-predetermined yet obvious and direct influence over the cards in the resultant reading.

If you are reading for yourself, shuffle the cards while concentrating on a question to which you need an answer, such as, "What do I need in order to grow?" or "What do I most need to work on in order to fulfil my destiny?" or "What limitations must I release in order to be happy and/or successful?" or "What blockages/obstacles do I need to overcome in order to realise my highest potentials?"

Frequently, the answer or guidance sought by the questioner at the time of the shuffling of the cards represents only a small portion of the total scope of the reading. The cards may suggest emotions, feelings and desires. They may stand for objects, situations or people. They may indicate duration of time, circumstances or a signpost in a certain direction. But overall, the interpretation of each card, singularly and in connection with the other cards around it, is limited only by the total responsiveness and competence of the interpreter. Therefore, the cards often reveal a great deal about the questioner herself rather than solely responding to the original question.

THE RIDER-WAITE DECK

Choosing Tarot cards is a deeply personal experience and choice. There are literally hundreds of different decks to choose from. Although I own around eight decks, personally I gravitate towards the Universal-Waite / Rider-Waite Tarot Deck, as it contains the imagery and symbols I most resonate with and can interpret with more ease than other, more complex *or* less intricate decks. In other words, it has the perfect blend of interpretable pictures, clear suits, and decipherable numbers (albeit in Roman numerals).

Any deck that you resonate with and are drawn towards is absolutely perfect, however I have chosen to outline a brief history of the Rider-Waite Deck here, as it is a common pack that can be found almost anywhere, and whose images grace the pages of this very book.

> The Tarot embodies the symbolical presentations of universal ideas, behind which lie all the implicits of the human mind, and it is in this sense that they contain secret doctrine, which is the realisation by the few of truths embedded in the consciousness of all, though they have not passed into express recognition by ordinary men. The theory is that this doctrine has already existed - that is to say, has been excogitated in the consciousness of an elect minority; that it has been perpetuated in secrecy from one to another and has been recorded in secret literatures, like those of Alchemy and Kabbalism; and behind the Secret Doctrine it is held that there is an experience or practice by which the Doctrine is justified.

A.E. Waite

Dr Arthur Edward Waite (1857-1942) was a genuine scholar of occultism who painstakingly researched and wrote a number of works including *The Key to the Tarot* and the *Holy Kabbalah*. Waite ultimately used symbolism as the key to the Tarot pack, writing, "The true Tarot is symbolism; it speaks no other language and offers no other signs. Given the inward meaning of its emblems, they do become a kind of alphabet which is capable of indefinite combinations and makes true sense in all. On the highest plane, it offers a key to the Mysteries."

Waite correctly surmised that The Fool, being unnumbered and representing zero, should not be placed between card numbers 20 and 21 as suggested by other Tarot scholars, but instead its more natural sequence lay before The Magician in attribution to the first letter of the Hebrew alphabet **, Aleph (see following table for corresponding Hebrew letters for each of the 22 Major Arcana cards).

In 1909, Waite, upon publishing The Key to the Tarot, needed an illustrator for the book and cards. A vividly illustrated 78-card Tarot pack known as the Rider deck was drawn up by Miss Pamela Colman Smith, under the initiative and supervision of Waite. Miss Smith, an American born in 1878 who had spent her childhood years in Jamaica, Kingston, London and New York, and a fellow member of the Order of The Golden Dawn, undertook for token payment the series of 78 allegorical paintings as described by Waite as a rectified Tarot pack. The designs were published by William Rider and Son, but success for her overall artistic endeavours eluded her and she died in 1951 penniless and obscure. Although she passed away disappointed that her paintings and writings failed to achieve success, she never stopped believing in herself, and her legacy and spirit lives on today in the Universal Waite Tarot Deck, which exemplifies the imagination, mysticism, ritual, fantasy and deep emotions of the undoubtedly talented artist. She would perhaps be all but forgotten were it not for her now-famous 78 Tarot drawings, and she would likely be pleased to know how many millions of hearts and souls the deck touches and illuminates still to this day.

The original Waite deck was published in 1910 by Rider & Company of London in conjunction with Waite's famous work: *The Key to the Tarot*. Several versions of this deck in varying quality are available at most book, new age and occult stores.

OTHER TAROT DECKS

In addition to the customary 22 symbolic pictures of the Major Arcana cards used for divination purposes, during the past two centuries various other designs have also appeared - and continue to appear. These art-rich decks have been prepared as a pictorial presentation of the times, and many include such scenes and imagery as science, literature, poetry, military events, dancers, folklore, industry, hunting and comedy. Especially prevalent in German Tarot decks are depictions of animals. Although there are French, Italian, Belgian, Swiss, American and German Tarots, the titles of the 22 emblematic designs are more frequently in French ^ than in any other language (except for the American versions which predominantly bear English titles).

** Hebrew Letter		**Waite Deck**	**^ French Name**
Aleph	0	The Fool	Le Fol / Le Mat
Beth	I	The Magician	Le Bataleur
Gimel	II	The High Priestess	La Papesse
Daleth	III	The Empress	La Imperatrice
Heh	IIII	The Emperor	L'Empereur
Vau	V	The Hierophant	Le Pape
Zain	VI	The Lovers	L'Amoreux
Cheth	VII	The Chariot	Le Chariot
Teth	VIII	Strength	La Force
Yod	VIIII	The Hermit	L'Ermite
Kaph	X	The Wheel of Fortune	La Roue de Fortune
Lamed	XI	Justice	La Justice
Mem	XII	The Hanged Man	Le Pendu
Nun	XIII	Death	La Mort
Samech	XIIII	Temperance	La Temperance
Ayin	XV	The Devil	Le Diable
Peh	XVI	The Tower	La Maison Dieu
Tzaddi	XVII	The Star	L'Etoile
Qoph	XVIII	The Moon	Le Lune
Resh	XVIIII	The Sun	Le Soleil
Shin	XX	Judgement	Le Jugement
Tau	XXI	The World	Le Monde

ASTROLOGY & THE TAROT

Tarot and astrology are inextricably linked. All the cards of the Major Arcana, which comprises 22 of the Tarot's 78 cards, are 'ruled by' or connected with either one of the twelve zodiac signs, one of the planets or luminaries, or one of the four elements.

The 22 Major Arcana cards contain the richest symbolism of all the cards in the Tarot deck, each carrying a myriad of messages for the reader to decipher. The symbolism contained within these images represents the archetypal aspects of your character. It also describes the Path your soul takes through each stage of life, revealing clues through which you can explore different parts of yourself. Each of the cards also represents an aspect of universal human experience and has a name that either directly conveys the meaning of the card, such as Strength or Justice, or depicts individuals that represent these human archetypes, such as The Hermit or The Empress. The illustrations on each card contain one or more figures and tuning into a card's imagery enables you to grasp its meaning intuitively. Consider the demeanour of the characters, if anything is obscured or veiled, whether it is day or night, daybreak or nightfall, the background, any symbols, the buildings, the colours, the animals, the vegetation, the weather and the season. Every card has its own story to impart, and through entering that story you can gain deeper insights into the full picture of your journey so far, as well as lighting up your Path ahead.

The following are the cards which correspond to each zodiac sign. (Please note that these may differ between various schools of thought. These are my interpretations and correspondences only, but they do align with the general consensus among most Tarot scholars.)

ARIES ★ No. 4 ~ The Emperor
TAURUS ★ No. 5 ~ The Hierophant
GEMINI ★ No. 6 ~ The Lovers
CANCER ★ No. 7 ~ The Chariot
LEO ★ No. 8 ~ Strength
VIRGO ★ No. 9 ~ The Hermit
LIBRA ★ No. 11 ~ Justice
SCORPIO ★ No. 13 ~ Death
SAGITTARIUS ★ No. 14 ~ Temperance
CAPRICORN ★ No. 15 ~ The Devil
AQUARIUS ★ No. 17 ~ The Star
PISCES ★ No. 18 ~ The Moon

Additionally, because every Major Arcana card has a link with at least one zodiac sign, element or planet; each sign will have at least two Tarot cards to which it essentially vibrates. These cards will have special meaning for your particular sign, planetary influence and elemental forces, and can carry powerful messages and lessons for you to reflect upon. They are as follows:

ARIES ★ The Emperor, The Tower & Judgement
TAURUS ★ The Hierophant, The Empress & The World
GEMINI ★ The Lovers, The Magician & The Fool
CANCER ★ The Chariot & The High Priestess
LEO ★ Strength, The Sun & Judgement
VIRGO ★ The Hermit, The Magician & The World
LIBRA ★ Justice, The Empress & The Fool
SCORPIO ★ Death, Judgement, The Tower & The High Priestess
SAGITTARIUS ★ Temperance, Wheel of Fortune & Judgement
CAPRICORN ★ The Devil & The World
AQUARIUS ★ The Star, The Fool & The World
PISCES ★ The Moon, The Hanged Man & Wheel of Fortune & The High Priestess

THE 36 DECANS & THE TAROT

Decans are thirty-six groups of stars that rise in a particular order on the horizon throughout each Earth rotation. These decans were developed in Egypt thousands of years ago. The rising of each decan marked the beginning of a new 'decanal hour' of the night for these ancient people, and eventually three decans were assigned to each zodiac sign. Each decan covers ten degrees of the zodiac wheel, and is ruled by different planetary rulers that rule over the other two signs of the same element (and a traditional ruler, when only seven of the planetary bodies were known). Decans continued to be used throughout the Ages, in astrology and in magic, but many modern astrologers, for whatever reasons, tend to disregard them. Consult the following for which decan your birth date falls under, and then the next list will tell you which are your three Tarot cards (which includes cards from the whole 78).

FIRST DECAN ARIES	★ March 21 - 30
SECOND DECAN ARIES	★ March 31 - April 9
THIRD DECAN ARIES	★ April 10 - 19
FIRST DECAN TAURUS	★ April 20 - 30
SECOND DECAN TAURUS	★ May 1 - 11
THIRD DECAN TAURUS	★ May 12 - 20
FIRST DECAN GEMINI	★ May 21 - 31
SECOND DECAN GEMINI	★ June 1 - 10
THIRD DECAN GEMINI	★ June 11 - 20
FIRST DECAN CANCER	★ June 21 - July 1
SECOND DECAN CANCER	★ July 2 - 12
THIRD DECAN CANCER	★ July 13 - 22
FIRST DECAN LEO	★ July 23 - August 2
SECOND DECAN LEO	★ July 23 - August 2
THIRD DECAN LEO	★ August 13 - 22
FIRST DECAN VIRGO	★ August 23 - September 1
SECOND DECAN VIRGO	★ September 2 - 13
THIRD DECAN VIRGO	★ September 14 - 22
FIRST DECAN LIBRA	★ September 23 - October 2
SECOND DECAN LIBRA	★ October 3 - 13
THIRD DECAN LIBRA	★ October 14 - 22
FIRST DECAN SCORPIO	★ October 23 - November 2
SECOND DECAN SCORPIO	★ November 3 - 11
THIRD DECAN SCORPIO	★ November 12 - 21
FIRST DECAN SAGITTARIUS	★ November 22 - December 1
SECOND DECAN SAGITTARIUS	★ December 2 - 12
THIRD DECAN SAGITTARIUS	★ December 13 - 21

FIRST DECAN CAPRICORN	★	December 22 - 31
SECOND DECAN CAPRICORN	★	January 1 - 10
THIRD DECAN CAPRICORN	★	January 11 - 19
FIRST DECAN AQUARIUS	★	January 20 - 30
SECOND DECAN AQUARIUS	★	January 31 - February 9
THIRD DECAN AQUARIUS	★	February 10 - 18
FIRST DECAN PISCES	★	February 19 - 29
SECOND DECAN PISCES	★	March 1 - 10
THIRD DECAN PISCES	★	March 11 - 20

THE 36 DECANS & CORRESPONDING CARDS

DECAN & SIGN	MAJOR ARCANA	COURT	MINOR ARCANA
1 Aries	The Emperor	Queen of Wands	Two of Wands
2 Aries	The Emperor	Queen of Wands	Three of Wands
3 Aries	The Emperor	King of Pentacles	Four of Wands
1 Taurus	The Hierophant	King of Pentacles	Five of Pentacles
2 Taurus	The Hierophant	King of Pentacles	Six of Pentacles
3 Taurus	The Hierophant	Knight of Swords	Seven of Pentacles
1 Gemini	The Lovers	Knight of Swords	Eight of Swords
2 Gemini	The Lovers	Knight of Swords	Nine of Swords
3 Gemini	The Lovers	Queen of Cups	Ten of Swords
1 Cancer	The Chariot	Queen of Cups	Two of Cups
2 Cancer	The Chariot	Queen of Cups	Three of Cups
3 Cancer	The Chariot	King of Wands	Four of Cups
1 Leo	Strength	King of Wands	Five of Wands
2 Leo	Strength	King of Wands	Six of Wands
3 Leo	Strength	Knight of Pentacles	Seven of Wands
1 Virgo	The Hermit	Knight of Pentacles	Eight of Pentacles
2 Virgo	The Hermit	Knight of Pentacles	Nine of Pentacles
3 Virgo	The Hermit	Queen of Swords	Ten of Pentacles
1 Libra	Justice	Queen of Swords	Two of Swords
2 Libra	Justice	Queen of Swords	Three of Swords
3 Libra	Justice	King of Cups	Four of Swords
1 Scorpio	Death	King of Cups	Five of Cups
2 Scorpio	Death	King of Cups	Six of Cups
3 Scorpio	Death	Knight of Wands	Seven of Cups
1 Sagittarius	Temperance	Knight of Wands	Eight of Wands
2 Sagittarius	Temperance	Knight of Wands	Nine of Wands
3 Sagittarius	Temperance	Queen of Pentacles	Ten of Wands
1 Capricorn	The Devil	Queen of Pentacles	Two of Pentacles
2 Capricorn	The Devil	Queen of Pentacles	Three of Pentacles
3 Capricorn	The Devil	King of Swords	Four of Pentacles
1 Aquarius	The Star	King of Swords	Five of Swords
2 Aquarius	The Star	King of Swords	Six of Swords
3 Aquarius	The Star	Knight of Cups	Seven of Swords
1 Pisces	The Moon	Knight of Cups	Eight of Cups
2 Pisces	The Moon	Knight of Cups	Nine of Cups
3 Pisces	The Moon	Queen of Wands	Ten of Cups

THE ASTROLOGICAL ELEMENTS & THE TAROT:
The suits & their corresponding elements

WANDS ★ The Fire Element

Aries, Leo, Sagittarius

The Tarot Wands (known in some old decks as Rods, Staves or Batons) are connected with growth, creativity, enterprise, ambition, progress, initiative, advancement, work/labour, action, adventure, energy, vitality, willpower, reputation, fame, efficiency, achievement, challenge and all creative matters. The Wands represent the Fire element, and their fire is mainly influenced by the planet Mars, which activates travel and work energy, and sexual force, but they also partake the energies of Jupiter - the fire of benevolent warmth and expansion - and incorporate the fire of the Sun, radiating confidence and wellbeing in all directions. Being of the Fire realm, the Wands are also associated with dynamic action, inspiration, passion and determination. Like fire itself, they signify the ignition and generation of warmth and energy, while also burning off the dross and impurities of life. Fire creates light and heat, but it can too readily burn and easily rage out of control, which can lead to destruction, ruin and havoc. However, the energy of fire can also be transformative. It needs fuel in order to be effective, and if this vital fuel is sourced only from the feelings, flames can be swiftly burned out. Therefore, the ultimate source of fuel for this brand of fire lies within the self's sense of connection with the spirit - as this is a deep well that never runs dry. The narrative of the fiery Suit of Wands propels you forward and defines your actions and motivations in life. It tells of the need to create change and movement, always beginning with the initial spark that sets the flames of passion ablaze. If Wands predominate in a reading, there's a high chance you are actively engaged in accomplishing your goals. They deal with the physical and spiritual life force - positive conflict, struggle and passion all being part of its expression. They reveal how active, dynamic, animated, enthusiastic and passionate we are, and how these are experienced and expressed by us. There are often elements of struggle with the Wands suit, because energy needs to move freely and spontaneously, and any blockages to this have to be shifted. Conflicts within the Wands cards are generally not considered serious, and lead to a deeper, more profound sense of Self once they are resolved. They also govern inspiration and invention, and the spark that can appear out of the blue to light the way forward. In a deck of playing cards, the Wands correspond to the suit of Clubs.

PENTACLES ★ The Earth Element

Taurus, Virgo, Capricorn

Pentacles generally represent material and financial matters, and is the suit of the merchant or tradesperson. This may take the form of money, career, foundations, establishments, business development, or monetary gain. The Pentacle, or five-pointed star, that symbolises Earth in nature magic is often displayed as a central feature on the Suit of Pentacles cards. The Pentacles (known in some old decks as

Coins or Discs) represent the Earth element - the energy that keeps us grounded, and the physical or material side of life. They represent the outer manifestation of our spiritual nature, and signify fertility and fecundity in all its forms - sensuality, sensual pleasures, sex and procreation, and the grounding and anchoring of creative energy. The Pentacles tell you about your relationship with the material world, resources, status, tangible assets, and also with your work. Being of the Earth realm, the Pentacles are also associated with prosperity, hard work, financial progress and practical concerns. They can represent the mastery of life's material aspects, or the ambition and striving directed towards achieving them. In essence, the Pentacles are connected with matters that are financial, economic, monetary, or concerning stability. They highlight your attitudes to wealth, work, possessions and success. Dealing with the practicalities of life, they reflect our thinking and actions around more Earthly issues, and can inform us of areas where we seek greater stability in our lives. You experience the story of the Pentacles through your relationship with the tangible, physical aspects of yourself - through your attitudes towards your body, sensuality, success, work and worldly goods. A healthy approach towards all of these provides you with a sense of confidence that deepens your perspective on life. Focusing on this suit can help us become more grounded and can reconnect you to life and creativity through linking your Earthy nature to your spiritual essence. The Pentacles provide a solid framework that can be used as a springboard to attainment. Without the foundation of the Pentacles, the effectiveness of the other suits and their elemental correspondences (emotional water, intellectual air and enterprising fire) would be hindered. In a deck of playing cards, the Pentacles correspond to the suit of Diamonds.

SWORDS ★ The Air Element

Gemini, Libra, Aquarius

The Swords correspond with the Air element and are an especially interesting and meaningful metaphor. Swords, or the mind, organise by dividing, and quite literally cutting through things. Being of the Air element, the Swords are associated with ideas, the intellect, mental activity, thought processes, and mental insights, attitudes and clarity, as well as representing courage, boldness, force, strength, aggression and ambition. Air cannot be seen, gripped, grasped or commanded of, and can only be felt with subtle 'other' senses - the higher mind being one of them. We know the air is there through its apparent physical presence such as wisps of wind, but we cannot see it, touch it or even embrace it. In this way, the Swords suit can signify a certain elusiveness, something that can somehow evade us. But it is nonetheless a powerful force. These cards represent activity, progress and accomplishment for good or bad, sometimes misfortune and disaster. This is the suit of leaders and warriors. With the Air suit, illusions are recognised and shattered in the pursuit of an inner kernel of truth, knowledge and wisdom that the Swords embody - but the quest is fraught with painful lessons and is not always easy. These challenges will lead to greater understanding. The story of Swords begins with the core connection to the all-wise, all-seeing eye of the spirit. This Divine essence first manifests itself in the mind and then thoughts create form. Everything you see results from an initial thought that was put into action. As well as relating to the conscious direction of the intellect and will, the Swords also reveal hidden motivations and attitudes that can influence a situation. Cards from this suit advise us to either go to the core of the problem or to cut ourselves free in order to start afresh. Considered to be powerful and potentially destructive and dangerous, the Tarot Swords can indicate battles and enemies, but they can also be used constructively, to summon courage and a more conscious quality of mind. Even though they have long had a reputation as harbingers of unhappiness and discomfort, the suit still has a useful purpose. Without the ability to use reason and logic we risk being constantly swept away by our emotions, with all the potential for disaster that this could bring. The Swords can therefore assist in bringing about increased clarity and foresight, which we can use to avert trouble that may be brewing, and nip explosiveness in the bud. The Swords may be connected with hostility, sorrows, loss, struggle, action, change, bitterness, power, oppression, malice and conflict, but they are also associated with fortitude, decisiveness, audacity, tact, fairness, strength, bravery, ambition, force and truth, as well as with ideas and communication. Swords are almost always double-edged, which symbolises the fine balance that is needed between the intellect and power, and how these two forces can be used for good or evil. Overall, the Suit of Swords reveals our state of mind. In a deck of playing cards, Swords correspond to Spades.

CUPS ★ The Water Element

Cancer, Scorpio, Pisces

Cups generally represent love, passions, feelings, humanity, emotions, gaiety and joy. The Cups correspond with the Water element and are an especially interesting and meaningful metaphor. Cups are vessels which can hold water, which is a symbol of pleasure and happiness. Water is life-enhancing and sustaining when it flows freely; if trapped or contained for too long, it becomes stagnant, blocked and unhealthy. And, like our emotions and feelings, water can change shape to fit any channel or container and can transform into other forms, such as ice or steam. The Cups reveal the flow of our emotions, how turbulent or calm our inner seas are, how we express ourselves and how this all influences the relationships we have with others. Their narrative tells the tale of our inner life and reveals hidden feelings. The symbol of the Cup resembles a chalice or sacred drinking vessel and brings to mind the Holy Grail or the cup of life. Consequently, the issues of the Cups cards have a spiritual quality. The Cups are connected with the unconscious, artistic abilities, fantasy, feelings, attachments, intuition, love, pleasure, emotions, harmony, sensitivity, fertility, happiness and unity. The decorative imagery and themes that run through the suit of Cups are fish, mermaids and of course water. The fish is a symbol of creative imagination, and the element of Water represents the feelings and the depths of the unconscious mind. The Cups deal with the emotional level of consciousness and are associated with connections, love, feelings, expression and relationships. The Cups suit can indicate that we are being ruled by our hearts rather than our heads, our emotions rather than our intellects, and therefore reflect instinctive responses and habitual reactions to situations. The Cups are also linked to romanticism, fantasy, imagination and creativity. The Suit of Cups connects us to the wellspring of the spiritual source, helping us to develop our emotions, develop intuition, and understand how we attract particular energies, relationships and events into our lives. The negative aspect of this suit includes being overly emotional, relying too much on one's feelings, becoming disengaged or dispassionate, fantasising and holding unrealistic expectations of yourself or others. All of these may manifest as repressed emotions, an inability to properly express yourself, and a lack of creativity, self-confidence or self-belief. In a deck of playing cards, the Cups correspond to the suit of Hearts.

THE CHAKRAS & THE TAROT CONNECTION

The word 'chakra' comes from the Sanskrit and means 'wheel', disc' or 'circle'. Chakras are vitally important to your physical health, emotional wellbeing and spiritual growth, and are regarded as a complete integrated system that works holistically. The chakras are funnel-shaped spinning energy vortexes of multicoloured light. These swirling vortexes of energy absorb and distribute life-force, the subtle energy known as *prana*. The seven master chakras - Root, Sacral, Solar Plexus, Heart, Throat, Third Eye and Crown - lie in the centre line of the body, with the first five embedded within the spinal column. Each chakra vibrates at a different vibrational frequency and on a different note, and responds to specific life issues or 'thought forms'.

The lower body chakras deal with physical issues. As we move up the body, the chakras correspond to increasingly spiritual concerns. As a consequence, each chakra's energy vibrates at a different rate, depending on whether they govern earthbound or ethereal issues. The lower chakras have slower and denser vibrations, while the higher chakras spin at faster speeds with higher vibrations.

Each chakra responds to specific life issues or 'thought forms'. The first, or Root Chakra, near the base of the spine, regulates issues of survival and fulfilment of our physical needs for food and shelter. The second, or Sacral Chakra, corresponds to physical desires or appetites. The third, or Solar Plexus Chakra, is connected with issues of power and control. The fourth, or Heart Chakra, deals with matter of love and the heart. The fifth, or Throat Chakra, corresponds to our beliefs, thoughts, and actions involving communication. The sixth, or Third Eye Chakra, governs spiritual sight and clairvoyance. The seventh, or Crown Chakra, lets in universal and Divine knowledge, and is a receiver of wisdom, guidance and understanding.

There are literally hundreds of smaller chakras and they are all interrelated in a very complex system throughout the human body. In addition, other non-physical chakras lie outside the physical body, the best known of which are the Earth Star chakra, located beneath the feet, and the Soul Star chakra, located above the head.

The major chakras, the moderators of subtle energy, are envisioned in the Vedas (the primary source of Hindu philosophy) as sacred lotus flowers, with each chakra having a lotus with a different number of petals.

Because the chakras have no physical manifestation and cannot be located using any scientific instrument, they have tended to be viewed with scepticism by many Western medical professionals, a distinction they share with energy points in acupuncture and the notion of meridians. Instead, they are believed to have been sensed intuitively by many people over many centuries, and indeed people in yoga positions and in deep meditation have reported experiencing the sensation of a surge of energy rising from the base of the spine and emerging through the top of the head. Some people have even said they have seen points of blue light when their *kundalini* energy has risen from the lowest chakra to the highest, as well as experiencing a profound sense of happiness and ecstasy.

In summary, the Universal Life Force enters the body through the Crown chakra at the top of the head. As it works its way through the body, it flows through the other centres. As it spreads to the Base chakra, it is said to arouse the kundalini energy, which yogis believe sleeps in a coiled serpentine form.

Once one examines the meaning between the 22 Major Arcana cards and the Tarot, they can see how I have made a link between each of these life experiences, areas and needs, and a Tarot Card. Some Tarot cards resonate with more than one chakra as that card may encompass more than one archetypal human experience or desire. Please see the descriptions for all 22 cards for their individual corresponding chakras. I have listed the chakra correspondence so that one may meditate on a particular card as well as tuning into that card's meaning in conjunction with working to balance that particular energy centre.

The seven master chakras are:

Root ★ Base of Spine ★ Red ★ Earth ★ Security & Survival

Sacral ★ Below the Navel ★ Orange ★ Water ★ Physical, Sexual, Creative & Material Desires

Solar Plexus ★ Behind the Navel ★ Yellow ★ Fire ★ Personal Power, Confidence and Control

Heart ★ Heart Region ★ Green ★ Air ★ Love & Compassion

Throat ★ Throat Region ★ Light Blue ★ Sound/Ether ★ Communication & Self-Expression

Third Eye ★ Between the Eyes ★ Dark Blue ★ Light ★ Clairvoyance, Wisdom, Intuition & Vision

Crown ★ Top of Head ★ Purple ★ Thought/Knowing ★ Spiritual Wisdom & Enlightenment

★ ROOT / BASE CHAKRA ★ The Base chakra, otherwise known as the Root chakra, is located at the base of the spine. Its Sanskrit name is *muladhara*, and its symbol is a four-petalled crimson lotus flower around a yellow square containing a downward-pointing white triangle. Harmony in this chakra is expressed as groundedness, stability and reliability. When this chakra is balanced, you are caring, focused, self-confident, secure, strong and happy, but out of balance it can make you sexually predatory or frigid, manipulative or guilt-ridden. It corresponds to the adrenal glands and the coccygeal nerve plexus.

★ SACRAL CHAKRA ★ The Sacral chakra is located around the sexual and reproductive organ region. Its Sanskrit name is *svadhisthana*, and its symbol is a six-petalled orange lotus flower containing a second lotus flower and an upward-pointing crescent Moon in a white circle. Balance in this chakra is expressed as originality, creativity, vitality and a healthy sexual appetite (libido). It corresponds to the sex glands and the sacral nerve plexus.

★ SOLAR PLEXUS CHAKRA ★ The Solar Plexus chakra is located at the diaphragm. Its Sanskrit name is *manipura*, and its symbol is a ten-petal yellow lotus flower whose centre contains a red downward-pointing triangle. Balance in this chakra is expressed as self-confidence, a feeling of personal empowerment, logical thought processes and goal manifestation. It corresponds to the pancreas and the solar nerve plexus.

★ HEART CHAKRA ★ The Heart chakra is located in the region of the physical heart. Its Sanskrit name is *anahata*, and its symbol is a twelve-petal green/grey lotus flower whose centre contains a green circle and two intersecting triangles making up a six-pointed star representing balance (six is also the number of Venus, the planetary energy with which the Heart chakra is linked). This chakra blockage is especially significant because it is the central energy centre, uniting the upper and lower chakras. Among other things, a blockage can manifest as a lack of overall emotional fulfilment and difficulty receiving or being in a state of love. Balance in this chakra is expressed as unconditional love for ourselves and others, as well as openness to give, accept and receive compassion. It corresponds to the thymus and the cardiac nerve plexus.

★ THROAT CHAKRA ★ The Throat chakra is located at the base of the throat. Its Sanskrit name is *vishuddha*, and its symbol is a sixteen-petal blue lotus flower whose centre contains a downward-pointing triangle within which is a circle representing the full Moon. Balance in this chakra is expressed as easy communication with ourselves and others on all levels. It corresponds to the thyroid and parathyroid glands and the pharyngeal nerve plexus.

★ THIRD EYE CHAKRA ★ The Third Eye chakra is located between and just above the physical eyes. Its Sanskrit name is *ajna*, and its symbol is two large white lotus petals on each side of a white circle, within which is a downward-pointing triangle. Balance in this chakra is expressed as developed and sound senses of intuition, clairvoyance, clairaudience and clairsentience. It corresponds to the pituitary gland and the carotid nerve plexus.

★ CROWN CHAKRA ★ The Crown chakra is located just above the crown of the head and does not, therefore have a 'physical' position. Its Sanskrit name is *sahasrara*, and its symbol is the thousand-petal white lotus flower. This is the level of super-consciousness or *samadhi*, a plane beyond time, space and consciousness. Balance in this chakra is expressed as cosmic connection and Divine awareness. It corresponds to the pineal gland and the cerebral cortex nerve plexus.

THE ZODIAC SIGNS & THEIR CONNECTION WITH THE CHAKRAS

ARIES & LEO ★ Solar Plexus
TAURUS & LIBRA ★ Heart
GEMINI & VIRGO ★ Throat
CANCER & SCORPIO ★ Sacral
SAGITTARIUS & PISCES ★ Third Eye
CAPRICORN ★ Base
AQUARIUS ★ Crown

AT A GLANCE ★ BASIC MEANINGS

Zero ★ The Fool ★ KEYWORDS ★ Beginnings, Innocence, Exploration ★ DIVINATORY MESSAGES ★ A fresh start, optimism, child-like confidence. Denotes spiritual strength and protection as a man makes choices on life's journey. The Fool, or Jester, indicates spiritual progress, learning life's lessons, and important choices or changes involving courage or wisdom. It can also mean insights gained through recklessness. Care must be taken to avoid foolish decisions. Other KEY THEMES are ★ Folly, leisure, tendency to be guided by one's inner authority, thoughtlessness, extravagance, immaturity, enthusiasm, blind zest, foolishness, frivolity, spontaneity, pleasure, lack of discipline, rashness, frenzy, unrestrained excess, failure to listen to advice from other people, carelessness in promises, craze, passion, mania, and the beginning of a wild adventure!

No. 1 ★ The Magician ★ KEYWORDS ★ Initiative, Will, Independence ★ DIVINATORY MESSAGES ★ You have more power and versatility than you realise. Denotes duality, the union of personal and Divine power, sometimes used selfishly for devious ends. The Magician tells you to look for new beginnings and opportunities that make the most of your talents. Although this card symbolises willpower and thought turned into action and skill, it can also suggest guile and trickery. Other KEY THEMES are ★ Originality, creativity, the ability to utilise one's capabilities to accomplish something, imagination, self-reliance, self-confidence, craftiness, the ability to influence other people, and determination to see a task through to completion.

No. 2 ★ The High Priestess ★ KEYWORDS ★ Intuition, Wisdom, Knowledge, Mystery ★ DIVINATORY MESSAGES ★ Take note of your dreams, intuition and inner guidance. Trust your instincts. Representing the inner life, spiritual enlightenment, silence, intuition, philosophy, learning, creative talents and cultural advancement, The High Priestess denotes inner perceptions, esoteric knowledge, occult studies, spiritual protection, and arcane secrets. Other KEY THEMES are ★ Sound judgement, serene knowledge, understanding, penetration, education, ability to guide and teach others, foresight, self-reliance, the tendency to avoid emotional entanglements, and hidden emotions.

No. 3 ★ The Empress ★ KEYWORDS ★ Nurturance, Fertility, Earth Mother, Emotional and Material Wealth ★ DIVINATORY MESSAGES ★ The Empress symbolises creativity and abundance on every level. Representative of intuitive emotions, feelings, artistic inspiration, nature, harmony, abundance, growth, protective love and fertility, this card has themes of femininity, harmony, creativity, warmth, love, material plenitude, and happy marriage. Other KEY THEMES are ★ Feminine progress and development, fruitfulness, emotional security, attainment, mother, sister, wife, feminine influences, children, accomplishment, female guiles, evolution, the ability to motivate others, level-headedness, decisiveness, and healthy attachments to loved ones.

No. 4 ★ The Emperor ★ KEYWORDS ★ Discipline, Authority, Structure, Influence, Power ★ DIVINATORY MESSAGES ★ Accept your authority and acknowledge your power. Represents the dominant male force, temporal power, governing energy, logical thought, intellectual faculties, and analysis. It is also symbolic of worldly status, wealth, knowledge through experience, self-discipline, business acumen, stoic wisdom, and mental activity. Other KEY THEMES are ★ Accomplishment, confidence, stability, an indomitable spirit, attainment of goals, firmness, leadership, initiative, paternity and patriarchal influences, brother, father, husband, male influences, direct pressure, strength of one's convictions, domination of reason and intelligence over emotions and passions, desire to increase domination in every direction, a capable person who is knowledgeable and competent, and the willingness to listen to counsel but then follows one's own convictions.

No. 5 ★ The Hierophant ★ KEYWORDS ★ Advice, Wisdom, Questing, Counsel, Tradition ★ DIVINATORY MESSAGES ★ Adopt a conventional and cautious approach to situations. The Hierophant stands for inspirational genius, spiritual guidance, traditional teaching, ethical integrity, enlightenment, mentoring, conventional behaviour, morals, a desire for social approval, and self-honesty and truth. Other KEY THEMES are ★ Ritualism, ceremonies, servitude, overt reserve, mercy, humility, kindness, goodness, forgiveness, inspiration, alliance, compassion, conformity, the tendency to cling to outdated principles and ideas, and a person with a deep sense of tradition, past heritage and accepted societal rules.

No. 6 ★ The Lovers ★ KEYWORDS ★ Choices, Options, Complementary Opposites, Decisions ★ DIVINATORY MESSAGES ★ A strong emotional bond or a choice to be made. The Lovers card represents the duality of the individual, choices, the weighing up of future actions in light of present circumstances, struggles between profane and sacred love, and ultimately a moment of decision. The Lovers can indicate a difficult choice between an idealistic love and a physical attraction, intuitive decisions, harmony, friendship, affection, and a complicated moral choice between opposing factors. Other KEY THEMES are ★ Unanimity, love, beauty, perfection, trials overcome, trust, honour, beginning of a possible romance, deep feelings, infatuation, being put to the test, yearning, temptation, possible predicaments, and an affair of meaningful consequence.

No. 7 ★ The Chariot ★ KEYWORDS ★ Victory, Willpower, Control, Progress ★ DIVINATORY MESSAGES ★ Face up to hard work and difficult experiences with willpower. The Chariot represents people controlling and mastering their primal animal passions and desires, and the balancing of negative and positive forces to achieve success and triumph. It denotes success, prestige and wealth through sustained effort after conquering a difficulty or adversity, and also signifies patience, endurance, sudden good news, and fast travel. Other KEY THEMES are ★ Conflicting influences, turmoil, vengeance, a possible voyage or journey, escape, fleeing from reality, rushing into a decision, riding the crest of success or popularity, urgency to gain control over one's emotions, determination to mix hard work with times of productive solitude, and the achievement of greatness when physical and mental powers are maintained in balance and effectively put to work.

No. 8 ★ Strength ★ KEYWORDS ★ Gentle Force, Courage, Inner Fortitude, Spirit, Power ★ DIVINATORY MESSAGES ★ Draw on your strength of purpose to beat the odds and triumph. This is a positive card, representing moral force of purity, the triumph of the spirit, and the mind's domination over material trials and adversities. Strength has no real negative meanings and it denotes might, courage and power used wisely - love conquering hate, the spiritual conquering the material, and sometimes a once-in-a-lifetime opportunity that must be taken. Other KEY THEMES are ★ Conviction, energy used wisely, defiance, innate abilities utilised efficiently, mind over matter, conquest, heroism, virility, the strength to endure despite obstacles, tireless efforts, and liberation.

No. 9 ★ The Hermit ★ KEYWORDS ★ Withdrawal, Retreat, Solitude, Contemplation, Inner Journeying ★ DIVINATORY MESSAGES ★ The Hermit is symbolic of some form of enlightenment, whether spiritual or educational. You need to take some time out. The Hermit represents the explorer or traveller in search of wisdom, truth and illumination, guided by his own 'inner light' and protected by his spiritual strength. The Hermit denotes retreat, solitude, an enlightening journey, wise counsel and a sudden insight which may solve a problem. Other KEY THEMES are ★ Counsel, knowledge, prudence, discretion, caution, vigilance, circumspection, self-denial, the tendency to withhold emotions, failure to face facts, possessing secrets which may or may not be revealed, and the tendency to dwell within this wealth of knowledge as something worthwhile without seeking to utilise the information towards some goal or practical application.

No. 10 ★ Wheel of Fortune ★ KEYWORDS ★ Change, Acceptance, Fate, Free Will, Destiny ★ DIVINATORY MESSAGES ★ A situation is about to alter. Nothing stays the same. The Wheel of Fortune represents the law of retribution and karma, the gaining of wisdom and balance through evolution, and the unexpected capriciousness of fate. It can indicate a sudden change in fortune - usually for the better - sometimes creating difficulties or setbacks that in time could prove beneficial, or that could be the result of past efforts. Other KEY THEMES are ★ Outcomes, a godsend, special gain or unusual loss, culmination or conclusion, approaching the end of a problem, inevitability, unanticipated events, advancement for better or worse, progress, and that which shall remain the same unless one is alert to unexpected opportunities.

No. 11 ★ Justice ★ KEYWORDS ★ Fairness, Morality, Balance, Karma ★ DIVINATORY MESSAGES ★ Behave in a fair and balanced manner. Allow Karma to reign supreme. This card represents balanced judgement and control, successful and positive outcomes in educational or legal matters, and denotes harmony of both character and mind. A balanced outlook, a favourable legal decision, honesty, integrity and the vindication of truth are also indicated. Other KEY THEMES are ★ Reasonableness, proper balance, equity, righteousness, virtue, honour, just rewards, good intentions, well-meaning actions, advice, poise, impartiality, and someone who doesn't take unfair advantage of people or situations.

No. 12 ★ The Hanged Man ★ KEYWORDS ★ Suspension, Sacrifice, New Perspectives, Faith, Transition, Surrender ★ DIVINATORY MESSAGES ★ You need to view a situation from a different angle. The Hanged Man represents a willing sacrifice entailing suffering and loss or hardship, but that can transform your life, and bring inner peace and wisdom. It indicates a temporary standstill, a suspension of life's chaos, and brings spiritual enlightenment, forgiveness, epiphanies, illumination, the reversal of a way of life, occult powers, and inner strength. Other KEY THEMES are ★ Reversal of the mind, abandonment, renunciation, the changing of life's forces, the period of respite between significant events, the need for some kind of readjustment, repentance or improvement, spiritual rebirth, the approach of new life circumstances, and a pause.

No. 13 ★ Death ★ KEYWORDS ★ Change, Renewal, Transformation, Endings, Beginnings ★ DIVINATORY MESSAGES ★ A time of powerful psychological change and transformation. A deeply spiritual card, the Death card does not indicate physical death but rather a sudden overturning of the old life to make way for the soul to be reborn. It denotes rebirth, regeneration, and perhaps a shock or destruction that will ultimately lead to a new, clearer Path. It can signify a creative or artistic struggle that ends in triumph and the end of a troublesome period or relationship which makes way for fresh growth to occur. Other KEY THEMES are ★ A clearing of the way for new experiences, the loss of a familiar situation or friendship, the loss of income or financial security, and the rising of a new dawn and self.

No. 14 ★ Temperance ★ KEYWORDS ★ Moderation, Balance, Blending ★ DIVINATORY MESSAGES ★ Bring more balance and moderation into your life. Temperance represents the purification of the soul by spiritual grace, the combining of the active with the passive, and the unifying of both male and female aspects. It is symbolic of balance, blending, peace, energy, creative inspiration, future harmony, combining the spiritual and the material, compromise, good sense, and a balanced attitude to life. Other KEY THEMES are ★ Patience, that which can be accomplished through self-control and frugality, accommodation, flow, management, fusion, union, consolidation, ability to recognise and utilise the material and intellectual manifestations available to oneself, a person without excessive tendencies (a calming influence) who is well-liked, highly regarded and exudes confidence and complicity, but possibly too temperate and moderate to achieve a goal presently out of reach and requiring considerable assertiveness.

No. 15 ★ The Devil ★ KEYWORDS ★ Temptation, Excesses, Entrapment, Bondage ★ DIVINATORY MESSAGES ★ You feel enslaved by a situation or addiction, but you can break free from it. The Devil represents great negative power and influence, materialism, temptations that lead one astray, physical and carnal desires, upheavals, revolutions, and an inexorable event or change. It can denote a strong power which is being used for destructive, selfish or unwise ends, which stems from fear, ignorance, greed, violence or superstition, or a life dominated by physical appetites, material gain or hedonistic pleasures, as well as a lack of sensitivity and empathy. Other KEY THEMES are ★ Subordination, ravage, malevolence, subservience, downfall, lack of success, weird experiences, bad outside influence or advice, black magic, seeming inability to reach one's goals, dependence upon another person which leads to unhappiness, the temptation to evil, self-destruction, violence, shock, self-punishment, the tearing apart of one's self-expression, an ill-temper, lack of principles, and destructive, harmful or unethical behaviours.

No. 16 ★ The Tower ★ KEYWORDS ★ Collapse, Upheaval, Ruin, Awakening, Rebuilding ★ DIVINATORY MESSAGES ★ Sudden and dramatic events could unexpectedly cause loss or a change of fortune. But it is a chance for renewal and rebuilding. The Tower represents sudden catastrophe or change that brings eventual happiness and the opportunity to reassess or rebuild. It signifies the shattering of illusions, a cleansing catharsis or the closing of a karmic circle. It can also indicate a sudden flash of inspiration and the beginning of enlightenment, and a shock or disruption to one's life pattern which is for the better in the long run. Other KEY THEMES are ★ Complete and sudden change, a breaking down of old beliefs, abandonment of past relationships, the severing of a significant friendship or relationship, bankruptcy, termination, havoc, breakdown, downfall, undoing, divorce, the loss of stability, trust or security, setback, and the eventual personal breakthrough into new areas.

No. 17 ★ The Star ★ KEYWORDS ★ Renewed Hope, Inspiration, Dreams, Optimism ★ DIVINATORY MESSAGES ★ A favourable card indicating that a dream could come true or a difficult situation is improving. Recovery from illness. Hope, faith and a bright future. The Star represents the refreshing of the mind and spirit after a period of darkness - through trust, hope, selfless love and encouragement - bringing fresh hope, spiritual inspiration and growth. It denotes renewed optimism, rebirth, strength and guidance, a love of others, good friends, unselfish help given, and an inspired and fresh input or effort. Other KEY THEMES are ★ Good omen, bright prospects, mixing of the past and the present, promising opportunities, insight, spiritual love, ascending star, culmination of knowledge and work from the past and present reaping rewards, satisfaction and pleasure, the proper balancing of desire and work, hope and effort, and love and expression, and results that will soon come to pass from energies expended.

No. 18 ★ The Moon ★ KEYWORDS ★ Hidden Depths, Betrayals, Illusions, the Subconscious ★ DIVINATORY MESSAGES ★ Things are not as they seem. There is a chance of deception and confusion. The Moon signifies the unconscious, the dream state, imagination, uncertainty, mystery, an emotional crisis that is caused by the repression of emotions, fluctuations, hidden forces, intuition, hallucinations, illusions, undercurrents, betrayal and deception. Other KEY THEMES are ★ Twilight, obscurity, trickery, dishonesty, danger, error, caution, warning, ulterior motives, insincerity, false friends or relationships, double dealing, craftiness, false pretences, liabilities, being taken advantage of, superficiality, unknown enemies, the meeting of many divergent influences, falling into a trap, being misled, failure to see or avoid the dangers which surround one, and the very real chance of making a mistake or error of judgement.

No. 19 ★ The Sun ★ KEYWORDS ★ Success, Joy, Vitality, Radiance ★ DIVINATORY MESSAGES ★ You will soon have joy, creativity, fulfilment, accomplishment and contentment. A positive card, The Sun represents the warmth of a sunny day, purity, joy, innocence, a childlike faith, energy, courage and strength. It denotes harmony in relationships, realising an ambition, successful achievement in any field and against the odds, completed studies, blessings, health, material comforts, contentment, the gift of gratitude, and material, spiritual and emotional needs satisfied. Other KEY THEMES are ★ Favourable omen, satisfaction, fulfilling relationships, flowing generosity, unselfish sentiment, warmth, sincerity, pleasure in daily existence, high spirits, Earthly happiness, uncomplicated joy, the rewards of a new friend, pleasure derived from simple things, achievement in the arts, liberation, appreciation of everything, and the ability to accept life as it comes and to live contentedly and with the flow.

No. 20 ★ Judgement ★ KEYWORDS ★ Evaluation, Atonement, Self-assessment, Opportunities, New Directions ★ DIVINATORY MESSAGES ★ Don't judge others or yourself too harshly. A chance for personal accountability and redemption. Some form of rebirth is possible. A very powerful and highly spiritual card, Judgement represents the eternal spirit, redemption, forgiveness, a second chance, moving forward, and a reincarnation or new lease on life. It symbolises the end of one period in life's journey and the beginning of another, rewards for past efforts, release, change and renewal, justified pride in achievements, a worthy life, and a spiritual awakening resulting in success. Other KEY THEMES are ★ The need to repent and forgive, the moment to account for the manner in which we have used our opportunities, rejuvenation, rebirth, improvement, development, promotion, the desire for immortality, legal judgements in one's favour, the positive outcome of a personal conflict, and that success will come if one is responsible and honest with oneself.

No. 21 ★ The World ★ KEYWORDS ★ Completion, Attainment, Fulfilment, Success ★ DIVINATORY MESSAGES ★ Life has come full circle. Otherwise known as the Universe, this card denotes overall worldly success and triumphant achievement, as well as marking the end of a cycle and the beginning of another. The World is a positive card which represents lessons learned, material and spiritual triumphs, a happy conclusion, or the end of a phase in life. It is the material wish card, representing profound success and reward, which also signifies joy, happiness, accomplishment, and a dream come true at last. Other KEY THEMES are ★ Perfection, ultimate change, the end result of all efforts, assurance, synthesis, triumph, and eternal life.

AT A GLANCE ★ SYMBOLISM & IMAGERY

(Please note that the following descriptions are guided by the Universal/Rider-Waite Tarot Deck, and variations may occur subtly or substantially between different Tarot decks.)

THE FOOL

A young man wearing a fool's cap and dressed in colourful attire wanders aimlessly, paying no attention to a dog barking at his feet. He is alone and unopposed. He wears a collar of pompoms suggesting frivolity. In his hand, and resting over his shoulder, he carries a stick symbolising his desire and will. The stick is attached to a bundle bearing his previous experiences which he guards as a valuable possession for future use. Having severed his dependency upon others, his face expresses naivety, innocence and blind trust. In his other hand, he loosely clasps a staff and, oblivious to details, pays little attention to the direction in which he is walking. Bushes of opportunity seem to spring up before him, symbolic of a new world of unlimited possibilities and uninhibited self-expression. The sack he carries may also be emblematic of his faults, which he refuses to confront or accept, but which he still carries as baggage. The Fool personifies the sprit and enthusiasm of youth possessed by the boundless and abundant range of new horizons which await those who are setting forth on a fresh undertaking. Overall, The Fool is a youthful, carefree and adventurous character.

THE MAGICIAN

A magician stands before a table on which various objects have been placed, including a sword, perhaps symbolic of obstacles and difficulties, a coin signifying accomplishment and realisation of efforts, a cup representing passions and emotions, and a wand, symbolising enterprise and will. A double-ended phallic wand of creativity is held in The Magician's hand and pointed both towards the heavens and towards the Earth. The Magician's hat is shaped in the horizontal figure eight, the ancient occult number ascribed to Hermes and suggestive of inner knowledge and the combining of heavenly and Earthly forces into eternal and lasting fulfilment. His uplifted hand draws the power from above and, through the unity of his willpower and creative potential, he brings things into material manifestation through the downward pointing other hand. This duality indicates that all things are derived from above to create all things in our physical experience. The Magician possesses the capability of employing the diverse objects on his table so as to succeed in thought, word and action. He perceives life as a perpetual game of limitless opportunity which offers circumstances upon which personal control can be exerted to bring about one's full potential and realisation.

THE HIGH PRIESTESS

The High Priestess is seated within the precincts of her own special temple. In her lap, sits a book of knowledge and esoteric wisdom which records past events from the conscious, subconscious, super-conscious and Universal minds. Dressed in long-flowing attire with an impressive cloak wrapped around the nape of her neck and a veil of sorts flowing down from her crown, The High Priestess is the eternal feminine goddess of the ancient world, bestowing both knowledge and wisdom to those around her. Embodying the perfect woman and feminine essence, The High Priestess wears a crown to denote her stature in life. Sometimes referred to as Isis, the ancient Egyptian Lunar goddess of fertility, she is capable of absorbing and retaining substantial amounts of diverse, factual details but applies her knowledge in elusive, shadowy and mysterious ways. As indicated by the rolled-up scroll or book in her lap, The High Priestess is the protector of wisdom and guardian of secrets, as well as the discerning dispenser of special insights to others. She is a teacher and a guide, and subtly communicates the silent whispers of her deep intuition.

THE EMPRESS

The Empress is a matronly woman seated upon her throne wearing a crown on her head, and staring ahead with resolute, calm assurance and stability. In her hand, she holds a sceptre of authority while her other hand grasps a shield depicting the symbol of the planet Venus, whose very essence she stands for. The Empress symbolises the idea of feminine productivity and nurturance. The imagery of this card, in all its greenery and richness of crops, suggests fertility, fruitfulness, abundance, plenitude, and tender motherly love. The Empress is the quintessential caring and providing Earth Mother.

THE EMPEROR

A regal-looking man of middle to older age with a beard and moustache and long flowing hair, sits upon his throne surveying his domain. He wears an unpretentious crown because he does not need to make obvious display of his exalted position. In his hand, he grasps a ceremonial sceptre indicating the active influence, power and authority he has over all matters which come before him. Exuding confidence, accomplishment and worldly self-assurance, The Emperor's robes are ornamental and accordingly regally befitting of his superior status and experienced position. His throne is decorated with four Rams' heads, representing Aries, the sign associated with this card.

THE HIEROPHANT

A solemn-looking man dressed in a flowing religious robe and wearing a ceremonial miter on his head, sits on a chair and clasps a triple cross which represents the creative powers that pervade the Divine, intellectual and physical worlds. Behind him are two columns representing on one side the law and on the other side the right to obey or disobey. This indicates a theme of duality which enables one to choose mercy or severity, and conformity or freedom. The crown symbolises the material, formative and creative worlds, echoing the symbolism of his staff. The Hierophant represents that which is orthodox and traditional even to the point of ineffectuality. He counsels the right thing to do in a moral sense, and it is up to the seeker whether to heed that advice or choose the less conventional path of non-compliance. His wisdom teaches that adhering to heritage and entrenched social norms are often more important than the practicality and necessity of change needed in the present.

THE LOVERS

A fresh-faced winged angelic youth hovers above a male and female, both naked and both with golden hair, signifying youth and alluding to naïvety. The Lovers represents all that is essential in the interaction of love and affection between human beings. Some interpretations suggest that the card symbolises the choice between vice and virtue, and that a decision must be made between the two. The overhead Sun radiates its light and energy over the figures below, and serves as a source of wisdom and creation. This is a card of great sympathy, warmth, need and devotion and it is suggestive of an emotional experience with meaningful outcomes and implications. But it hints at the ever-present danger, in a romance so deep and beautiful, of possible trickery through blindness, and making the wrong decision or errors in judgement which may have bearings on future experiences.

THE CHARIOT

A crowned conqueror stands erect in a cubical Chariot supported by four columns and covered with a luxurious canopy. He bears a sceptre in his hand and wears a suit of armour with facial epaulets on each side. On his shoulders appear the faces of Thummim and Urim, seekers of the Divine will of God through an oracular medium. The Chariot is drawn by two sphinxes (or horses in some decks), representing the mixture of adversity and the union of the positive and the negative forces which abound in one's life. The sphinxes appear to be pulling in different directions, or at least facing in them, compelling the charioteer to control them. The Chariot represents the material currents which carry us all towards our destiny, but it advises that to reach our goals and attain our victory, we must keep our horses under control using our willpower; the horses being opposite in nature, emphasise that progress is only achieved through the attentive supervision over divergent forces. The conqueror in his Chariot vanquishes those before him and he strikes out against all elementary forces to achieve triumph.

STRENGTH

A woman courageously holds open the jaws of a lion which has sought to defy or overpower her. The beast appears stunned and the force required by the lady appears minimal, suggestive of the true inner strength that she possesses. Above the woman hovers the same horizontal figure eight as The Magician wears, signifying an eternal essence of everlasting fortitude. The lion represents outside influential forces that may be jeopardising the lady and serves as a caution to the words and actions of others; he also represents temptations which may appear, requiring firm control, willpower, inner strength and a resolute determination to overcome. This card, although it depicts a woman, represents all of humanity, in both a collective and personal sense, and the mighty feats we can accomplish through the sheer strength of our convictions, gentle but firm resolve, and tireless, steady efforts.

THE HERMIT

An aged, bearded man in a voluminous habit holds a lantern in his hand up high to light up his Path ahead. He walks with a staff in his hand for support as he travels the Path of initiation and inner knowledge. He is ready to come to the assistance of his fellow human with counsel and advice, but not before he has had a period of retreat, withdrawal and introspection. The Hermit is the guardian of time and patience, a wise man who dispenses wisdom and truths from the eternal well of knowledge which both precedes him and stretches out before him. He is the Ancient One in cowled robe whose is keeper and eventual divulger of the knowledge of the ages for the benefit of himself and of others. His lantern illuminates esoteric learnings, but at times this knowledge may be so overwhelming that he carries it as a burden. At his best, he uses his gained insights to shed light upon the Path not only for himself, but for others too.

THE WHEEL OF FORTUNE

The Wheel of Fortune contains six spokes indicating that each stage of the life experience is across the wheel from its opposite. On either side of the wheel a creature ascends and a creature descends, one appearing to descend into misfortune while the other appears to be rising towards good fortune. These animals are depicted in the perpetual motion of a continuously changing Universe and the flow of the human life journey, while the sphinx sitting at the top seeks to maintain equilibrium. The Wheel of Fortune is symbolic of a revolving circle which dispenses both sorrows and joys, life and death, good and evil, black and white, signifying that within all elements and phases of life there is a positive *and* a negative. The Wheel is a circle without beginning or end, and from it we can derive the symbols of perpetual eternity and the continuous motions of progress and change. The simultaneous ascent and descent is suggestive of evolution and involution towards the destinies of fortune, probabilities, inevitabilities, chance, fate, and predestined outcomes. The sphinx at the top of the wheel signifies the principle of balance and stability by which we have the power to alter our supposed fate through the use of our free will.

JUSTICE

The crowned female figure of Justice, said to depict Astraea, Goddess of Justice in Greek mythology, is seated between the pillars of positive and negative, mercy and punishment, forgiveness and vengeance. One of the cardinal virtues, in one hand she holds the scales of Justice suggesting equitableness and fairness. In the other hand, she grasps a double-edged sword, endowing her with the ability to determine right from wrong, and indicating that sometimes action from both ways successfully overcomes a trying situation. Her face resolute and firm in conviction, Justice is capable of the fair administration of manners, courtesy and morals in light of the person or circumstances involved. Representing the pillars of principled strength and integrity, although she wears no blindfold, Justice still remains fair and unbiased, and does not permit temptation, preconceptions or ignorance to misguide her.

THE HANGED MAN

A young man hangs upside down from a wooden beam, his feet tied with a cord and his hands bound behind his back. His arms are bent at the elbows and form the shape of triangles. His eyes are open and he appears fully aware and conscious of his surroundings; his face is serene, suggesting acceptance of and surrender to his current situation. We see in the Hanged Man the moment of suspension at which truth and realisation are revealed to us if we only yield to them. For often when we are vulnerable and yielding, the cloaks of secrecy are removed, and the inner self is exposed. Although the man is still earthbound, he has attained some measure of relief through this temporary standstill between transitions in his life. He understands and accepts that all he can do in this situation is submit to the flow and be patient as he awaits the next stage.

DEATH

The skeleton in this card, which may be either male or female, represents change, transitions and rebirth. The Tarot Death card stands for the ending of something in the present which will bear a fruitful outcome in the events of the future. The energy of the skeletal figure serves as a breaking force to loosen the chains which bind and hold back change. This card represents the transitional phenomena of decay and death that are modified to create renewal and new life. The finality of the past is removed from the future through the irrevocable sweep of the scythe. The fear of change often overshadows the promise of new directions and the wondrous opportunities these present. But as death ultimately teaches us all, once the current Path is swept away and cleared, it is only natural that transformation and regeneration will follow.

TEMPERANCE

This card depicts the virtue of Temperance as a winged angel robed in a long-flowing garment and pouring liquid from one vessel to another. Just above her shoulders rests thick flowing golden hair which falls in curls, framing her pleasant and calm face. The essence of life flows between the two containers, symbolising the flowing of the past through the present and into the future. The vessels represent moderation and frugality, and the pouring of the liquid from the higher urn to the lower one without spilling its contents, is suggestive of discipline and balance. Behind the angel are hills and shrubbery which indicate the unlimited opportunities one can realise through the successful combination of two elements and the exercising of self-restraint. The angel of Temperance possesses the powers of moderation, harmony, successful blending, and a conspicuous lack of excess in all areas of life. Secure and self-reliant, she is capable of living within modest but still comfortable means.

THE DEVIL

This card depicts a grotesque-looking horned, bat-winged demon holding a flaming torch - symbolising destruction and evil intent - in one hand and elevated on a pedestal. The Devil's other hand is upraised signifying his propensity for black magic, power and destruction. Two horned and tailed figures are tied by their necks with chains attached to a ringbolt and stand at his feet. The fact that the chains only loosely hang around the pair's necks, suggests that the bonds that bind us can be removed by ourselves through discipline, determination and willpower. The Devil is the bearer of shock, disaster, curses and misery. This card strongly indicates human suffering, subservience, ruin and desolation. He personifies the person who is devious and yields to temptations and compulsions with no regard for the consequences or the effect upon others. Overall, The Devil is a bad omen, bespeaking of unhappy circumstances and unfortunate situations that may befall one who is a slave to their obsessions and material desires, and most of all, who fails to break free.

THE TOWER

A tall tower with a crowned roof explodes due to an internally raging fire caused by a sudden, violent lightning flash, possibly originating directly from the Sun. Sometimes called the House of God, The Lightning Struck Tower, The Hospital, The Tower of Babel or Fire of Heaven, this card depicts two figures, a male and female, plummeting to the ground along with sparks and debris. The Tower ultimately represents the breaking down of previous conditions and the destruction of what was once regarded as stable and secure. The Tower is struck so that just the top is severed from the main structure, signifying a clean break from the past. This card suggests that something which was once thought as sound and solid, is now undergoing catastrophic but ultimately necessary collapse and change. It aims to teach us that even though disaster can strike at any time and without warning, that this apparent misfortune usually contains the seed of something that is for our own good. It then serves to offer us a chance to rebuild from the ruins.

THE STAR

A naked maiden kneeling on one knee by the side of a pond pours the waters of life from two urns - one into the pool and the other onto dry land, perhaps symbolising the conscious and unconscious minds, or spiritual and Earthly concerns. Her facial expression is one of satisfaction and hope. In the sky above hovers a huge star, the Star of the Magi, ablaze in golden yellow, and surrounded by seven smaller ones. These stars of hope and illumination ascend above the naked girl, and a bird and flowers abound, hinting at the birth of new life and promise. The bird is the sacred Ibis of thought while the stars represent the radiant cosmic energies shining upon the Earth to signal a fresh dawn. This card represents the coming of new opportunities and inspiration. Perhaps the most poignant message of this card is that it comes just after The Tower; when one considers both these cards' meanings, it is surely no coincidence.

THE MOON

The Moon is a mysterious card which signals dangers in the form of deception, illusions, betrayal, fantasies and hidden emotions. In this card, two canines - one a domesticated dog, representing the tamed side of human nature, and one a wolf, symbolising the wild, untamed side of human nature - howl at the Moon, from which drops of influence seem to be falling. On either side of the dogs, two towers appear, and in the foreground, a crab or crayfish hiding in the water of a pool begins to crawl out of its watery depths. This card suggests the presence of self-delusion, jealousy, prejudice, caution or danger in one's current life. Moonlight is indeed deceptive; the Moon demonstrates its power over the water, and there is likewise a great deal of outside influences revealed in this card. The dogs have adapted to life with humans but they remain a threat due to their susceptibility to the Lunar influence which pervades the dark, shadowy night. This is a card of warning, and indicates that events being presently experienced are being somehow obscured by undesirable - and often hidden - malices and menaces.

THE SUN

A huge Sun complete with round face and golden outstretched rays, shines down upon a naked child riding a white horse. The nakedness of the child indicates he has nothing to hide and he embodies pure, untainted joy, happiness and contentment. The Sun triumphs over him and resplendently shines out to touch all upon the Earth below. From the Sun's beams flow strong and positive Solar energies which permeate all living beings and give rise to feelings of brightness and satisfaction. Indeed, the day comes after night, just as The Sun appears after The Moon.

JUDGEMENT

This card depicts a winged angel, possibly Gabriel, with golden hair blowing on a trumpet to which is attached a banner bearing the design of a cross. Below, naked figures rise from coffins while on each side a naked man and woman also rise with clasped hands turned upwards towards the angel. These figures suggest the rising of negative and positive forces, and the stirrings of past doings that are now standing before the concept of Judgement. This card suggests not only the revival and reawakening of the individual concerned, but also a calling to atonement for that which has passed. We all commit sins in some form or another and one day we must be called to account for our past deeds. The rising figures indeed symbolise the cleansing away of the shrouds of times and actions passed - but not before admitting them and bringing them forth for Judgement first. Judgement teaches the wisdom that the deeper our emotions the more profound our redemption, and the greater our sorrows the more meaningful our appreciation for joys.

THE WORLD

A naked female figure is encircled by a flowing veil or cloth as she dances in the centre of a laurel wreath, signifying victory and achievement. In each hand, she holds a double-ended wand, representing the power she commands from all sides. Though her legs form a cross, one foot appears to be firmly planted on the ground and she is secure in her position. Elated but emanating a tranquil aura of joy and accomplishment, the female figure is in command of her dominion. The two wands represent the powers resulting from all the efforts described in the 21 preceding cards and the ultimate attainment of one's goals through the use of her conscious and subconscious will. In the four corners of this card are the four cherubic animals of the Apocalypse - a human, an eagle, a bull and a lion. These four corners may also suggest the four elements of Fire, Water, Earth and Air, which the animals represent, and which are now perfectly in-tune and balanced. All that has taken place before is now culminating in ultimate completion and overall fulfilment. You have finally arrived! Rejoice!

A JOURNEY THROUGH THE LIFE EXPERIENCE

What does each card tell you about the stage of your own life path?

Some cards are more 'evolved' or further along the Path than others. Starting with The Fool, who begins our Tarot journey (and in some schools of thought, ends it also), at number zero, and progressing through the Major Arcana in order, one becomes more and more enlightened and unfolds gradually, advancing him or herself like a flower blossoming. Each card is numbered except for The Fool (which can be regarded as either zero or 22), which is often considered to be the querent, the person setting out on the journey of enquiry. Here is a very simplistic rundown on the cards and what they mean for our progress or place on that Path:

The first six cards of the Major Arcana ~ THE FOOL, THE MAGICIAN, THE HIGH PRIESTESS, THE EMPRESS, THE EMPEROR, THE HIEROPHANT - show us as 'beginners' who have not yet been shaped by more mature societal forces.

The second six cards of the Major Arcana ~ THE LOVERS, THE CHARIOT, STRENGTH, THE HERMIT, WHEEL OF FORTUNE, JUSTICE - represent our intermediate steps, where we learn to apply our knowledge to new challenges.

The next five cards of the Major Arcana ~ THE HANGED MAN, DEATH, TEMPERANCE, THE DEVIL, THE TOWER - show our processes of wrestling with our inner demons and of beginning a process of regeneration and deeper learning.

The final five cards of the Major Arcana ~ THE STAR, THE MOON, THE SUN, JUDGEMENT, THE WORLD - signify our awareness of group consciousness and that we're pretty advanced life journeyers.

NUMBERS & THE TAROT DECK

The Tarot deck is divided into two sections: The Major Arcana and the Minor Arcana (note that the '2' is for balance). Each card bears a number. While the origins of the Tarot are steeped in mystery, two significant facts exist about the Tarot deck and its numbers: The Major Arcana consist of 22 cards and the Minor Arcana, 56. The numerological significance of this is that 56 adds up to 11 (5 + 6), a *master number*, and 22 is also a master number. This can't be a coincidence. The numbers on the cards are important symbols to be used for understanding one's destiny.

The master number 11 is the number of self-illumination through spiritual inspiration appropriate for the Major Arcana. The number 22 is the number that brings cosmic law into the material and physical world to build a new world of highest principles, which is the essence of the Major Arcana.

THE 22 MAJOR ARCANA

ARCANA ~ *Noun*. An inner secret or mystery; something hidden from the masses; one of the great secrets which the alchemists sought to discover.

It's perhaps no coincidence that the Major Arcana of the Tarot have 22 cards - zero through 21 to be exact - as the number 22 is a master number. In fact, 22 is considered the most powerful of all the numbers and is called the master builder number because it symbolises the potential for bringing spiritual understanding into physical form. Keywords for it are dreams made manifest, realisation, ancient wisdom, evolution, Universal love, the Divine imagination, vision, transformation, redemption and personal power. The 22 symbolises mastery and inspiration, and it utilises intuitive insights and creative expansion, coupled with practical methodology. It is ultimately concerned with spiritual ascension. The 22 is meant to serve the world in its mastery.

The Major Arcana cards describe major events and turning points in our lives (such as pregnancy, relationship and career changes, marriage, and personal crises or challenges). While these cards have universal meanings, each person brings their own personal interpretation to them. Each card will be read in a different way depending on who is reading it and what question the querent is asking.

The Major Arcana contains the richest symbolism of all the cards in the Tarot deck, each carrying a myriad of messages for the reader to decipher. The symbolism contained within these images represents the archetypal aspects of yourself. It also describes the Path your soul takes through each stage of life, revealing clues through which you can explore different parts of yourself.

Each of the cards represents an aspect of universal human experience and has a name that either directly conveys the meaning of the card, such as Strength or Justice, or depicts individuals or concepts that represent the human archetypes, such as The Hermit or The Empress. The illustrations on each card contains one or more figures or creatures and tuning in or tapping in to a card enables you to grasp its meaning intuitively. Every card has its own story to impart, and through entering that story you can gain deeper insights into the full picture, the journey so far or the journey to come.

THE MINOR ARCANA ADD UP TO 11

The Minor Arcana have 56 cards. If we add 5 + 6 we get to the master number 11. Eleven is the most intuitive of all the numbers. It symbolises illumination and intuitive understanding, especially of spiritual truths or principles. The 11 focuses energy on 'otherworldly' consciousness, but we can use that same energy to turn inwards to create inner conflicts and fears that manifest negatively in our outer lives. The number 11 symbolises truth found in faith, not in logic, and the Minor Arcana are all about how to live life in the everyday world.

The Minor Arcana is comprised of four suits of 14 cards each. The Lesser or Minor, Arcana cards of the Tarot deck correspond to the suits in an ordinary deck of playing cards. There are the usual 'pip' cards Ace to 10, and the court cards King, Queen, Page (Jack) plus the Knight which is placed between the Queen and Page. The Minor Arcana cards represent more ordinary day-to-day events and circumstances, and people.

THE TAROT NUMBERS

0 ★ Unformed, empty and full, free will, no karmic debt.

1 ★ New beginnings, initiation, purpose, courage, originality, the self. Aces are the number 1, and all Aces deal with the potential for beginnings, a new time, initiating a new start, or a birthing of some kind. These fresh starts can be through a stroke of fate, a personal decision, or a literal birth. In magic, alchemy and witchcraft, one stands for the Universe, the One, the Source of All, Unity. It is the first manifestation of creative light that will multiply into millions of unique parts, each separate and yet containing the power of the first. Oneness preserves the integrity of creation, and cannot be divided without losing its integrity. In the beginning, there was one: the absolute, the all in one, the one in all. This one is the "I" of the Universe, represented by a rod or, in alchemy, a serpent. It is the absolute symbol of masculinity, the active, engendering principle. Finally, there is the monad, considered by the Renaissance alchemists, philosophers and esoteric practitioners to be the great, unifying principle and soul of the world.

2 ★ Balance, relationship, duality, choice, polarity, contrast, psychic knowing, intuition. The number 2 deals with duality, balance, and relationships. In the Tarot, the 2 deals with choosing and comparing two people, options, viewpoints or situations. They refer to relating with others and this may be in business or personal life. In magic, alchemy and witchcraft, two stands for the Goddess and God, the perfect duality, projective and receptive energy, the couple, personal union with Deity, balance, and the mother/anima and father/animus principle. This number represents two forces opposing *or* complementing one another. It often stands for male and female, positive and negative, light and dark, and heaven and earth. In spiritual teaching, it can be used to represent the division between God and man, sometimes known as the 'Lover and the Beloved'. In alchemy, a separation from one into two is essential to release the vital energy that a polarity generates.

3 ★ Equilibrium, 2 + 1 = 3, Mind/Body/Spirit, creation. Creative and emotional expression, synthesis, celebration, happiness, joy. The 3 symbolises fun, joy, playfulness, celebration, and creative and emotional expression. Three denotes creative new enterprises or losses, and these involve others as well as yourself. In magic, alchemy and witchcraft, three stands for the Triple Goddess, the Lunar phases, the physical, mental and spiritual aspects of humans, the trinity and the sacred triangle, fertility and creation. Practically every religious or wisdom tradition has a trinity at its core. The three ingredients of alchemy are known as Salt, Mercury and Sulphur, or body, soul and spirit. With the operation of three forces, we have a living and dynamic situation. There are possibilities for change and growth. Two opposing forces can be reconciled by the third in a new and creative solution. Three encapsulates the essence and concept of a triangle.

4 ★ Elements, seasons, directions, crossroads, structure, determination, foundation, form and order. The number 4 represents foundations, stability and the status quo. It also deals with health and hard work. Fours bring safety, security and relief from problems. In magic, alchemy and witchcraft, four stands for the elements, the winds, the seasons, the square, the physical and material world. It is the most stable of numbers. Four stands for the four elements of Earth, Water, Fire and Air, the 'building blocks' of creation. Four signifies two sets of polarities, but although this creates tension, this tension can be used to create a house, for example, or lay out an arena for action. It can also create an enclosed area such as a philosophical rose garden. There are always battles where four is involved, but there is also potential for constructive work. The usual representation of four is the cross or the square. Four is associated with the four arms of the cross, a very common Earth symbol in ancient cultures and civilisations. Both the square and the cross have also been revered as power symbols which impart strength, will and inspiration. In astrology, the power and potential of four corresponds particularly to the zodiac signs Leo and Scorpio. It is essentially a feminine energy that is especially activated at night-time.

5 ★ Change, instability, rebellion, the maverick, adventure, quintessence, expansion, restlessness, vigour. The 5 is the number of change and adaptation, and in the Tarot, it usually means conflict and strife. The change that's required is what causes the conflict, and the 5s tell us that there is a need to adapt to unpleasant changes. Fives all denote challenges which may be desired or result from a loss of sorts. In magic, alchemy and witchcraft, five stands for the quintessence, the pentagram and pentacle, the physical senses, the elements plus Akasha (or spirit). It is a Goddess number, the fifth element unifying the other four: Earth, Air, Fire and Water. Five is about dynamic focus, a combination of two and three. It can be sparkling, sexual or charismatic, or on the other hand, a decisive act of destruction. It can also represent the quintessential element which is a distillation of all four basic elements. A five-pointed star, the pentagram (five points joined by one line) or a pentagon (a five-sided figure) are its main representations.

6 ★ Idealism, assistance, advice, problem-solving, matters of the heart, committed responsibility, truth, balance, perfection. The number 6 represents the benefit of giving to others, and assistance. The 6 is the number of service and responsibility.

Sixes suggest conclusions to minor matters, as well as denoting useful turning points. Six is the principle of reconciliation. In magic, alchemy and witchcraft, six represents the union of fire and water, brought into a harmonious relationship. Six is shown as a hexagon, or a six-pointed star made up of two interlaced triangles, which point above and below, symbolising unity between heaven and earth.

7 ★ Perception, inner journeying, insight, reflection, spirituality, manifestation, fortune, achievement. The number 7 deals with awareness and wisdom. It is the number of inner work, research or study, reflection and rejuvenation. In the Tarot, it signals changes brought about by wisdom and insights into a situation. Sevens signify some confusion and ambiguity however. In magic, alchemy and witchcraft, seven stands for the planets the ancients knew, the duration of the Lunar phases in days, power, protection, mystery, mysticism and magic, perfection, and is a sacred combination of numbers three and four. Seven signifies a full range of differences. It contains diversity within a recognisable order, like the spectrum of colours in the rainbow. The seven days of the week are a familiar version of this, each day with its own character and magical correspondences. Something that has seven components in it has an identity of its own, above and beyond the individual ingredients. For this reason, a group is said to function effectively only when it has seven members or more. The warring fours and harmonious threes, their sum equalling seven, find their first conjunction here. In some schools of alchemy, the power of seven has been described as the *Power of Fusion*. The power of seven is connected with oneness, community and Cosmic consciousness, and describes a poetic, mystic ability to tune in and to be at one with all life and All That Is.

8 ★ Power, organisation, materialism, mastery, infinity, success, inspiration, transcendence, opportunity, expansion. The 8 is the number of money, control and authority. In the Tarot, the 8 shows control or mastery over a situation (or lack of it), where self-reliance, autonomy or personal power might be required. Eights characterise freedom *and* restriction, plus decisions that need action. In magic, alchemy and witchcraft, eight stands for the number of the sabbats, the number of the God, and eternity. Eight stands for the octave. It is also the number of architecture and structure, where two sets of four can be combined elegantly together. The steps of the octave, which we associate mostly with notes in music and also possessing a vibrationally-connected connotation, are said to represent a cosmic order, in which you find a similar note at the top to that at the bottom, but at a different pitch or level. The octave is generally seen as a 'vertical' structure. Eight can be found in the octagon, or can be seen as two interlaced squares, or an eight-fold star. Ancient numerologists sometimes interpreted the potential of eight as an Energy which networks, connects, circuits and organises the Worlds. It represents the point at which the infinite and finite merge, where the spiritual materialises and matter spiritualises, where the unconscious becomes conscious and conscious becomes unconscious, and also where life follows death and death follows life. It is through the power of eight that Spirit dissolves into matter and matter can be transmuted into Spirit. In sacred geometry, the number eight is drawn up and down the staff of the caduceus symbol (two snakes entwined around a rod). This symbol is thought to

symbolise the circuits and cycles that support and perpetuate life; it is the spiral, the stairway and the spiritual DNA that leads from Heaven to Earth and back again, because eight and its two eternal circles, never really begin and never end. In this sense, it symbolises eternity and infinity.

9 ★ Vision, wisdom, intuition, attainment, power, influence, culmination, achievement, accomplishment, satisfaction. The number 9 is about endings, loss, grief, completion and fulfilment, as well as the wisdom and understanding that comes from the completion of the cycle. An intense number, filled with the energy of all the lower numbers, nines show situations that are either comfortable or uncomfortable. In magic, alchemy and witchcraft, nine is a number of the Goddess, the number of initiation, and as the last of the single numbers, it brings the sequence to a close. Nine is a significant and magical number. It equals three times three, and in mythology, we often find an original trio who have expanded to nine. Each point of the triangle can generate another triangle. In this sense, nine has an essentially expansive, lively form of energy that can include detail and diversity expanded from the basic three. Representations of nine usually combine the three triangles in some way. It represents completion - life flows in cycles of nine - nine years, nine months, nine days - and throughout life our major changes tend to happen with our personal nine year. Numbers one to nine are the basic vibrations and represent our nine basic experiences of life. These experiences relate to our inner world and also to our outer world, and with a deeper understanding of the correlations between our experiences and the identifying numbers one to nine, we have an excellent reference for all aspects of our self and our journey through life. In sacred geometry, the power of nine is linked to the power of three triangles, which is a common symbol for perfection and completion. Ancient alchemical lore states that to travel around the triangle twice you become wisdom - the completion of this law states that to travel around the triangle thrice you become Law. With the advent of nine, the full course for the journey of involution and evolution has now been set.

10 ★ Renewal, karmic completion, mastery, abundance, fullness, culmination. Completion; making way for the next phase. The number ten represents rebirth and renewal at the end of the cycle of Ace through ten. Ten has great numerical significance as we go into double figures at this point. It is a natural ceiling for the first 'ladder' of numbers. Ten has stability, and is the number of a set of principles of creation which manifest themselves in different forms of energy. Ten is a karmic number and means renewal is earned through work from the past. The sum of the first four numbers, $1 + 2 + 3 + 4$, ten is considered the great number of all things, the archetype of the Universe. According to Pythagoreans, ten is the most supreme number, since it encompasses all arithmetic and harmonious proportions. It represents Divine power. Ten is the number of the Sun, symbolising the cosmos, the paradigms of creation, completion and perfection. A very fortunate and 'holy' number (the Ten Commandments comes to mind), leading you to victory in situations where others fear to tread. It suggests vibrant and creative originality. If number one signifies the origin, beginning or initialisation, number ten indicates an outcome, end or fulfilment. With the occurrence of ten, whatever has been sown or

conceived by one can be harvested or born. So, this number includes, gathers and contains all those which have gone before it, and symbolically, it shows that fulfilment coincides with the end of a cycle. In the Tarot, tens indicate that lessons have been learned and mastery has been achieved, so a rebirth is about to occur or is necessary. Tens usually indicate that the outcome of a situation will be a complete success or a complete failure.

★ TREE OF LIFE & THE TAROT ★

I know that an ash tree stands called Yggdrasil, a high tree, soaked with shining loam; from there comes the dews which fall in the valley; ever green, it stands over the well of fate.

Seeress's Prophecy

Known in Scandinavian mythology as Yggdrasil the World Tree, and in Kabbalah as the Tree of Life *, this tree is an eternal green sacred ash which stood at the centre of the Norse spiritual cosmos and which overshadowed the entire Universe. Its branches, roots and trunk united heaven, Earth and the nether regions. The roots of Yggdrasil lay in Hel, while the trunk ascended through Midgard, the Earth. Rising through the mountain known as Asgard, it branched into the sky - its leaves were the clouds, its fruit the stars. In the Kabbalah, the Tree of Life consists of ten spheres, or sephiroth, through which, according to mystical tradition, the creation of the Universe came about. The sephiroth are aligned in three columns headed by the supernals - Kether, Chokmah and Binah - and together symbolise the process by which the 'Infinite Light' Ain Soph Aur becomes manifest in the Universe. The mystical path of self-knowledge, which the Tree of Life represents in all its stages and ascensions, entails the rediscovery of all the levels of one's being, ranging from Malkuth (physical reality) to the infinite Source. With this in mind, the medieval kabbalists divided the Tree of Life into three sections of the soul: Nephesch (the animal soul) corresponding to the sephiroth Yesod, Ruach (the middle soul) corresponding to the sephiroth from Hod to Chesed, and Neschamah (the spiritual soul) corresponding to the supernals, especially Binah. Practitioners of western magic, who use the Tree of Life as a glyph for the unconscious mind, sometimes distinguish the 'magical' path, which embraces all ten sephiroth, from the 'mystical' path of the Middle Pillar, which is an ascent from Malkuth through Yesod and Tiphareth to Kether on the central pillar of the Tree. Occultists also identify the 22 cards of the Major Arcana with the paths connecting the ten sephiroth. For each card, I have briefly outlined which path or connection that particular card has with the Yggdrasil.

The Sephiroth are each assigned a number which is significant to that path, and are as follows, beginning at the top of the Tree:

1 ★ Kether ~ Purest Existence. The Crown. The Cosmos.

2 ★ Chokmah ~ The Supernal Father. Wisdom. Energy without form - the great impregnator. The Zodiac.

3 ★ Binah ~ The Supernal Mother. Understanding. The roots of form. Saturn.

4 ★ Chesed ~ The Preserver. Mercy. Organisation and inspiration. Jupiter.

5 ★ Geburah ~ Strength and Severity. Force, catabolism, necessary destruction. Mars.

6 ★ Tiphareth ~ Beauty. Individuality. The Sun.

7 ★ Netzach ~ Victory. Intuition, dance, arts, emotions. Venus.

8 ★ Hod ~ Glory. Intellect, logical faculties. Mercury.

9 ★ Yesod ~ Foundation. Images, the machinery of the Universe. The Moon.

10 ★ Malkuth ~ Kingdom. Physical manifestation. The Earth.

* While the World Tree and the Tree of Life share many similarities, each providing complex structures for organising human experience and perceptions of the workings of the Universe, they are not identical in every way.

THE 22 MAJOR ARCANA CARDS & THE HUMAN LIFE EXPERIENCE

NOTE ★ Under the subtitle 'SYMBOLISM' for each card, I have described the imagery mainly from (but not restricted to) the Rider-Waite Tarot deck. Therefore, the symbols and images described are not found in all Tarot decks, and the images in different decks can and often do differ considerably.

★ THE FOOL ★

Ruled by Uranus & the Element of Air

Number ★ Zero (or 22 in some decks)
Astrological Signs ★ Aquarius, Gemini, Libra & Aries

Keywords ★ Beginnings, Innocence, Exploration

The Fool holds the wisdom of having seen and known the great Plan, a controlled folly of abandonment to the design of the Universe.

Paul Hougham

Magical Title ★ The Spirit of Ether
Divinity ★ Ouranos
Spiritual Value ★ The Fool can be used whenever you are seeking to stir, awaken, and use the energetic forces of the Universe. You can enhance your natural vitality and sense of wonder by reconnecting with these natural forces.

★ KEY THEMES ★

"Trusting Your Inner Elf"

Fresh Beginnings ★ Adventure ★ Quest ★ Excitement ★ Asserting Your Independence ★ Creative Solutions ★ Spontaneity ★ Egolessness ★ Innocence ★ The Need For Optimism ★ Naiveté ★ Unexpected Opportunities ★ Courage ★ Folly ★ Happy-Go-Lucky Mortal ★ About to Step Off a Cliff Into the Abyss ★ Impulse

Meditation ★ "I have the courage to step forward; I am not afraid of the unknown. I am Divinely protected."

★ *When Working with this Card* ★

MAIN ENERGIES ★ Innocence, Courage, Adventure, Faith
MAIN GOD OR GODDESS TO INVOKE ★ Mars
CANDLE COLOUR ★ White
MAGICAL TOOLS OR SYMBOLS ★ Staff, Travel Sack
CRYSTALS ★ Moss Agate, Clear Quartz, Apophyllite

ASSOCIATED BEINGS, GODS, GODDESSES & ARCHETYPES ★ Primal Humans, The Joker, The Outlaw, The Jester, The Wise Fool, Alecto, Mercury, Mars, Shu, Selk, Thoth, Circe, Anubis, Mystis, Hecate, Danu, Cerridwen, Nath, Tefnut, Mother Earth, the Child of the Great Mother, The Eternal Child.

ARCHETYPES ★ The Fool is the happy wanderer who sees the world through the eyes of an innocent. He represents each of us at our primal cores – naïve travellers through life, embarking on a grand adventure, essentially solo, out to learn whatever experiences are for our betterment and the overall highest good. The Fool is the Divine Child, Jung's *puer aeternus* or Eternal Child, the Hero or Heroine, the Wanderer, the Seeker.

> You're only given a little spark of madness. You mustn't lose it.
>
> **Robin Williams**

CHAKRAS ★ Use this card to balance and meditate upon the Sacral and Solar Plexus chakras.

Sacral ★ Below the Navel ★ Orange ★ Water ★ Physical, Sexual, Creative & Material Desires

Solar Plexus ★ Behind the Navel ★ Yellow ★ Fire ★ Personal Power, Confidence & Control

TREE OF LIFE ★ In western magic, which combines the Tarot paths of the Major Arcana with the ten sephiroth on the Tree of Life, the path of The Fool connects Kether and Chokmah.

> Go confidently in the direction of your dreams. Live the life you have imagined.
>
> **Henry David Thoreau**

NUMERIC SIGNIFICANCE ★ The Fool's number is zero. Since zero is not a 'natural' number - we don't use it for addition, subtraction or any basic mathematical purposes - it falls outside the sequence of ordinary numbers and is therefore unbound by rules of order. Zero is the number of innocence. Linked to The Fool, its magical qualities are those of complete trust. Zero inspires leaps of faith - take chances with an open heart and the Universe will support you. Zero is eternity, unbounded and endless, and paradoxically, it is also nothingness. Its symbol, the circle, suggests infinity, but it also conveys restriction - being encircled can leave no choice for room or movement. The Greenwich Meridian in London indicates the point from which time can be measured. On a plaque at that location are the words and figures: "Greenwich 00 ° oo ' E."

"Zero floats freely, outside time and place. The concept of zero implies a sort of non-existence ... It is the great divide, the vaporous border between two parallel universes ... It's not compelled to takes its place in a line-up with other numbers. That concept dovetails nicely with the thought of the Fool, free to come and go throughout the rest of the cards at will."

Corrine Kenner

THE FOOL'S JOURNEY ★ This is where the journey begins, with the Divine Child archetype. The Fool is like an infant who is sent from the higher forces to enlighten the human race. He is at the heart of the Major Arcana, and makes sense of the whole story. The Fool is *you* - and he resides somewhere in every card.

And in our willingness to step into the unknown, the field of all possibilities, we surrender ourselves to the Creative Mind that orchestrates the dance of the Universe.

Deepak Chopra

THE STORY ★ Wide-eyed and innocent as a newborn child, The Fool has descended from the celestial realms, eager to begin his mystical journey on the Path towards enlightenment. All is new to him and he has not yet learned to fear. Living from moment to moment, going forward without plan nor care, unaware of potential perils and joyful, in his luggage he carries the memories, instincts and experiences of past lives, waiting to be utilised afresh this time around. He carries a wand symbolising the pure faith of his actions, upon which sits a head that looks backwards, representing The Fool's past as he moves ever-forward. The dog leaping and bounding behind him symbolises the purity of the animal nature of our physical bodies and is seen in playful harmony with The Fool. The backdrop is suffused with green, the colour of growth, and the sky is filled with the fresh light of a spring season, signalling shining, new life. Like the court jesters who maintained his tradition, The Fool is truthful, and has no contaminating malice or desires.

Failure is unimportant. It takes courage to make a fool of yourself.

Charlie Chaplin

THE MESSAGE ★ The Fool, who is young in years, is the true spiritual guide, and this card's presence suggests that you are entering a new and exciting phase of your life. It is therefore important that you believe in yourself and realise that the benevolent and ever-expansive Universe wishes you to succeed. But he is also telling you to listen to your wiser self, and to think carefully before making any move, reminding you that a thoughtless action will inhibit your progress. Develop a sense of purpose and don't allow yourself to become hesitant or indecisive. You must prepare the ground very thoroughly and make certain that you see every aspect of your present situation clearly and with a calm, resolute mind. Now is the time for faith, belief and commitment to your deepest dreams. Step into - and up to - the challenge. Throw caution to the wind and let it carry you where it will.

Twenty years from now you will be more disappointed by the things that you didn't do than by the ones that you did do. So, throw off the bowlines. Sail away from the safe harbour. Catch the trade winds in your sails. Explore. Dream. Discover.

Mark Twain

THE AWAKENING ★ Do not over-analyse things; sometimes you just have to take chances and risks. This is not the time for sophistication or delving for hidden meanings in the words or actions of others. Be as a child or you will overlook the heaven that is on your Earth. Above all, do not look back, or attempt to anticipate happenings or events. This is a time for innocence and faith; take any necessary steps forward with confidence and hope.

We can be awake - *completely* awake. The process is very natural. It starts when we are children, helpless but aware of things, enjoying what is around us. Then we reach adolescence, still helpless but trying to at least *appear* independent. (Then) we become adults - self-sufficient individuals able and mature enough to help others as we have learned to help ourselves. But the adult is not the highest stage of development. The end of the cycle is that of the clear-minded, all-seeing Child. That is the level known as wisdom ... Return to the beginning; become a child again. The wise are Children Who Know, those whose minds are filled with the wisdom of the Great Nothing, the Way of the Universe.

Benjamin Hoff

THE LESSON ★ The Fool represents the Self on a journey, who grows and learns with each new encounter. He teaches that we must be open our vulnerabilities and frailties, and to plunge into the unknown anyway. As the whimsical and wide-eyed adventurer, he gives us the distinct and exquisite feeling that sometimes taking a leap of faith is the only mode of transportation we have available to us.

Come to the edge.
No, we will fall.
Come to the edge.
No, we will fall.
They came to the edge.
He pushed them, and they flew.

Guillaume Apollinaire

SYMBOLISM ★ The Fool card symbolises the state of potential from which all possibilities arise. It is the purest embodiment of the self on the quest for spiritual awakening. When The Fool appears in a Tarot spread, it suggests that you are about to embark on a journey that will fundamentally change you - either literally or by changing your outlook on life. You may not be certain of what lies ahead, but you must be willing to take the risk.

The Fool, or Jester, symbolises the ability to laugh, to play, and to make fun and light of yourself and others. He pinpoints truths no one else would dare express because he does so in an innocent, unmalicious, playful manner.

The Fool's staff represents the Suit of Wands, symbolic of passionate, fiery energy. He grasps the staff firmly, as he does all of life's opportunities, and although it is a symbol of power, The Fool uses it in a playful manner.

Above The Fool, and gracing the corner of the card, is the bright Sun, radiating its rays. The luminous sunshine accompanies The Fool because his presence dispels all darkness.

The Fool's cloak is usually blue, representing his inner search for wisdom and truth. And when he finds his enlightenment, he will be eager to communicate it to others.

OVERALL ★ CONNECTING IT ALL UP ★

> The beauty is that The Fool also interacts with our moments of joy and sorrow in the everyday events depicted in the Minor Arcana. More than just a friend, The Fool is our guide, master and hope.
>
> **J. Drane, R. Clifford & P. Johnson**

The Fool is usually the first card in the Tarot deck, the starting point of the Tarot experience. In some early decks, he appeared at the end of the Major Arcana rather than at the beginning, as he not only begins our journey but may also accompany us throughout it - this is essentially because he symbolises our very self. When he first sets out at the beginning of his Path, he is a stranger to his inner self and lives primarily in his conscious mind, but by the end of his journey he has glimpsed the deeper mysteries of his real self. The Fool seeks the truth, and turns his attention towards the spirit in search of it. There is in The Fool an element of the Divine trickster, and even though The Fool doesn't know what he is doing in the sense of logical thought, he moves from an impulse that arises out of the infinite possibilities emanating from the state represented by the number 'zero'. The Fool is simple, innocent, trusting and ignorant of the potential trials, setbacks and pitfalls that await him, and he is prepared to abandon his old ways and follow his quest by taking a leap into the unknown. Indeed, The Fool represents the need to let go of old ways and begin something new, untested and unexperienced. For those willing to follow The Fool's example and deviate from the path society has set out for us, this leap can bring joy, adventure, and finally, for those with the courage to continue even when the Path becomes fearsome, the leap will bring peace, knowledge and liberation.

Interestingly, in some early Tarot decks, The Fool appeared as a giant court jester, towering over those around him, his title the 'Fool of God'. The term has also been used for harmless madmen, idiots and fitful people, all of whom were thought to be in touch with a greater wisdom only because they were disconnected from the rest of us. This archetype persists in modern mythology also.

The card depicts The Fool wandering off, his few possessions slung over his shoulder in a small bag hung from a pilgrim's staff, oblivious to the chasm ahead, with his dog jumping at his leg. Symbolically, his bag carries his experiences. He does not abandon them, for he is not thoughtless, they simply do not control him in the way that *our* traumas or memories so often control our lives. The stick upon which his bag casually hangs, is, in some interpretations, actually a wand, a symbol of power and magic. The Fool card's image symbolises the instinctive life force that both holds him back and urges him on. Like its ruler Uranus, The Fool is the spirit of chaos, of the unexpected, but also about innocence and the simple joys of living. This card belongs anywhere in the deck, in combination with and between any of the other cards, offering an animating force to more static images and symbols. As such, he assists during times of transition, and also in times of difficult passage.

Containing all possibilities, The Fool represents the phenomenon of synchronicity or coincidences between happenings, and is the part of us that unconsciously connects to the greater Universal whole, so things are constantly happening to us that involve the unspoken and often unacknowledged links between our thoughts and the events outside of ourselves. If you are open to magic, you will accept these synchronicities on an intellectual level, and in turn will notice such events more frequently and learn to appreciate them more fully.

This card can be said to represent the human soul that is unselfconsciously happy to be alive, that does not yet reflect back upon itself, the spark of life that reincarnates again and again until it truly awakens to itself. Reincarnation is the secret key to The Fool, and The Fool is indeed the 'secret' key, or at least significantly the first door which opens us up to the rest of the Tarot experience. The Fool, whose awareness is limited to the present moment, moves from moment to moment, life to life, without intellectual consideration or care for what has gone before and what will be in the future. Representing innocence, The Fool is perpetually young and always starting afresh. He believes in himself and instinctively trusts his body and the general flow of life.

Astrologically, The Fool is ruled by the Air element, making it as free as the wind. Uranus, considered the most eccentric of the planets, gives the card's symbolism qualities of intellectual brilliance, intuitive flashes, lawlessness, reform, inventiveness and originality. Linked to this rebellious planet, it also promises mystery, a dash of genius, adventure, and a great opportunity to reinvent your life. It impels you to listen to your own inner guidance about following your dreams while still staying open to outside guidance and information; actively seek any insight you may need for your leap.

Although some divinatory meanings of this card are thoughtlessness, insecurity, folly, apathy, frivolity, extravagance, lack of discipline, immaturity, irrationality, hesitation, indecision, delirium, frenzy, enthusiasm and naivety, it also proclaims that nothing can harm you, whatever you do, so take a risk! It does, however, advise to look before you leap - a measured, calculated risk will reap the greatest rewards - and lessons. This card symbolises new beginnings in all senses, courageous leaps into some new phase of life, and is a particularly potent symbol when that jump is taken from some inner prompting and deep feeling rather than careful planning. Such is the nature of erratic and unpredictable Uranus.

Not limited by ordinary social conventions and uncomplicated and unanalytical by nature, The Fool is never afraid to believe in something Divine or greater than ego. Naturally flowing, trusting, naïve and spontaneous, The Fool often plunges into the cosmic experience without fear or expectation.

It is The Fool in each of us which urges us away from lethargy and towards enlightenment and transformation without fear of the future. The Fool is the part of you who, paradoxically, does not worry about being foolish but at the same time, is probably more open to the accusation. He represents the part of ourselves who simply doesn't care what other people think or how things might look. In this way, The Fool enjoys a charming, playful sense of life and a willingness to try new things, regardless of potential consequences or outcomes. He can be an agent of awakening and signifies a ripe time for our inner child to emerge.

The Fool is an adventurous card, always ready to change, and is a great agent of luck and possibility. It suggests that unconventional people will enter your life throughout your travels to share a part of your journey with you, and it also tells you to expect the unexpected at all crossroads. It signifies that an unexpected influence will soon come into play, such as the possibility of adventure or escape or sudden opportunity. Trust yourself, for even if he is afraid, The Fool is able to win others over with instinctive wit, innocent and kindness, opening up doors for opportunity to enter everywhere he goes. The Universe seems to favour those who are open and willing to be moved and carried along by its flow, and blesses them with growthful and delightful experiences.

The Fool's number is zero (or unnumbered, like the Joker in a deck of playing cards), the circle, the symbol of eternity, symbolising the ending of the journey back at the beginning, wise and transformed by your travels. It can also be regarded as unnumbered, and has been placed at number 22. The most complex and 'human' of the cards, The Fool, the innocent, the wise man, the trickster, embodying all of humanity's contradictions (male/female, good/evil, angel/devil, etc.), The Fool is a symbol of spirit, spontaneity, openness to life and receptivity to opportunities. Trusting that love flows through the Universe will allow your desires to emerge into reality. To really know The Fool is to one's 'inner elf', the eternal, innocent joker who lives just outside the restrictive boundaries of externally-imposed ideas of Self.

When working with this card, bear in mind that it is said to represent the person who is the subject or enquirer in the reading. Ask the subject, or yourself, what they or you hope to gain from your journey through the Tarot. It is also worth noting and reminding yourself that even a fool can have flashes of great wisdom and sudden lightning bolt thoughts, reminiscent of the brilliant but ever-unpredictable Uranus, ruler of this card.

★ HOW THIS CARD RELATES TO URANUS & THE ELEMENT OF AIR ★

The Fool, who doesn't care what society thinks, is assigned to Uranus,
the planet of rebellion and revolution.

Corrine Kenner

The Fool is a foolish man. And as such, he knows everything, but is unaware that he does. Or, he possesses all the gifts, all the truths, all the wisdom, all the joys, all the wonders of the seen and unseen worlds, but is not fully conscious of this. He must therefore submit himself to the various trials of life to develop his faculties and become an enlightened being. These are the lessons of the planet Uranus, and the element of Air, for both have the potential to become powerfully illuminating forces, which can light up the sky of any willing recipient's world with their knowledge. The Fool is an idealist, a master of initiative, change, the tearing down of the old to make room for the new - much like his planetary connection Uranus. Both are also regarded as freedom-seekers, rebels, and eccentrics, unable - or perhaps unwilling - to meet the social norms and expectations which surround them. Both are willing to take a chance on the extraordinary, and as quintessential free spirits, they will take the leap, lunging ahead without regard for the past, the present or the future. The Fool represents blind trust in the Universe, an innocent faith and knowing that cannot be seen or touched, and the Air element embodies this principle also, relying on the ethereal all-seeing wits of its own mind to take bold and unexpected leaps into the unknown. The Fool, albeit a character who is supposedly symbolically just starting out on the journey of life, is a beginner, but he also carries a wealth of wisdom, genius and insights within the bag slung over his shoulder. But, like the Air element and the planet Uranus, his talents must be tuned in, plugged in, electrified in some way, for their sparks to be of effect. If both can plug their innate knowledge and arcane, all-knowing wisdom into the power-point of the Universal stream of consciousness, then they can indeed light up the entire sky and fulfil - and share - their inborn abilities for deep cosmic understandings. The Fool, the Air element, and Uranus, being made up of the unknowable and ungraspable 'fifth element' of ether, each *know*, without question, that every being's soul's blueprint, past and future is already laid out in the Akashic Records *.

* In Eastern mysticism and occultism, the 'Akashic Records' are an all-pervading life principle or all-pervasive space of the cosmos. The akasha is the substance ether, a fifth element and the subtlest of all the elements, and in yoga the akasha is one of three universal principles along with *prana*, the Universal life force, and creative mind. It is said that everything that ever happens throughout the Universe - every emotion, thought, sound, action and so forth - is recorded permanently upon the akasha. The Akashic Records is a term coined in the late nineteenth century, from *akasha*, the Sanskrit word for 'aether', 'space', 'luminous' or 'sky', and is a cosmic compendium of thoughts, emotions and events that exist beyond time and space. The Akashic Record is believed by Theosophists to be a kind of life force which contains information on all that has occurred and all that will occur. These records of past and future events, ideas and actions, are believed to be encoded in a non-physical plane of existence known as the astral plane and were referred to as "indestructible tablets of the astral light" by H.V. Blavatsky, occultist, spirit medium, author and co-founder of the Theosophical Society in 1875.

✯ DIVINE MANIFESTATION USING THE FOOL ✯

You can Divinely manifest things in your experience through tapping into your inner Trust.

The Fool is a paradox, in that he is the end and the beginning. He is the Divine Child in all of us, yet possesses a certain faith, a distinct knowing, a strong trust that he has come forth into form to find and follow an authentic, true path. You can use The Fool for Divine Manifestation by tapping into your trusting, innocent, inner child, who knows exactly what to do. Meditate on this child, the person you were before you became tainted, conditioned, swayed by the people and the world around you. What is your ideal situation? How would you live a life that aligned perfectly with your highest self? For a moment, exclude all other people, obstacles, blocks and setbacks that may prevent you from achieving your Divine Life and highest self. In other words, what would your ideal life involve if you had all the money, approval and support from others, time, freedom and supreme health and vitality to achieve it? Is there any chance that you can take little leaps across the great chasm of life? The Fool, although a foolhardy adventurer who takes giant leaps, tells you to re-connect with your Inner Child, that spirit within whose candle stays alight all the days of your life, no matter how far off-course you get. It is this pure, unaffected spirit within who knows what you should do. Through meditation, listen to this voice's gentle whispers, telling you to take that leap of faith. And never fret, the Universe has your back. Whatever will be will be. Trust.

★ EXERCISES TO TAP INTO YOUR INNER FOOL ★

★ Choose one incident or time in your life where you have done something with blind faith (even if you were afraid). Have you ever taken a leap into the unknown, based on a whim, or is spontaneity something that comes quite naturally to you? Have you ever taken the plunge into something new and exciting? Have you ever chosen the path less travelled? What results did it yield? What lessons did it teach you? Are you glad that you took the chance? Would you do it again if you had your time over? Reflect about something you have done in your life that was based on fear and trust at the same time, something you have done out of the ordinary, out of your comfort zone, or completely against your character.

★ Think about your mild fears. Then, do something that you are afraid of, no matter how small. You will probably find that it wasn't as hard as you thought. Take one small step towards a big dream or desire that you currently have. Have confidence that the Divine will take care of the details for you, and has your back if you just take one small step into unknown, never-chartered-before territory. It can be wonderful swimming in the waters of faith, courage, flow and trust, and further endows you with the strength to undertake new, different adventures on an ongoing basis.

★ THE MAGICIAN ★

Ruled by Mercury

Number ★ 1
Astrological Signs ★ Aries, Gemini & Virgo

Keywords ★ Initiative, Will, Mindpower, Independence

Magical Title ★ Magus of Power
Divinity ★ Hermes
Spiritual Value ★ The Magician himself is the house in which the Divine Spirit dwells. He is the director of channelled energy. This card may be used when you need to fix your focus to accomplish a single purpose or intention. The Magician develops your internal visions and insights, and gives you the capacity to do something about your conditions to gain control over what is happening at any given moment. It can also help you to develop your intellectual mind, your creativity, your expression, and your interest in science and books.

★ KEY THEMES ★

"Dancing in the Fire of Life"

Opportunity ★ Initiative ★ Interesting Prospects ★ Free Will ★ New Ventures ★ Intelligence ★ Apprenticeship ★ Potential Talents or Qualities Shining Through ★ Ability to Convince Others ★ Originality ★ Spontaneity ★ Flexibility ★ Possibilities ★ Skill ★ Adaptability ★ Duplicity ★ Free Spirit ★ Power ★ Influence ★ Cunning

Meditation ★ "I have the willpower, magical tools and initiative to create my own experiences. I am spiritually, mentally, emotionally, psychically and physically equipped to exercise my unique brand of personal power to manipulate the inner and outer worlds to suit my needs, for the ultimate benefit of all. I will use this power wisely."

★ *When Working with this Card* ★

MAIN ENERGIES ★ Personal Power, Initiative, Will, Independence
MAIN GOD OR GODDESS TO INVOKE ★ Mercury / Hermes / Thoth
CANDLE COLOUR ★ Orange
MAGICAL TOOLS OR SYMBOLS ★ Pentacle, Wand
CRYSTALS ★ Labradorite, Amber, Merlinite, Emerald, Tiger's Eye

ASSOCIATED BEINGS, GODS, GODDESSES & ARCHETYPES ★ Wizards, Ancestral Spirits, Archangel Uriel, Logos, the Trickster of Mountebank, Daimones *, Hermes ^, Mercury, Thoth, Odin, Danu, Lugh, Ogma, Gwydion, the Morrigan, Lleu, Minerva, Luna, the Dagda, the Alchemist, the Magus, Merlin.

ARCHETYPES ★ The Magician is the skilled and cunning master of all he encounters. He represents an individual in control and charge of life's techniques and tools, and is the strong-willed powerful game-player and game-changer. He is the Magus, the Mystic, the Alchemist, the Shaman, the Trickster, the Psychopomp, the Wizard.

* In Greek mythology, daimones are a type of spirit or intelligence between gods and humans. Daimones means 'divine beings' and they include various classes of entities, such as guardian spirits of places, tutelary spirits, genii, demigods, and ministering spirits. They can be either good or evil in nature (a good daimon is called an *agathodaimon*).

^ Hermes, the Greek messenger god, known as Mercury in the Roman pantheon, represents wisdom, cunning, magic, spiritual illumination, mischief, and skill with words and expression. Wings on his feet sped him on his missions as the communicator between the gods or between the gods and mortals. Known as the gatekeeper, the patron of the traveller, and as a god of healing, Hermes carries a caduceus which he uses as his magic wand. Clever, crafty and sly, he is the trickster, guide, scoundrel and magician, who deceives with his eloquent wit and spellbinding charm.

CHAKRAS ★ Use this card to balance and meditate upon the Sacral, Third Eye and Crown chakas.

Sacral ★ Below the Navel ★ Orange ★ Water ★ Physical, Sexual, Creative & Material Desires

Third Eye ★ Between the Eyes ★ Dark Blue ★ Light ★ Clairvoyance, Wisdom, Intuition & Vision

Crown ★ Top of Head ★ Purple ★ Thought/Knowing ★ Spiritual Wisdom & Enlightenment

TREE OF LIFE ★ In western magic, which combines the Tarot paths of the Major Arcana with the ten sephiroth on the Tree of Life, The Magician represents the path from Binah to Kether (The Magician raises one hand aloft to draw down the creative energies of Kether, which may then be transmitted further down the Tree). As he is also linked mythically to Toth, in this capacity as the Logos of the Universe and a higher form of Hermes/Mercury, The Magician is associated with Hod, lower down the Tree.

NUMERIC SIGNIFICANCE ★ The number one represents the source of all existence. Oneness preserves the integrity of creation, and cannot be divided without losing its integrity. In the beginning, there was one: the absolute, the all in one, the one in all. This one is the "I" of the Universe, represented by a rod or, in alchemy, a serpent. It is the absolute symbol of masculinity, the active, engendering principle. Alchemists talk about one truth, one matter, one process: "One is the All, and by it the All, and in it the All, and if it does not contain the All it is nothing." It is usually represented as a point or circle. Finally, there is the monad, considered by the

Renaissance alchemists, philosophers and esoteric practitioners to be the great, unifying principle and soul of the world. Ruled by the Sun, number 1, which is truly indivisible, signifies power, stoutness of heart, independence, action and responsibility, as does the Magician whose number it is. Number one represents beginning and the primal cause. A symbol of creation and the human species, it is depicted in the standing stone, the upright staff and the erect phallus. In the Native American Earth Count, one represents Grandfather Sun and fire, the spark of life. A very powerful number, it represents unity and wholeness. In Pythagorean theory one represents the masculine principle, and is the first masculine number and the number of beginnings, and is therefore considered to be the number of the Universe and the highest order. In sacred geometry, one is linked to the Greek primordial Monad, which, when interpreted, means 'Divine Fire', 'Divine Spark' or 'Logos of Life'. The number one, just like the Magician with which it resonates in the Tarot, stands for all that is strong, individual, original, wilful and creative.

THE FOOL'S JOURNEY ★ Here's where The Fool discovers his creativity and talent for using various tools to achieve his goals. The Jungian archetype for The Magician is the Trickster, such as the Native American coyote.

I am Thoth, master of divine words, he who acts as interpreter to all the gods.

Thoth, Ancient Magician God

THE STORY ★ The Magician is an effective, powerful man with a strong focus upon goals. He makes plans and then fulfils them. He is a skilled and clever character, who performs occult rituals, pouring energy from his extended hand which erupts into a pillar of living fire. As fire can transform what is added to it, this shaman can transform one thing into another: clay into brick, water into steam, fire into embers. While The Fool before him symbolises the unconscious, untainted mind, The Magician is the embodiment of conscious knowledge, with its ability to know and therefore manipulate the outside physical world. Like The Fool, The Magician wears a pointed hat, the apex of which alludes to the ability to draw down cosmic forces. On the table (or altar) before him lie a Pentacle, Cup, Sword and Wand; each is a token of his use of and mastery over the four elements. The Magician offers a choice of directions and the opportunity to take one of them; the Cup represents the realm of feeling and relationships; the Sword is connected with the mind and the logical, rational world; the Wand symbolises creativity and imagination; and the Pentacle is associated with the material, the body and the physical world. Opportunities are available in each, or all, of these areas. He represents vigour and talent in any chosen area, which are backed up by a strong urge or pull. Overall, The Magician represents desires made manifest on Earth through the power of thought. He is the mediator between the spiritual and the physical worlds, and with initiative and cunning, he decides which ideas will be made real.

Great heart will not be denied.

J. R. R. Tolkien

THE MESSAGE ★ You are ready! Indeed, this card signals an effective commencement of a project which is grounded in reality. You realise that you can bring about desired effects through using specific tools that are at your disposal. This gives you a special sense of power, and enables you to choose a specific goal or path and work towards it. Even though your methods and motives may focus on self-interest and grandiosity, you have the resources or the ability to manifest them. Life is indeed *magical*.

> Do not go where the path may lead, go instead where there is no path and leave a trail.
>
> **Ralph Waldo Emerson**

THE AWAKENING ★ You are undertaking or achieving something new, and are starting a period in your life where you can exert your free spirit and willpower. If your willpower is consciously and assertively directed, you can now accomplish all that you visualise. The Magician impels you to go forward into the world and use your skill and intelligence to produce magical results.

> The tools or objects used in making magic are essential, although they are just tools. They hold no inherent power within themselves, but focus and refine the power within you. They are visual and manual aides or symbols to help in contacting the subconscious mind and persuading it to work the magic you desire. Any magical implement is an expression of a magician's will and the ability to carry out that will.
>
> **D.J. Conway**

THE LESSON ★ Generally, The Magician signifies fresh beginnings, the start of a new phase or cycle, and a directed sense of purpose. The Magician is a card of potential which points to the importance of a new enterprise. It's time to forget false modesty and to strike out in a new, dynamic, bold direction. Capitalise on your imaginative and creative skills. The fresh start The Magician implies should not be entered into lightly - there's often an element of trickery or doubt surrounding this card, however it is particularly auspicious for business ventures and financial matters because it shows that you have what it takes to succeed; indeed, all the necessary tools are at your disposal.

> Strong reasons make strong actions.
>
> **William Shakespeare**

SYMBOLISM ★ From the as-yet-untapped potential of The Fool, The Magician emerges as the determination to make things happen. This card therefore denotes confidence, decisiveness and an awareness of one's personal power and effect. You actually have the knowledge, skills and experience at hand but you must now concentrate on using these skills and also on marketing them. There is a suggestion that even if you don't feel confident, you should do your best to appear so, and you may need to use an element of trickery to achieve this - or to get what you want.

Its symbolism is youthful and dynamic, hinting at the vast creative forces being channelled through the body of The Magician with the help of the tools that are laid out before him, using these elements for the manifestation of his desires.

The Wand the Magician is pointing towards the sky symbolises his use of it to access Universal forces in order to amplify the power of his will and intentions.

The Magician's right hand, the symbol of action, points downwards to the four Tarot tools anchoring the energy. The inspiration gained through his spiritual connection with the Universal forces needs Earthly energy, so his body acts as a conduit for these ends.

In most cards, he is represented as a travelling entertainer, a 'showman', part mountebank, part wise-man, and possibly also a trickster and illusionist. The Magician, in medieval Europe, lived on the fringes of the law and was regarded with a mixture of fascination and suspicion by the authorities and the people. He is always number One - at centre stage and in the spotlight. This apparent forthrightness can be misleading, for there is always something going on behind the scenes - sometimes even deception. The image exudes originality and confidence, which associates it with positive action, cleverness, cunning, individuality and creativity.

OVERALL ★ CONNECTING IT ALL UP ★

The first step to becoming is to will it.

Mother Teresa

Traditionally The Magician is ruled by Aries, tying in with the fact that both Aries and The Magician are number one in their respective astrological and Tarot sequences. As such, The Magician represents the ego, sitting like the Sun at the centre of the personality, with the fire of will manifesting his desires into reality through the power of initiative.

The Magician's number is 1, the symbol of a new beginning, and the brim of his hat forms a number 8, the symbol of infinity and eternal life. He is depicted wearing a long robe and standing before a table, upon which lies a Cup, Wand, Sword and Pentacle, representing the four suits of the Minor Arcana, and the elements of Water, Fire, Air and Earth, which in turn stand for feeling, intuition, thought and sensation, the four functions of human consciousness. The four types of divination used that correspond with each element are (respectively): hydromancy, pyromancy, aeromancy, and geomancy. He holds a wand in his hand, and sometimes appears with a serpent coiled around his waist, combined to signify a person of authority with the power to do good. Surrounding him are greenery and flowers. He holds the wand towards the heavens, to symbolise the purity of his higher aspirations, while the other hand points downwards, towards Earth and matter.

The Magician is often dressed in white and red to represent spiritual purity and passion, demonstrating the essential duality of his nature. He is connected with the Greek Hermes, messenger of the Gods; he stands for the link between the gods and men, and this can also be perceived as the link between the conscious and the unconscious mind.

The Magician represents a child, an adolescent, a young boy or girl, a student, a person who is young at heart, open-minded, inquisitive, and dynamic; someone with a youthful temperament or demeanour, whatever their age; somebody who undertakes or achieves something new, or who is starting a period in their life where they can exert their free-spirited essence.

The alchemy of Fire is The Magician's great secret. His activating power changes one thing into another; he represents the toolmaker, the wand-pointer and the shaman. Of all early humankind techniques, fire was the most powerful and versatile. Recent archaeological research suggests that fire has been intelligently used for as many as five million years. It allowed ancient and primitive people to turn grain into bread, clay into bricks, and matter into ashes. As groups congregated around the central hearth fire, its warmth and light could protect them, as well as evoking a magical sense of sacred power embodied within the flames. The Magician as shaman demonstrates the channelling of healing heat - the Fire of the Universe coming through the human being. Like any shaman, The Magician is a mediator between two worlds - the inner, spiritual plane and the outer, physical plane.

Without The Magician's connection to magic and the sacred rites of Fire, the ego becomes egocentric and regards itself as the centre of the Universe. The Magician's stance in this card allows for eye-to-eye contact with Divinity, while simultaneously touching the more physical elements of Water and Earth - the Cup and Pentacle on his table. He knows that the ego must mediate between nature and the Divine and finally come to understand that the two are in fact *one*.

The Magician symbolises the complex nature of the world, of life and reality. He tells us that the Universe is a formidable cosmic game, and that reality is an illusion, a projection of our consciousness, and not to be trusted without question. He appears wise but he is also artful and cunning; his sideways glance puts us on our guard. In a spiritual context, The Magician shows that it is time to put intuition and psychic abilities to practical use. The Magician can also announce the arrival of an important man into the life of a woman, and in this case, he will be amusing and intelligent.

This card stands for the availability of options in many areas, and offers the enthusiasm to follow hunches or one's intuition. When it appears in a reading, it means you have the gift of energy; you are motivated to do, to act, to go forth. You may feel goal-directed now, with a strong sense of purpose and direction. There is warmth to your personality, a radiant self-confidence that impels you to take a stand, affirm an idea you believe in, or undertake something creative in order to get what you want. What you want may be personal and self-centred, or it may be directed by a higher will that you are channelling. The Magician knows that creative achievement demands a certain diligence, self-discipline, craftiness and wiliness, and that if one wants to manifest something worthwhile, then they need to visualise the goal and work toward it without getting distracted. In the arts of healing and magic, intention is *everything*. So, hold the end result in view and get to work. All ideas need a channel to bring them down to Earth, to make them real on the physical plane, otherwise they may fade away into the ether, unrealised and unmanifested. Indeed, you must remember that The Magician works with both forms and the formless, and with The

Magician on your side, you should be able to accomplish whatever you set out to achieve.

The Magician stands for a teacher-guide, a person who offers education and enlightenment to all pupils attending the first lesson in the School of Life. The energy embodied in The Magician is that of purpose, action, intention, potential, skill, craftiness, creativity and will. The Magician tells us that we all have the ability to get on with life, as long as we acknowledge and accept there are obstacles to be overcome. He also challenges us not to be deceived by the transient, material world. He indicates an important new beginning, suggesting a time of action, skill, potential and creative initiative. The tools needed for the onward journey are available, but steps may not yet have been taken towards achievement of the goal. This card suggests new opportunities for intellectual or creative pursuits and the possibilities for new adventure and fulfilment. It is time to bring all aspects of our life together - love, emotions, finances and morality - and to prepare for changes in moving forward.

The Magician suggests also that you should be more aware of your weaknesses - self-awareness is an important element of psychological wholeness. Do not rush into decisions, as impulsiveness may cause trouble in the future, but aim to be calm and practical. Be aware that you are in a position to influence others now *and* in the long-term, but discretion is vital. Your originality and compassion are highlighted here, but beware of being too clever or manipulative.

This card signals that now is the right time to begin new projects. If you have any doubts about your ability to manifest your dreams, leave them behind. In fact, the more self-confidence you cultivate, the more success you experience. Although you may not be feeling ready to move forward upon your Path, you're actually more prepared than you realise. Your life experiences have trained you for this moment, and the opportunities that are now presenting themselves to you are magical. It is not necessary to take any more classes or read any more books, which only serve as further delays to your walking through that golden door that is open for you right now! Take focused action with respect to any plans you may have been preparing for.

When working alongside The Magician in your Tarot journey, ask yourself how you can begin to shift your focus in life from external things to your inner self, as by looking inward you can discover even greater treasures than the material world can offer. Its divinatory meanings are originality, individuality, positive action, creativity, self-reliance, imagination, self-confidence, spontaneity, ingenuity, flexibility, self-control, deception and mastery. Generally, he signifies new beginnings, the start of a fresh cycle, a sense of purpose, willpower and initiative. The Magician is a card of potential, showing the importance of a new enterprise. The Magician is ultimately imparting the message that a great reserve of power and energy is available, and it is up to the seeker (you) how it will be used. Powerfully, he shows us that life is a magical act, and our mind the magician. Go forth and make your claim because you are ready and magical circumstances abound!

★ HOW THIS CARD RELATES TO MERCURY ★

The Magician, the master of banter and fast talk, is assigned to Mercury, the planet of speed and communication. You'll often see him pointing heavenward, conveying messages from the heavens above to the Earth below ... Mercury comes to life in the form of the Magician - the master of space, time, and cosmic energy.

Corrine Kenner

In Rome, the archetypal Magician was known as Mercury (in Greece, he was known as Hermes). Trickery, cunning and cleverness are the key links between Mercury and The Magician. Both get by on their wits, and while not always resorting to deception, they have an uncanny way of morphing, distorting and twisting their essences in order to obtain that which they desire - much like a real magician. The Magician's meaning suggests that the mind is more powerful than matter, and that we can change our world by changing our perceptions of it. Mercury and The Magician are also the Master Charmers, and can disappear into the ether if someone or something threatens to tie down their essentially free and difficult-to-pin-down nature. The Magician is a channel for transformation and change, in every sense of the words, and as such he conducts energy from the ether through his body, using that power to manifest and manipulate his own reality. He embodies the Hermetic maxim, "As above, so below," demonstrating that we are both the microcosm *and* the macrocosm. There are no emotions involved in this principle, for both are concerned with the mind as well as activity and manifestation. Neither the Magician nor Mercury care about your acceptance, nor your understanding, they simply want you to come along for the adventure - and get lost in alchemical wonderlands with them if you so choose. Take their hands, and they will do one of two things - help you transform yourself through new ways of doing, thinking about or seeing things, or they will shape shift, leaving you standing in the cold lab of reality, bewildered and alone - but nevertheless somehow changed for the better.

★ DIVINE MANIFESTATION USING THE MAGICIAN ★

You can Divinely manifest things in your experience through tapping into your inner Will.

The Magician is your inner Alchemist, who knows the way through his innate knowledge of magic, spells, and invocations. He seeks, accesses and hand-picks resources of all kinds, using his willpower and initiative. He has a profound knowledge of the Gods, Goddesses, Angels, Ascended Masters, and Ancient Ones, and asks their assistance when necessary. But the Magician in you knows instinctively that in seeking the aid of these Divine Helpers, that you are simply accessing the God or Goddess in *yourself*. To use the full powers of the Magician in your daily life, I would suggest setting up a personal altar, table, room, space or corner of your home or garden, and dedicating it to your Magic Self. Whenever you are feeling like raising some energy or becoming a channel for Divine Manifestation, simply go to your special area and state your intention, goal, wish or desire. Some magical tools and symbols for this area could be: a special cloth, something to represent each of the five elements (fire, earth, air, water, spirit - for example, a wand, pentacle, candles, incense, feathers, a god or goddess statuette, chalice, cauldron), crystals, woods, plants, herbs, and much, much more (the only limit is your imagination, and to this, the Magician knows there is no limit). Replenish and use the area often enough so that the energy does not become stagnant. Movement is good, even if you just move the tools around from time to time, or state your wish by holding a crystal in your hands and breathing into it three times. Re-charge your magical tools and cloth under the Full Moon or the Sun once a month. Once you have stated your intentions or dreams once, you can leave it at that, or you can repeat your desires as often as you like. The Magician is independent and a power unto himself, so you make the rules; after all, your Inner Magician is running this show! Ask, Believe, Receive. Be wise. Have fun. Now go forth and create!

★ EXERCISES TO TAP INTO YOUR INNER MAGICIAN ★

★ Write down your strongest desire, goal or wish at this current time. Then reflect upon how you can use your willpower, initiative and inner resources to take the first step along the path towards your goal. Next, write a little list of smaller goals that will lead to the big one. Once you have written down a few steps you could take, begin *now* by taking at least two of those steps.

★ The Magician represents the first step in your practical work. You have probably already taken this first step by determining what, more than anything else, you want to be, do or have. You have set the mark at which you are aiming the entire energy of your life. Think about the resources (internal and external) and innate talents you have at your disposal, and how they could help you achieve this goal. Write them down! Resources could be anything from a philosophical attitude, free time while the kids are at school, a basic knowledge of the law of attraction, perseverance, ability to save small amounts of money steadily, and even other people such as your children, your partner, a boss at work, or a close friend who has achieved something similar. How can you better access or use these resources so that you can develop further along the Path towards your desire?

★ THE HIGH PRIESTESS ★

Ruled by the Moon & the Element of Water

Number ★ 2
Astrological Signs ★ Cancer, Scorpio, Pisces & Virgo

Tarot readers often recognise themselves in the High Priestess. She's a mystic, seated at the gateway between this world and the next. She knows the secrets of the Universe, but she shares them only with the wise.

Corine Kenner

Keywords ★ Intuition, Wisdom, Knowledge, Mystery

Magical Title ★ The Princess of the Silver Star
Divinity ★ Pontos

Spiritual Value ★ The High Priestess is the purest root-essence of consciousness, the direct connection from the highest awareness, across the Abyss, to the middle consciousness. She is the great feminine force controlling the very source of life, gathering into herself all the vitalising forces and holding them in suspension until the time of release. This Arcanum can be used when you are having difficulties discerning the hidden elements of a situation or problem, or when you need to let go of certain emotions, turmoil, entanglements, or things you have become stuck in. It is especially useful when you are experiencing periods of tension, confusion, or anxiety. This card is also helpful during times of difficulties in achieving inner peace, seeking serenity, or when you are aspiring to tap into your truest inner self. The High Priestess can provide inspiration to help you develop your skills of mediumship or psychometry.

★ KEY THEMES ★

"Embracing Your Inner Mysteries"

Desire for Esoteric Understanding ★ Seeking to Uncover Mysteries and Secrets ★ Mystical Powers ★ Dreams ★ Psychic Abilities ★ Unconscious Mind ★ Reliance on Instincts ★ Patience ★ Guided by Intuition ★ Careful Consideration Before Action ★ Inner Calm ★ Knowledge that is Both Inborn and Acquired ★ Experience ★ Forethought ★ Wisdom ★ Purity of Intent ★ Thoughtful Reflection ★ Secret Knowledge

Meditation ★ "I possess a wealth of arcane wisdom, knowledge, secrets and mysteries, which I choose to share with discretion and discernment to those who are ready and willing to receive it. I trust my intuition when selecting these Chosen Ones."

★ *When Working with this Card* ★

MAIN ENERGIES ★ Wisdom, Compassion, Enlightenment
MAIN GOD OR GODDESS TO INVOKE ★ Athena
CANDLE COLOUR ★ Violet / Silver
MAGICAL TOOL OR SYMBOL ★ Book of Shadows
CRYSTALS ★ Amethyst, Purple Flourite, Moonstone, Pearl, Opal

ASSOCIATED BEINGS, GODS, GODDESSES & ARCHETYPES ★ Nature Spirits, the Anima, the Gatekeeper, Elementals, Daimones, Selene, Isis, Sophia, Mut, Artemis, Diana, Brigid, Oshun, Nephthys, Yemaya, Acantha, Athene, Hippo, Therma, Neptune, Poseidon, Venus, Luna, Gidja, Arianrhod, Ceridwen, Lady of the Lake, the Guardian, the Medium, the Poet, Delphi: Oracle of Knowledge.

ARCHETYPES ★ The name The High Priestess means literally "the chief feminine elder." This label symbolises the original receptive, reproductive and form-building power in the Universe. She is the enigmatic keeper of mystical keys and gateways. Secretive and guarded, she knows the supreme spiritual secrets life holds – but she shares them only with the wise. She is the Magical Helper, the Mystic, the Writer or the Scribe, the Psychic, the Shaman, the Visionary, the Witch, the Guide.

CHAKRAS ★ Use this card to balance and meditate upon the Third Eye and Crown chakras.

Third Eye ★ Between the Eyes ★ Dark Blue ★ Light ★ Clairvoyance, Wisdom, Intuition & Vision

Crown ★ Top of Head ★ Purple ★ Thought/Knowing ★ Spiritual Wisdom & Enlightenment

TREE OF LIFE ★ In western magic, which combines the Tarot paths of the Major Arcana with the ten sephiroth on the Tree of Life, the path of The High Priestess connects Tiphareth and Kether.

No one can give wiser advice than yourself.

Marcus Tullius Cicero

NUMERIC SIGNIFICANCE ★ Two represents duality and its Roman numeral representation is II, like the black and white pillars on either side of the High Priestess. Two is ruled by the Moon, the planet which fosters harmony by favouring love, union, cooperation, compromise, passivity, diplomacy, tact, negotiation, settlements, and all mutually beneficial ventures. In the context of numerology, two is a soul vibration, making these people sensitive to everything around them. Just like The High Priestess, two is linked to the instinctive, creative and unconscious minds. The number two is essentially a feminine energy which is sensitively tuned to empathy, instinct, caring and intuition. It represents the first divergence from the unity represented by the number one, and as such, signifies the first opportunity for diversity and conflict. On the other hand, it represents the first flowering of the creative principle, and is a symbol of fertility, for male and female, positive and negative, spirit and matter, and also for that part of ourselves that enables us to turn and look at ourselves, allowing for self-reflection and therefore, greater conscious awareness of self. Duality, the number two, or the Duad as it was called by Pythagoreans, represents both diversity and equality or justice. This idea of diversity originates from the idea of two opposites, such as good and evil, night and day, joy and pain, love and hate, riches and poverty. Yet, at the same time, both sides of a question must be always heard, so the number two also stands for concord, harmony, response, balance and sympathy. When early humankind became aware of the binary rhythms upon which the great symphony of nature is based, and which is at the heart of nature itself, it became aware of everything which is double: sky and Earth, male and female, hot and cold, day and night, high and low, life and death, Sun and Moon, inside and outside, pure and impure, good and evil. And so it is with the High Priestess - a deeply aware, wise, instinctive woman who bases all judgement on her firm but flowing intuitive functions.

> Water was the first mirror, and because mirroring is duplication or reflection, the symbolism of water is closely related to the meanings of the number two.
>
> **Paul Foster Case**

THE FOOL'S JOURNEY ★ Although The Magician can control the material world, another world is out there - the hidden, intuitive side of everything. The High Priestess sits between logic and spirit and is associated with the Jungian archetype of the Wise Woman, such as Grandmother Spider in Navajo myth.

> The best and most beautiful things in the world cannot be seen
> or even touched - they must be felt with the heart.
>
> **Helen Keller**

THE STORY ★ The High Priestess is a private, all-seeing and spiritual woman with hidden depths and a deep, albeit veiled, compassion for others. Passive and quiet, she represents a vessel of memory and holy female wisdom. Her powers are so great that they are almost beyond actions, her timeless secrets communicated through an inner voice, and only those wise enough to retreat into silence and undertake thoughtful study will know them. The crown The High Priestess wears as headdress, is reminiscent of the waxing and waning Moon and the natural rhythms of the feminine cycle. These crescent horns of fertility connect her to the Lunar cycle - the waxing Moon forms one horn, the waning its opposite. It doesn't seem to be mere coincidence that the Greek word *delphi* is linked to the word 'uterus' and connects The High Priestess (and women) with prophecy, insights, divination and oracles. The High Priestess effortlessly directs her psychic abilities in harmony with the desires of the Universe that is her child.

> Intuition is a spiritual faculty, and does not explain, but simply points the way.
>
> **Florence Scovel Shinn**

THE MESSAGE ★ The High Priestess is the Seer who tunes into everything happening anywhere, anytime. She represents dreaming consciousness, latent psychic abilities, and the modes of our innermost perceptions. She embodies the highest spiritual values, representing an open door to the sacred realms of mysticism and magic. The High Priestess is telling you to learn from emotional situations. The answers you seek lie in your emotions and feelings, so trust your intuition and the power of your natural psychic abilities. Also, by paying special attention to your dreams and any intuitive messages you receive, you will be accurately guided by them. When she appears in a reading it means your intuition is functioning more strongly than your intellect. A wisdom is activated in you that is older and deeper than your ordinary mode of thinking. She signifies decision-making with an awareness of the hidden and the visible aspects of the situation. Stay open to your emotions and your feelings in order to come into contact with what you already know. Study spiritual topics, and remember that silence and solitude can be golden, as they yield the answers you seek.

THE AWAKENING ★ Selective in your desire for knowledge, you aspire to know and hold the key to life's mysteries, the essential, primordial principles and secrets that are the unique and sacred nature of life on Earth. Silent, secretive, clairvoyant and enlightened, The High Priestess can guide us through the dark wood of ignorance, indicating that reason alone cannot guide us. Her task is to show us the way to the inner world of the collective unconscious. She has a book of wisdom on her lap, with its most esoteric secrets hidden under the edge of her cloak; behind her is the veil between the inner and outer worlds, or the spiritual and the material planes. And although we, as travellers on the Tarot journey, may not yet be ready to part this veil, we are being shown that it exists. Her overall appearance is a message to go quietly within yourself to become aware of your eternal connection to All That Is, and the strength you gain from this knowledge will bring profound insights.

> The main lesson you should learn from The High Priestess is that your personal field of subconsciousness is materially connected with even the most distant of stars, (and) through your personal subconsciousness, you have access to the inexhaustible Universal supply of original material, and you may make it what you will.
>
> **Paul Foster Case**

THE LESSON ★ The High Priestess imparts a simple yet meaningful message: Look for the answers to questions within your heart. Trust your insights, intuition and gut feelings, and act on your hunches. As she also represents learning, she indicates you should undertake a period of study - either formal, or that which comes about through your experience of life. It can suggest the start of training in the Tarot, clairvoyance, astrology, and other mystical studies which rely on intuitive application or psychic attunement. She may also represent unnoticed 'power behind the throne', which indicates hidden influences at work and secrets that may be revealed later. Something may not be currently known to you and you are not in possession of all the facts, so she advises that you wait until these are more fully uncovered to you before making any further moves. She could also indicate a female teacher or mentor will enter your life soon, or that you yourself will have some knowledge and wisdom to share with and teach to others. If you are in the process of trying to answer an important question about your life, The High Priestess invites you to relax and listen to your inner voice. Take a deep breath, and imagine an open, illuminated space in the centre of your chest where all wisdom resides, and let the answer come to you.

SYMBOLISM ★ The High Priestess sits between two pillars representing severity and mercy. Her robes are patterned with pomegranates, suggesting the mystery and richness of life and death. Her robe, her posture, the scroll she holds in her hand, and her crown, symbolise intuition and the ability to listen to, and act upon, inner authority and guidance. Symbolising all that is subtle and 'hidden', she holds the keys to the mysteries of life. She carries the knowledge of occult wisdom, which is accessed through her connection with the deep emotional self, and whereas The Magician in the preceding card manifests his power in more tangible ways and using physical tools, The High Priestess contains the power within *herself*, using her abilities for spiritual growth rather than outward expressions of her forces, and uses only her mind and feelings to achieve this.

The staff she grasps appears to connect both the heavens and the Earth, and symbolises that The High Priestess is the gateway to the conscious mind through the subconscious. She is able to access both spiritual and Earthly mysteries.

Upon her chest, sits a cross. The cross is a symbol of healing, an integrating of the spiritual (vertical) and material (horizontal) dimensions in unity.

The symbols of the temple in which she sits are also revealing. The temple was built thousands of years ago during the reign of King Solomon, and had pillars named 'Boaz' and 'Jachin' (two characters of renown in ancient Judaism), representing the masculine and feminine elements and identified on this card as the initials 'B' and 'J'.

The peacock pictured in some cards symbolises The High Priestess's ability to choose to display her beauty, or to keep it hidden from view.

OVERALL ★ CONNECTING IT ALL UP ★

The wiser a man is, the less talkative will he be.

Ali ibn Abi Talib

The High Priestess is depicted as a regal-looking young lady sitting between two pillars, which represent opposing forces such as life and death; she acts between them. She has always had a spiritual meaning, and in older decks was known as the Female Pope or The Papess. She rules the shadowy world of the unconscious mind and imagination, and symbolises the creative process of gestation; indeed, the foetus must remain in the womb until it is ripe to birth itself, and nothing should be done to precipitate this moment. The lady shown on the card often wears virginal white, signifying unfulfilled potential. In some decks she appears holding a pomegranate, the many-seeded fruit of fertility, suggesting promise for the future. The High Priestess is connected with the Crescent Moon, which symbolises a new cycle of creativity, and she has links with Persephone, goddess of the underworld, and the

Egyptian Lunar goddess Isis (in some cards The High Priestess is depicted wearing the horned crown of Isis).

This card can be a challenging card to interpret because of its hidden, elusive and shadowy quality. Her links with the underworld and the unconscious can suggest that she doesn't reveal her secrets easily. Despite its lack of apparent clarity, its divinatory meanings can be perceived as wisdom, sound judgement, serenity, common sense, penetration, foresight, objectivity, perception, intuition, self-reliance, emotionlessness, and platonic relationships.

When this card appears in a reading, it is necessary to seek understanding and solutions on an intuitive level rather than applying the rational mind. The mysterious world of The High Priestess is one of dreams and intuition, which are mediums through which she can best be approached in the search for meaningful answers. These answers may also come in the form of a secret which will be revealed to you. But some secrets need to be decoded first, in order to be deciphered. In this way, The High Priestess has a lock, but she also provides the key to those who seek it.

She also symbolises a budding potential, indicating that perhaps something is yet to come to fruition and it will only be realised and fulfilled at the right time and place. Her connection with gestation reinforces this, giving the strong message that tells you to make sure the time is ripe before you take action. There is no need to race into action. Take time to gain more insight, as things may not be as they appear on the surface.

If you are a female, The High Priestess is telling you to be confident in your approach to life, its problems and what it has to offer. You are far stronger than you may realise, but must avoid overbearing behaviour. You can maximise your potential by thinking before you speak, and making sure of your grounding before you commit yourself to anything. You may also benefit from higher study and knowledge.

If you are a male, The High Priestess is telling you that you need to become more aware of your feminine side, and allow yourself a freer flow of emotions. You should also listen to your intuition and heed its guidance; it could be a greater help than you realise. Often this card describes a strong feminine influence, and in a man's reading it can represent the most important woman in his life.

Regardless of gender, when this card shows up, it is compelling you to withdraw from the chaos and noise of daily life and seek counsel from your guides and angels. Meanwhile, know that everything you need to know will be revealed in time; you just need to foster patience and be led by your inner knowing.

Know that The High Priestess only exists to help you and respond to your every question. While galaxies swirl above you, pose your query without any attachment to the answer you will receive. In time she will take her hands from behind her back, and in them will be the symbol of your answer.

★ HOW THIS CARD RELATES TO THE MOON & THE ELEMENT OF WATER ★

The High Priestess, the archetypal psychic, is assigned to the Moon,
the luminous orb of reflection and intuition.

Corrine Kenner

Without question, this is the card of intuition, secret knowledge and veiled wisdom, all which have strong Lunar connections and are strongly associated with the Water element. The Moon and that over which it presides, the Earth's waters, both have qualities of ebbing, waxing, flowing and waning, just as instinctual knowing does across the broad and profound spectrum of human perceptions. As the High Priestess is the embodiment of the Moon, the luminary orb of intuition, reflection and illuminating insights, she sometimes keeps her face obstructed from view to preserve the wisdom she shares with a select few. When she is ready to shine, she indeed does, and her Lunar rays can light up the bleakest of landscapes.

★ DIVINE MANIFESTATION USING THE HIGH PRIESTESS ★

You can Divinely manifest things in your experience through tapping into your Intuition.

The High Priestess uses her innate and naturally flowing wisdom and discernment to achieve your spiritual progress. She knows that everything you desire is to achieve the same ultimate goal: you will feel happy in the receiving of it. Her advice to you therefore, is to *be happy now*. If like attracts like and our thoughts are like magnets, whatever you are thinking or feeling, you are by default attracting into your life experience. So often we think it is money we want, or marriage, or joyful work, or children. But what we are *really* wanting out of these things is the feelings of happiness and pleasure they will give us, so if we are desiring money, love, joyful work or children, then what we are really wanting are the feelings they will give us, which could be respectively: security, being loved, fulfilment, and satisfaction. It is really important to use the gentle art of wisdom and discernment when pursuing our goals and dreams, and rather than objectifying them into material categories such as money, love, work or children, we should instead turn our focus to the feelings that they will add to our lives. Only then will you realise that it is not the object that you are chasing, but rather the inner experience you will attain by having it. Once you have decided the feeling behind your deepest desires, your next task is to switch the focus to enhancing and increasing that feeling or emotion in ourselves. Only then can we become a magnet to our desires. In other words, to attract love, you have to radiate love; to attract money, we have to feel rich; to attract fertility, we have to act how we would if we were already pregnant. The examples - and indeed the possibilities - when we practice this and become refined experts at it, are infinite. In her Divine Wisdom, the High Priestess knows that you are so much closer to your desires than you think you are, for all you need to do to bridge the gap, is to feel the way you will feel upon attaining your desire *now*. Then sit back, open the channels, be alert to opportunities and signs, and allow it to come into your experience.

★ EXERCISES TO TAP INTO YOUR INNER HIGH PRIESTESS ★

★ The Four Types of Psychic Ability ~ It helps to determine which one you are for greater self-understanding. Which one are you?

Clairvoyance ★ Means 'clear-seeing'. This describes the ability to see spirit forms. These appear either as a materialisation or in the mind's eye.

Clairaudience ★ Means 'clear-hearing'. This describes the gift of clear hearing and describes one who can hear spirit voices and noises, either inside the head or as external sounds.

Clairsentience ★ Means 'clear-feeling'. This might be experienced as the ability to tune into the atmosphere in a space, or to experience other people's distress as though it were happening to the clairsentient herself. Examples are hunches and intuition.

Claircognisance ★ Means 'clear-knowing'. This is the least well-known of the four psychic talents. It describes the ability to know things without being told and to receive fully formed ideas.

Some ideas you can use for stimulating & determining your psychic ability:

★ Ask the wind for information about a future event. Close your eyes and listen to what the wind and the leaves are saying, as if they are voices.

★ At the beginning of each week, make a positive prediction of something that will happen to a family member or a global event during the week ahead.

★ When you are in another part of the house from your partner, child or pet, call them in your mind. Keep calling softly but clearly and see how long it takes them to respond.

★ Think of a family member or friend you have not seen for a while and look at a photo of them or hold an item of theirs. Say, "Call me or mail me," and picture them carrying out the action. Repeat this five more times during the same day.

★ Focus on a candle flame in a room with no breeze. Concentrate on making the flame rise up or move in a chosen direction.

★ THE EMPRESS ★

Ruled by Venus

Number ★ 3
Astrological Signs ★ Taurus & Libra

There are three things that will endure – faith, hope and love –
and the greatest of these is love.

Paul, 1 Corinthians 13:13

Keywords ★ Nurturance, Fertility, Security, Abundance, Emotional Wealth

Magical Title ★ Universal Mother, Daughter of the Mighty Ones
Divinity ★ Demeter

Spiritual Value ★ The Empress is the root-essence of emotion in its purest form. She is an aspect of Isis, suggesting the creative and positive side of Nature, and expresses the Egyptian trilogy of Isis, Hathor, and Nephthys. You can use this Arcanum when you feel isolated from the world or somehow cut off from your environment. It can help you correct a feeling of inner alienation which may have become an obstacle to your expression and communication with others. Together The Empress and The Emperor (the following card) function as Anima and Animus.

★ KEY THEMES ★

"The All-Providing Supreme Nurturer"

Creation ★ Fertility ★ Emotional Wealth ★ Motherhood ★ Happy, Stable Relationships ★ Growth ★ Lavish Abundance ★ Birthing and Fostering Dreams ★ Art ★ Creativity ★ Affinity with Nature ★ Security ★ Pleasure ★ Harmony ★ Material Comforts ★ Fruitfulness ★ Ripeness ★ Mother ★ Wife

Meditation ★ "I am the lover, the provider, the nurturer and the carer, who bestows myself and others with a free and steady flow of feminine gifts. Abundance, fertility, plenitude and natural Earthly wisdom are my way of life."

★ *When Working with this Card* ★

MAIN ENERGIES ★ Love, Nurturance, Kindness, Generosity
MAIN GOD OR GODDESS TO INVOKE ★ Hathor
CANDLE COLOUR ★ Green
MAGICAL TOOL OR SYMBOL ★ Cornucopia
CRYSTALS ★ Diamond, Green Aventurine, Rose Quartz, Jade, Citrine, Emerald, Aquamarine

ASSOCIATED BEINGS, GODS, GODDESSES & ARCHETYPES ★ Angels, Jupiter, Dionysus, Venus, Demeter, Bes, Anauel, Lakshmi, Euthenia, Artemis, Rosmerta, Gaia, Inanna, Diana, Bast/Bastet, Diakoku, Epona, Ishtar, Hera, Freya, Aditi, Boann, Brigid, the Lady of Flowers, Branwen, Aje, Tsai Shen, Ceres, Mut, Hathor (the Mother of the Universe), the Earth Mother, the Matriarch, the Goddess of Giving.

ARCHETYPES ★ The Empress is the archetypal mother, the supreme nurturer who creates, nourishes and tends to all her creations, including humankind. She is the abundant, flowing life-force of the physical, material plane. She is the Artist, the Creator, the Mother, the Queen, and the Goddess.

CHAKRAS ★ Use this card to balance and meditate upon the Root, Sacral and Heart chakras.

Root ★ Base of Spine ★ Red ★ Earth ★ Security & Survival

Sacral ★ Below the Navel ★ Orange ★ Water ★ Physical, Sexual, Creative & Material Desires

Heart ★ Heart Region ★ Green ★ Air ★ Love & Compassion

TREE OF LIFE ★ In western magic, which combines the Tarot paths of the Major Arcana with the ten sephiroth on the Tree of Life, the path of The Empress connects Binah and Chokmah.

> Beauty is in the heart of the beholder.
>
> **H.G. Wells**

NUMERIC SIGNIFICANCE ★ According to many schools of thought, the number three reigns everywhere in the Universe, just as The Empress's principles of abundance, life and love do. Practically every religious or wisdom tradition has a trinity at its core. The three ingredients of alchemy are known as Salt, Mercury and Sulphur, or body, soul and spirit. With the operation of three forces, we have a living and dynamic situation. There are possibilities for change and growth. Two opposing forces can be reconciled by the third in a new and creative solution. Ruled by Jupiter, three is a lucky number which enhances optimism, self-expression and sociability. Associated with spring, and consequently beginnings, new ventures and fertile phases, three is the number of flowering and expansion. Number one contains the idea, number two is the pair which comes together to carry it out, and number three bears the fruit. Three symbolises the creative process that begins after one becomes two and starts to culminate into 'ten thousand things' - the essence of creation. The number three, or the Triad, was esteemed by many ancient philosophers as the perfect number. From an early age, the idea of 'three wishes' becomes a part of our mythology, it is a part of our collective lore that 'things happen in threes', and it is regarded as powerful and sacred as it represents the manifestation of life itself. It represents the three common stages we all encounter: birth, life and death; and the vessels through which we experience these: body, mind and spirit. There are three primary colours - red, blue and yellow - from which all other colours originate. The Pythagoreans believed in three worlds - the Inferior, the Superior and the Supreme - while followers of Socrates and Plato acknowledged three great principles - Matter, Idea and God. There are three dimensions of space - height, length and breadth; three stages of time - past, present and future; three states of matter - solid, liquid and gaseous; and three kingdoms of nature - animal, vegetable and mineral. Three is a magical number associated with the triple Goddess who moves through the experiences of maiden, mother and crone, and is linked to the Waxing, Full and Waning phases of the Moon. Indeed, the Tarot's Empress embodies all of these principles and concepts.

THE FOOL'S JOURNEY ★ Now that he's learned about his own two sides, The Fool meets the first of the parental archetypes. The Empress is The Fool's Earthly mother. She represents the more accessible, more benign aspects of the female archetype. The Empress is pure emotion, motherhood, love, gentleness, sexuality, passions, fertility, healing, feeling and giving. According to Jungian theory, The Empress is the anima, or the feminine side of the self. The Empress is symbolic of the Earth Mother or nurturer - the archetypal feminine principle in its role of abounding sensual fruitfulness. As such, she signifies benevolence, creation and ripeness. In the sequence of the soul's journey through the Major Arcana, The Empress is the worldly child of The Magician and The High Priestess.

The Empress can be linked to the Full Moon, which, upon reaching its shining bright potential, must slowly fade into the darkness and become a mere sliver. The Fool learns from his Earthly mother about nature, its rhythms and cycles of growth, death and rebirth, and the idea that these cycles are present within all humans. She also imparts wisdom to her 'son' about women and their ways and needs, and how he can care for and nurture himself. She leads by example, and from her The Fool learns how to attend to and respect his own body and needs, and also how to love and cherish others. Attached as he may be to his Empress Earth Mother, he eventually needs to leave her and make his own way in the world if he is to reach his own potential (in this way, The Empress does also have a bittersweet quality, in that she encompasses the loss that most mothers feel when their offspring leave the nest and launch themselves into their own lives).

> The Empress is the deep knowing that every nut, stone
> and leaf is an expression of the Divine plan.
>
> **Paul Hougham**

THE STORY ★ The Empress represents the Great Mother, in all her simplicity and purity. She promises abundance, birth, growth, harmony, community, and relationship. She can represent the Earth from which all life is born, and to which it returns at the end of its cycle. The first Empress-type statues were the small pregnant 'Venus' figurines from the Ice Age in Europe and Russia (at least 30,000 BC). These tiny goddess figures are pregnant to bursting point and generally without distinctive features of face, hands or feet - the emphasis clearly lay upon their full breasts and bellies. Much feminine wisdom has faded with the rise of patriarchal societies in our modern world, but we still hold the basis for these mysteries within our bodies. The Empress in her contemporary 'seductress' pose symbolises the unconscious knowledge contemporary women share of the ancient mysteries and female reverence, of healing and transformation, that live on in our much-diminished but ever-pure Divinity. The Empress feels her connection to the Earth. She knows - has always known - the mystery of procreation, the potential for growing and nurturing life, the sacred act of birthing, and the communal life close to the soil - a time when people did not make war, but spent their leisure time making love and art. The Empress is a sensual, practical woman who appreciates good, wholesome, hearty food, nature and a pleasantly simple life. She is nurturing and generous, and teaches that you need to foster your dreams and desires. If the card preceding this, The High Priestess, holds the secrets of life, then The Empress is what gives that life soul and emotion, for she represents the understanding and the power of that life. The Empress's potency lies primarily in feelings, as she is able to exploit both the riches of the heart and the psyche.

There are three ingredients in the good life: learning, earning and yearning.

Christopher Darlington Morley

THE MESSAGE ★ The Empress, the archetypal fertile Earth Mother, can help bring daydreams to fruition in a world where logic and intuition should dwell together as heaven and Earth do. As such, The Empress is telling you to give birth to your dreams, to nurture yourself and others, spend time in nature, and indulge in creative and artistic endeavours. She suggests a possible pregnancy, a harmonious home environment and progress with your plans. She encourages you to enjoy material comforts and sexual fulfilment but to be wary of overindulgence. Enjoy the beautiful things in life, knowing that you deserve to be exquisitely and Divinely provided for.

THE AWAKENING ★ The realisation that life is inherently a creative process motivates you to explore what brings you harmony. The upsurge of energy and passion that arises with this awakening, attracts cooperation in others, as well as abundance. The Empress helps you to understand that growth occurs only when you nurture your dreams. Have an open and sympathetic heart and your wishes will be provided for. Exert your power with a loving hand and then creativity, productivity, heaven and Earth will all exist for you on the same plane. The Empress dreams a dream that all her unconditionally loved children, whom sprouted from her seed, be fortunate and know the abundance that is their birthright. When agriculture became agribusiness, the life-giving qualities of The Empress seemed lost, and work became the tedium it is for most people today - cut off from any real meaning. The time we stopped loving the Earth as our Mother, and the female as her representative, was the day we left the Garden. The Mother, The Empress, beckons us to return to her before we destroy ourselves. She asks to be re-awakened within us all, so that we might once more experience the bounty, joy and purpose of life on the planet.

> A woman is the full circle. Within her is the power to create, nurture and transform.
>
> **Diane Mariechild**

THE LESSON ★ This is a warmly emotional card, suggesting love, luxury and comfort. When The Empress appears in a reading, you are coming into touch with your ancient sensual nature. She brings out your artistic side, opens up your love of beauty, and heightens your aesthetic appreciation. The Empress represents 'prosperity thinking' and the power of positive imagination. This is a materially and practically inclined card rather than psychically- or spiritually-oriented one, although it does have links with the Divine feminine. She instils the faith that your hopes *will* come to fruition, finances *will* improve, green leaves *will* sprout, shows you examples and symbols that fertility *will* abound, and you *will* begin to feel more confident as you reap the rewards of your efforts. Ask the Great Earth Mother for what you need, for she is the unerring All-Provider. And keep in mind that Venus (Ishtar-Aphrodite), the ruler of this card, is the Wishing Star.

SYMBOLISM ★ The Empress is the third numbered card in the Major Arcana. The number three is indicative of synthesis and harmony, childbirth and maternal productivity. The Empress is shown as an Earth Mother, gentle and caring, surrounded by comfort and plenitude. She wears a crown of twelve stars - one for every month of the year, and every sign of the zodiac. She has been called 'the star-crowned empress, herself the morning star'. This is a direct identification with the goddess Venus, otherwise known as 'the morning star', who, as well as her famed associations with love, is also a deity connected with fruitfulness and harvest.

The left hand of The Empress points towards the sky and the heavens. Her right hand holds a spectre pointing to the ground, symbolising her anchorage to the Earth. She also holds a protective shield with the symbol of an eagle, and is normally depicted in natural surroundings with a stream flowing behind her. The position of her hands connects her with The Magician card and shows that she is the primal creative force, representing motherhood and security, in a way that ultimately brings together heaven and Earth.

OVERALL ★ CONNECTING IT ALL UP ★

> The Earth is our mother ... This we know. All things are connected. Humankind has not woven the web of life. We are but one thread within it. Whatever we do to the web, we do to ourselves.
>
> **Chief Seattle**

The Empress, as the Earth Mother, sometimes appears in a field of corn, symbolising her link with nature. She has a strong connection with motherhood and is portrayed as pregnant, or at least wearing a flowing outfit which hints at it. The Empress nurtures and nourishes, representing any process that involves physical growth and sustenance. Unlike the shadowy, mysterious symbolism of The High Priestess, The Empress dwells in daylight. She is connected with the Greek god Demeter, who brought the crops to fruition and tended the Earth so that mankind could eat.

Still other cards depict a beautiful, serene woman with long, flowing fair hair that resembles the golden fields of corn, dotted with poppies, surrounding her. A waterfall and forest can be seen beyond the rich fields, and at her feet a horn of plenty overflows with fruit, symbolising the Earth's abundant bounty. The Empress is a symbol of potential possibly fulfilled by the hint of pregnancy that her loose and flowing robe suggests. Her robe is adorned with seeded-pomegranates, her lap contains a sheaf of corn, and she wears a necklace of ten pearls, symbolising the ten planets that comprise the Solar system. The twelve stars in her crown represent the twelve months of the year, the twelve signs of the zodiac, and the twelve hours each of day and night; she wears a necklace with four stones, standing for the four seasons of life: birth, blossom, fruition and decay; indeed, all these life stages and processes are presided over by The Empress, and this imagery points to natural cycles, growth, abundance, fertility, and the ever-present possibilities of new life.

The Empress represents a time of passion, a period during which we approach life through feelings and pleasure rather than thought and ideas. This passion can be either sexual or motherly; either way, it is deeply experienced. Marriage, children, and issues involving motherhood and creativity will be positively affected when this card shows up.

The Empress reveals that it is time for birth, whether literal or creative. Whatever has been gestating in the previous card, The High Priestess, is now ready to be born. When she appears in a spread, she denotes a time of growth, of flourishing crops, creative ideas and all things reaching their full maturity. Your creativity and hard work will bring you great rewards, according to this card. You have the Midas touch right now, so anything that you give your loving attention and nurturance to will flourish. This card points to prosperity, material and domestic comforts, security and protection. It is obviously a maternal card so may also indicate childhood, motherhood, reassurance, nurturing and a firm foundation for future progress.

The Empress tells you that your financial position will improve, but you must be circumspect and do everything you can to increase your money in a safe way; she never encourages risk-taking. Emotional security may flourish with this card's presence, business partnerships will be successful, and harmony in your home life will increase - it is even an opportune time to 'add' to your home if you are wishing to do so, as she has some bearing on procreation.

Ultimately, The Empress represents happy, stable relationships, growth and fertility. This card is a symbol of fulfilled potential, creative pursuits, the satisfaction of nurturing something to fruition (as well as the pain of its loss), and symbolises love, marriage and motherhood. Its divinatory meanings are feminine progress, fruitfulness, pregnancy, security, mother, sister, wife, marriage, children, feminine influence, practicality, accomplishment, nurturing, and the ability to gently motivate others.

★ HOW THIS CARD RELATES TO VENUS ★

The Empress, wife and mother, is assigned to Venus, the planet of love and attraction ... The Empress is an archetypal mother who constantly generates new life. Perpetually pregnant, she's a symbol of fertility and growth.

Corrine Kenner

Venus is associated with love, beauty, art, harmony, affection, desire, relating, relationships, pleasure, acceptance, social graces, vanity, sociability, persuasion, luxury, unison, aesthetics, outward style, indulgence, refinement, values, comfort, resources, enjoyment, agreeableness, good humour, symmetry, proportion, mutuality and sympathy. These are all concerns or qualities of the beautiful, pleasure-seeking, abundance-bestowing, fertility-blessing Empress, and indeed in the Rider-Waite deck card image, the symbol for Venus is inscribed upon the heart-shaped shield sitting beside The Empress, suggesting Venus's energy and presence in all her experiences. In keeping with her role as the Morning and Evening Star, Venus rules two signs: Taurus and Libra, and influences their corresponding houses: the second house of money, luxury, aesthetics, comfort and possessions, and the seventh house of marriage, business partnerships, and personal relationships.

★ DIVINE MANIFESTATION USING THE EMPRESS ★

You can Divinely manifest things in your experience through tapping into your inner Creative Artist.

The Empress is the All-provider, who teaches you that abundance is everywhere, if you only open your eyes and your spirit to its vast range of sources. To fully optimise the lessons learned from the Empress, it is important that you examine any lack mentality or scarcity thinking that has been holding you back. Where you are at right now in *every* area of your life - finances, education, relationships, self-love, et cetera - is a direct result of your thinking. If you lack in any area, it is simply a matter of turning the lack into abundance through changing your thinking. You may not have control over your external circumstances, but you always have control over how you use and direct your mind. The Empress teaches us to have a conscious awareness of the correlation between what we are thinking and what we are receiving in the form of our experiences. In other words, through the law of attraction, we are attracting into our lives whatever we are thinking about. This Law is infallible and perfect. If we want to attract riches both inner and outer in our life experience, we each individually hold the key to The Empress's ever-flowing, ever-providing and abundant cornucopia. She provides everything we need, if we can allow our scarcity patterns of thinking to fall away and let the abundance-mentality flood our minds. As well as fine-tuning our thoughts, we can extend our inner wealth outwards, in the form of gratitude, generosity, sharing, and love. There is no lack, only a perception of it, because we have deviated so far from the natural laws in our modern 'human condition'. As above, so below. As within, so without. Be mindful of your thoughts and how they connect with what you are creating in your life.

★ EXERCISES TO TAP INTO YOUR INNER EMPRESS ★

★ Read a book or an article about the Law of Attraction (LOA), a truly amazing phenomenon, with the power to change your life forever. The LOA embodies the pervading force of the Universe, whose primary principle is *abundance*, which is one of The Empress's keywords. Learn everything you can about it and apply its principles in your daily life and thinking; it will richly enhance your life.

★ Manifest something small, like a free item, a gift in the mail, a silver coin, a song on the radio, or a feather, by using the principles you have learned about the Law of Attraction. Write down what you wish to manifest, give it some deep thought, and set the conscious intention that it will happen (don't allow a smidge of doubt to enter your mind as this will contaminate the process; just trust), then place your envelope in a handbag pocket and refer back to it at a later time to determine if it manifested in your experience. If it indeed did, this will give you the confidence that the LOA works. And if you start with the small things, then your faith will grow into asking and receiving ever bigger things. The possibilities are endless; the Universal supply is limitless.

★ THE EMPEROR ★

Ruled by Aries

Number ★ 4
Astrological Signs ★ Aries & Scorpio

Keywords ★ Discipline, Authority, Structure, Influence, Power

Magical Title ★ Chief Among the Mighty, The Son of Morning
Divinity ★ Ares
Spiritual Value ★ The Emperor provides the great energising force to enable you to break free from limiting beliefs or situations, particularly those that you feel trap you. This Arcanum can be used to call upon a higher, perhaps more authoritative part of your being, to ask it to release that part of your character that belongs to the 'old self' that you are trying to transcend. You can use The Emperor's great powers to give you the courage to break free from any difficulties. Together The Emperor and The Empress (the preceding card) function as Animus and Anima.

The Emperor is the centredness with which we might behold the Great Plan.

Paul Hougham

★ KEY THEMES ★

"Trusting Your Inner Authority"

Father ★ Boss ★ Material Wealth ★ Leadership ★ Authority ★ The Power to Influence ★ Organisation ★ Logic ★ Structure ★ Certainty ★ Discipline ★ Temporal Power ★ Action ★ Energy ★ Assertiveness ★ Material and Moral Power ★ Strength of Character ★ Concrete Realism ★ Objectivity ★ Willpower ★ Stoicism ★ Material Status

Meditation ★ "I light the way for others through my natural leadership, resoluteness, iron will, strength, authority, holding true to my beliefs and having the courage of my convictions. Influence, power and dynamism are my way of life, and I am a willing and able guide and supreme example to anyone seeking my counsel."

★ *When Working with this Card* ★

MAIN ENERGIES ★ Power, Authority, Stability, Discipline, Knowing, Empowerment
MAIN GOD OR GODDESS TO INVOKE ★ Saturn
CANDLE COLOUR ★ Brown
MAGICAL TOOL OR SYMBOL ★ Thor's Hammer, Sword
CRYSTALS ★ Jet, Smoky Quartz, Bloodstone, Black Obsidian, Heliodor, Red Jasper, Tiger's Eye, Hematite

ASSOCIATED BEINGS, GODS, GODDESSES & ARCHETYPES ★ The Animus, the Dictator, Archangels, Transhumans, Horus, Saturn, Zeus, Jupiter, Bran, the Great Giver, the Midas, the Father.

ARCHETYPES ★ The Emperor is the authoritative protector, ruler and provider who rules the physical, material world. A father figure, he commands structure out of chaos so that civilisation may prosper. He is the King, the Judge, the Patriarch, the Visionary, the Ruler.

CHAKRAS ★ Use this card to balance and meditate upon the Root, Sacral, Solar Plexus and Throat chakras.

Root ★ Base of Spine ★ Red ★ Earth ★ Security & Survival

Sacral ★ Below the Navel ★ Orange ★ Water ★ Physical, Sexual, Creative & Material Desires

Solar Plexus ★ Behind the Navel ★ Yellow ★ Fire ★ Personal Power, Confidence & Control

Throat ★ Throat Region ★ Light Blue ★ Sound/Ether ★ Communication & Self-Expression

TREE OF LIFE ★ In western magic, which combines the Tarot paths of the Major Arcana with the ten sephiroth on the Tree of Life, the path of The Emperor connects Tiphareth and Chokmah.

> A leader is a dealer in hope.
>
> **Napoleon Bonoparte**

NUMERIC SIGNIFICANCE ★ Four, the number of The Emperor, stands for the four elements of Earth, Water, Fire and Air, the 'building blocks' of creation. Four symbolises structure, stability, integrity and security, because four points come together to form a solid. Four signifies two sets of polarities, but although this creates tension, this tension can be used to create a house, for example, or lay out an arena for action. It can also create an enclosed area such as a philosophical rose garden. There are always battles where four is involved, but there is also potential for constructive work. The usual representation of four is the cross or the square. Four is associated with the four arms of the cross, a very common Earth symbol in ancient cultures and civilisations. Both the square and the cross have also been revered as power symbols which impart strength, will and inspiration. The Quaternary, the number four, or the Tetrad, was regarded by many ancients as symbolic of truth, while the Greeks considered it to be the root of all things. Traditionally the number of the Earth - there are four seasons and four primal elements (Fire, Earth, Air, Water) - four can be said to represent many other things also: the four liberal sciences were considered to be astronomy, geometry, music and arithmetic, four accepted states of death, judgement, heaven and hell, four compass point directions, four winds, four Archangels guarding the Earth (Uriel, Michael, Raphael and Gabriel) and four humours (phlegmatic, melancholic, choleric and sanguine), four limbs of the human body, Four Noble Truths (in Buddhism), the perfect number according to Pythagoras, being the source of ten (1 + 2 + 3 + 4 = 10), and significantly, the four suits of the Minor Arcana (Wands, Swords, Pentacles, Cups) - the number four brings structure and order, which is demonstrated perfectly in the square, an equal-sided, balanced, stable and dependable shape. It is the number of reality, logic and reason. The essence of man's threefold nature - mind, body and spirit - is brought to the material plane, to form a square, symbolising reality and solidity.

THE FOOL'S JOURNEY ★ Just as The Empress is the feminine, The Emperor represents the masculine side of each of us, the animus. This card is about responsibility, authority, and reason, all ideas we associate with a father figure. The Empress is The Fool's mother, The Emperor his father. Leaving behind the natural feminine softness of his mother, The Fool comes across The Emperor, who complements The Empress absolutely by portraying the opposite characteristics. The Emperor is a mature man who is seated upon a brilliant gold carved throne adorned with the heads of eagles. The powerful eagle is a regal bird that is symbolically and literally able to fly higher than any other, with the keenest eyesight of all the birds.

The Emperor wears a gold Crown, a symbol of status and authority. While The Empress reclines comfortably on soft cushions, The Emperor sits bolt upright upon his grand throne, ready for action, conjuring up an impression of power, influence and wealth. As The Empress is the mother, so The Emperor is the father, the giver of life, the 'owner' who has sown the Divine seed. His task is to teach The Fool how to handle the material side of life, and how to live in and deal with the world of men. Instructing him on matters of authority and administration, and imparting guidelines on moral and ethical behaviours, The Emperor teaches wisdom of a worldly nature and is essential to The Fool's development. The Emperor is the dynamic symbol of drive, ambition and fame, and he teaches The Fool about the channelling of energies to make ideas solid and workable. He denotes a time to take control of life in a material and concrete sense.

> If your actions inspire others to dream more, learn more,
> do more, or become more, you are a leader.
>
> **John Quincy Adams**

THE STORY ★ The Emperor is the archetypal male, relating to the zodiac sign Aries and its ruling planet Mars. He is the imposing and stern, but fair, father figure. He has acquired the skills and authority to play the game of life successfully. He can be dictatorial at times, may view life in a serious manner and not possess a great sense of humour, but he can be depended upon for his steadfast nature, reliable character and worldly-wise advice.

THE MESSAGE ★ Where the fire of the preceding female Empress card is shamanistic, healing and sensual, the fire of The Emperor is warlike, ascetic and domineering. In astrological terms The Magician's fire is Arien: "I Am," while The

Emperor's fire is Leonine: "I Will." Fiery nonetheless, hence its connection with Aries, the impulsive, independent, strong-willed, bossy, authoritive leader of the zodiac. The Emperor symbolises the intellect - the creative, powerful building tool of the human mind - having detached itself from nature, the heart and the emotions, and makes it function now in an autonomous, orderly, dissociated manner. The Emperor, through his stern rulership and overseeing of others, is keen to make his ideas and plans solid and tangible. He signifies that although your dreams are valid and sound, they still need guidelines and structure so that they can manifest effectively. It therefore is important to create a detailed plan for how you wish to proceed, and maintain firm and authoritative control over how that plan is implemented; it is imperative that you cultivate logic, discipline and organisation. When The Emperor appears in a reading, it implies you are up against a patriarchal structure of some kind, and probably have to deal with rigidity, confrontation with authority, or someone who is in a position of power over you (e.g. a boss, a father, a governmental head) who is egotistical, self-centred, out of touch with his feelings, and is not easy to get along with. Perhaps he represents *you*, and the realisation that perhaps your intellect has become rigid, your beliefs fixed, your creativity stunted in some way - whatever the case, you may just need the right outlet and support from other cards on the Tarot journey, to be way-showers, in order to loosen up and express your feelings with more flow.

Overall, The Emperor is a powerful man who is in a strong position. As such he stands for material status and Earthly wisdom, rather than psychic or spiritual knowledge. He is influential because he has confidence in his abilities and personal power, and a great sense of self-control.

THE AWAKENING ★ You feel a need to protect what you have gained, and develop strength of character through setting firm boundaries and recognising that there are rules for playing the game of life. The Emperor teaches you - and you are rapidly learning - to start to take control of your own Path. The Emperor, however, has climbed the mountain and even claimed it as his own, but doing this has reduced the number of options available to him, therefore rendering his life rather lonely. He has been a pioneer and a leader, becoming the master of his material world, and with his great reasoning abilities he has triumphed over emotion and passion. As a true patriarch, he lacks female intuition, but no such 'weakness' would be acknowledged by him for fear he may lose footing or authority. Dedicated, disciplined and stable, he has no difficulty in getting others to carry out his orders. Ambitious, he will begin innovative projects that are not always as staid and conservative as he himself appears. If old patterns must be broken, he will consider his options as he wishes to be perceived as benevolent and thoughtful as well as infallible. Though sometimes bossy and domineering, he will always remain responsible, reliable, solid, and, ultimately, charismatic.

THE LESSON ★ See the whole picture clearly before you act, as if you stood atop The Emperor's mountain. Most of all, what is needed here is a return to the consciousness represented by The Empress card - the goddess of archaic, gentle wisdom and compassionate understanding. The childlike wisdom of The Fool - the first Tarot card - can also help loosen up The Emperor's firm grip on his need to control his world. But despite his firm austerity and discipline over your life, the Emperor has his part to play, and we do need him to show us that we do need to build a strong foundation under our castles in the air sooner or later.

> If you have built castles in the air, your work need not be lost. That is where they should be. Now put the foundations under them.
>
> **Henry David Thoreau**

SYMBOLISM ★ Whereas The Empress is viewed as the mother figure, The Emperor is the archetypal father, representing authority that commands respect and obedience. The Emperor, a regal man of middle-age appearance, and dressed in ornate robes surveying a barren domain, governs the qualities of leadership and his role is to create stability and structure, lay down boundaries, exert power, and to make and enforce rules and laws. His rules will keep you safe and secure and his guidance is firm but fair.

Many Tarot decks show The Emperor seated on a throne carved with a Ram's head atop, signifying its link with the zodiac sign Aries. At his feet is a shield bearing the device of an imperial eagle, a symbol of worldly power and aspiration.

Only one side of his face is seen, which suggests he is only concerned with one side of life. His expression is stern and unbending, indicating high honour, unwavering ambition, control, influence, and that he takes himself seriously. His posture also indicates his focused intent; he leans to the left, holding his shield, as if he is either listening closely or is about to spring into action.

The Emperor wears the rich robes of a king and holds a royal spectre in his right hand, sometimes with another Ram's head, giving him a regal air of authority.

OVERALL ★ CONNECTING IT ALL UP ★

> Obstacles cannot crush me. Every obstacle yields to stern resolve. He who is fixed on a star does not change his mind.
>
> **Leonardo Da Vinci**

The Emperor's main divinatory meanings are worldly power, masculinity, potent creativity, worldly gain and achievement, confidence, stability, authority, wealth, an indomitable spirit, warrior tendencies, patriarchal figure, father, brother, husband, male influence, domination of intelligence, and reason over emotion and passion. He also indicates the desire to be a success, the making of wise choices, security, fatherhood, and the respect of others. The Emperor card signifies high honour, the achievement of ambition and it may show an influential male whose help may be required. It also represents a man in control of any given situation.

The Emperor is the certainty of life, of successful power. He has an air of power and dignity. He generally sits on a throne, holding symbols of power such as an orb and sceptre, and in some decks, he carries a sword, signifying masculine potency and temporal authority. The Emperor's power is a worldly one, a strong will to impose his rules and to exercise his sovereignty over the material, concrete, tangible reality of this world. He possesses a robust character strengthened with certainties and convictions; he achieves, produces and protects. His intelligence is supreme; it is the practical and logical intelligence often seen in those in positions of power.

The Emperor represents authority figures, such as the Father, your boss, head of an organisation, or an alpha male. Don't expect fun and frolicking when this card appears, as it represents a symbol that imposes rules which must be obeyed. He is a disciplined, successful and sometimes dogmatic man, who believes only what he can see and what he can prove.

In contrast to The Empress, a symbol of maternal influence, The Emperor symbolises paternal dominance, presiding over the realms of finance, politics and material resources. While The Empress attends to the human need for emotional and physical nourishment, The Emperor strives for advancement in the wider world, employing the masculine energy required to build cities and make laws. He also indicates the kind of energy required to transform ideas into reality. However, inclined he is to act, starting things and not finishing them are key features.

The appearance of The Emperor in any reading indicates that the time is right to pay attention to the practical, material side of life. As he is connected to the elements connected with business, amassing resources, politics and making money, it is likely that when he shows up in a reading, the forming of a company, the beginning of a new business, or the purchase of property is imminent. He may also be strongly indicative of an important person appearing in your life who could prove to be a significant influence. Also, you should feel empowered to take a leadership role in your career and any projects that you're working on, and remember to cultivate structure and order so that you can move from the preparation stage into the execution of your plans. Believe in your ability to be a positive and diplomatic leader and above all, get organised so that you can be more structured and your goals can manifest.

The Emperor is giving you confidence and saying that success will come provided that you channel your energy and use it positively. He is old and wise, and has himself learned that premature, impetuous action does not pay off - and warns you against it. He encourages you to be firm but not ruthless; assertive tendencies must be controlled and you must exercise patience when dealing with others. The Emperor reminds you that being in a powerful position increases the amount of responsibility you carry. Further, he encourages females to become assertive and independent.

★ HOW THIS CARD RELATES TO ARIES ★

The Emperor, master and commander, is assigned to Aries, the sign of leadership. Look for the images of the Aries Ram on your Emperor card.

Corrine Kenner

The leader of the pack, the Emperor typifies the Aries personality: bold, courageous, decisive, confident, fearless, masculine, and in firm control. A master and commander, a no-nonsense visionary, and an aspiring as well as accomplished conquestor, The Emperor is strong, direct, forceful and pioneering in his rule. Like

Aries, The Emperor rules with his head, not his heart. He never questions himself, is hot-headed and brash, and he forges ahead into new territories with all the vigour of a youthful warrior. An initiator and self-starter, the motivated Emperor and Aries both share the qualities of passion and power.

The Emperor is authoritative, bossy, wilful, self-assured and doesn't indulge in petty emotions - much like the spirit of the Ram who rules over this card. And although idealistic, arduous and adventurous, the typical Arien is, like the Tarot's Emperor, ultimately ruled by reason over emotions, and logic over intuition. Aries is, after all, the born ruler who is always - and desires to be - in steely control, admired, respected and above all, an effective, headstrong, and quintessential leader. Considering this, The Emperor and the Aries could well be one and the same.

★ DIVINE MANIFESTATION USING THE EMPEROR ★

You can Divinely manifest things in your experience through tapping into your inner Authority.

The Emperor is the Wise Ruler who helps you make the decisions about the material aspects of your life. Sometimes we need sound, practical, unemotionally-based advice, and the Emperor can give you this. We all have a personal Emperor in our lives, in the form of our inner authority. When we are decisive, efficient and orderly, we are harnessing the Emperor's cool power. But for the most part, we base our decisions, relationships and working life on our emotions, which can cloud our judgement. The Emperor puts the control back into your hands, so that you can get back to important material concerns in your life, such as protecting loved ones through providing a stable home, career advancement, financial ascension, and the acquisition of things that make life comfortable. Too often in our society we are taught that to strive for material possessions is a bad thing, a wrong thing. But if we can embody the balance and moderation of the equally-wise Temperance card, combined with the Emperor, we can have our cake and eat it too. The Emperor's biggest lesson is that you need to build a foundation under those daydreams using practical, sound common sense and fore-planned, laid out steps. Now get to work.

★ EXERCISES TO TAP INTO YOUR INNER EMPEROR ★

★ Is there someone in your life who you feel you need to stand up to, or who is exerting their power over you (overtly or otherwise) and you are feeling a bit helpless? If so, think of that person and generate the feelings of The Emperor as you visualise yourself asserting your needs or feelings to that person, with confidence, authority and power. Do not literally confront the person in question, as you may not be ready to do so at this time and the timing might be off, which will only serve to discourage you. For now, just visualise yourself feeling powerful and authoritative around that person. Hold this feeling for as long as you can. When you are next around the person, try acting like this (without words) and you may find that their power over you simply falls away and dissolves. Sometimes pretending or faking it can be just as empowering as actually facing up to the person or the fear.

★ Is there an area in your life you feel you have lost control over, or would like to regain more power over? Ask the Emperor for his guidance in gently but surely ushering a sense of control back into your life. His wise counsel and sense of stability and structure will help you to rebuild your strength in whatever area of your life is calling for it.

★ THE HIEROPHANT ★

Ruled by Taurus

Number ★ 5
Astrological Sign ★ Taurus

Keywords ★ Advice, Wisdom, Questing, Enlightenment

Magical Title ★ Magus of the Eternal Gods
Divinity ★ Zeus

Spiritual Value ★ The primary function of The Hierophant is to link together the Great Above to that which is Below. He is the Great Teacher of the Mysteries, helping to bring you understanding as a connection between sensory experiences and your inner illumination. While The Emperor (the preceding card) is the 'doer', the Hierophant is the 'thinker', the reflective, mystical aspect of the masculine. This card frequently indicates the hidden guardianship of the Masters, and therefore bestows Divine wisdom, manifestation, explanation, and teaching. This card may be used when you want to act, but are unsure what your true heart's desire is. The Hierophant can help you to develop generosity of spirit, sincerity, order, organisation, justice, courtesy, tact, and refinement.

The teacher is one who is willing to take us by the hand and share
out of the abundance of his or her sojourn and study.

J. Drane, R. Clifford & P. Johnson

★ KEY THEMES ★

"Spiritual Guide and Counsellor"

Search for Meaning in Life ★ Longing for Spiritual Enlightenment ★ Mentors and Guides ★ Traditional Viewpoints or Methods ★ Schools, Spiritual Institutions and Organisations ★ Spiritual Wisdom and Development ★ Questing ★ Learning ★ Benevolence ★ Stability ★ Rigidity ★ An Experienced, Older Man ★ Sense of Right and Wrong

Meditation ★ "I seek to do the right thing, to uphold tradition, and choose the high moral ground on all issues. I impart my knowledge, wisdom and spiritual lessons to others through both my gentle example and wise counsel, and in doing so spread a message of peace and compassion."

★ *When Working with this Card* ★

MAIN ENERGIES ★ Spiritual Knowledge, Compassion, Guidance, Trust
MAIN GOD OR GODDESS TO INVOKE ★ Sophia
CANDLE COLOUR ★ White
MAGICAL TOOL OR SYMBOL ★ Pillar Candles

CRYSTALS ★ Amethyst, Purple Fluorite, Emerald, White Howlite, Aquamarine

ASSOCIATED BEINGS, GODS, GODDESSES & ARCHETYPES ★ Divine Universal Being, Archangels, Holy Spirit, the Pope, Christ, Logos, the Zodiac, Sophia, Osiris, Holy Wisdom, the Wise Old One, the Father, the Gatekeeper, the High Priest.

ARCHETYPES ★ The Hierophant is a symbol of traditional guidance, authority and influence. He's the head of a hierarchy, determined to maintain his religious and cultural traditions and illuminate others with these insights and guidelines. He is the Guardian, the Herald, the Guide, the Teacher, the Shaman, the Visionary, the Wounded Healer.

CHAKRAS ★ Use this card to balance and meditate upon the Heart, Throat and Crown chakras.

Heart ★ Heart Region ★ Green ★ Air ★ Love & Compassion

Throat ★ Throat Region ★ Light Blue ★ Sound/Ether ★ Communication & Self-Expression

Crown ★ Top of Head ★ Purple ★ Thought/Knowing ★ Spiritual Wisdom & Enlightenment

TREE OF LIFE ★ In western magic, which combines the Tarot paths of the Major Arcana with the ten sephiroth on the Tree of Life, the path of The Hierophant connects Chesed and Chokmah.

NUMERIC SIGNIFICANCE ★ The Hierophant's number is five, a significant number in that metaphysicians suggest it symbolises the fifth element - spirit. This number, symbolised by the five-pointed star pentacle, is an intellectual vibration and is connected with freedom and movement, spirit, energy, travel, adventure and creativity. The Yogis of Tibet, the Indians of North America and the Taoists of China are just a few of the many varied cultures which have revered the number five as a power of Nature, seeing it as an expression of the vital, Universal life-force which sustains, pervades, connects and interweaves throughout everything that exists. The power of five was also regarded by these cultures as the 'gate of heaven' and as 'a doorway to the collective'. The Greeks considered the pentagram as a sacred symbol of light and vitality. The quincunx, the Pentad, or the number five was regarded by the followers of Pythagoras, as well as other philosophers, as the symbol of health and prosperity, but on the whole, it seems universally to have symbolised marriage, fecundity and propagation, this belief probably having its origin in the idea of five being the union of three and two, or a male and female number (in Ancient Rome, its significance was emphasised by the burning of five tapers during the marriage ceremony). A fifth element indeed exists, and was described by Plutarch in the 1st century AD, in these words: "If we assume that the World in which we live is the only one there is ... then it is itself made up of, as it were, five worlds which make

Harmony of it: one is the Earth, another Water, the third Fire, the fourth Air, and the fifth Sky, with the last one being called Light by some and Ether by others and by yet others, Quintessence." The Hierophant embodies the spiritual principle of the number five.

Number five takes us beyond the material plane and into the realms of mind and spirit, into ideas, abstracts and mental constructs. In the Western esoteric traditions, five relates to the fifth element, which is ether. This is symbolised by the pentagram, or five-pointed star, which is a potent magical symbol.

Theresa Morey

THE FOOL'S JOURNEY ★ Here is where The Fool learns about society's larger traditional values, which are represented by The Hierophant, sometimes called the Pope. The Fool learns about his heritage and communal roots, and Jungian theorists assign the archetype of the persona to this card, the social mask we all wear when we are out in the world. Sometimes this mask is worn to enable us to fit in with social convention. The concept of our outer persona's mask is also associated with your astrological Ascendant, or the mask you wear in public.

The Hierophant is the sacred light of our inner priest tracking the development of compassion as we emerge into the love and wisdom of the elder, the ever-young grandfather.

Paul Hougham

THE STORY ★ The Hierophant represents spiritual wisdom and is the mediator between heaven and Earth. He is a great teacher, always compassionate and fair. A sympathetic ruler, he listens and is merciful. He has breadth of vision and is able to encompass and understand all facets of human needs and desires. He emphasises the importance of learning and the role of the individual in society. He is depicted in the Tarot as an old man - wise, placid, patient and merciful - whose guidance is practical but follows, without question, the dogma as taught by his predecessors. His goals are the maintaining of social mores, and the assured position of his religion or spiritual leaning. This 'father confessor' can be relied upon for advice and support, within the guidelines of his training. And while he faithfully lays down the codified laws and principles contained in his book, his unremitting daily study and practice of those traditions still impart to him some of the occult knowledge upon which his religion was originally based.

Knowledge speaks, but wisdom listens.

Jimi Hendrix

THE MESSAGE ★ The Hierophant indicates you are searching for a deeper meaning to your life. To find this, seek out mentors, role-models, advisors, guides, experts, and like-minded kindred spirits.

> Don't impose on me what you know,
> I want to explore the unknown
> and be the source of my own discoveries.
> ... The world of your truth can be my limitation;
> Don't instruct me; let's walk together.
> Let my richness begin where yours ends.
> ... You believe that every human being
> can love and create.
> I understand, then, your fear
> when I ask you to live according to your wisdom.
> You will not know who I am
> By listening to yourself.
> Don't instruct me; let me be.
> Your failure is that I be identical to you.

Umberto Maturana, *The Student's Prayer*

THE AWAKENING ★ As The Hierophant sets you thinking about the deeper meaning of life, you are beginning to question the purpose of your existence, and this leads you to explore your spiritual nature. A guide or mentor helps to set you on this Path, and you discover a rich connection with a source of all-embracing love. Although he is seen as a spiritual teacher, in this context The Hierophant teaches spiritual ethics and thought within a more traditionally religious framework, and implies conservatism as well as a preference for the established method and order. If this card represents a situation, it is one in which the querent should take the tried and tested approach. It is not a time to fly in the face of reason or to act unconventionally. Instead, you should act in a sensible, honest and trustworthy manner. Rules and traditions are based on the sincere desire of our predecessors to preserve what was useful in their time. But your interests are not always best served by blind obedience, and the repression of your right to free thought may result in oppressive conformity. But in some situations, religious and spiritual moral values may comfort, teach and sustain you. In any case, The Hierophant urges us to listen to our conscience and uphold our moral responsibilities.

> The greatest good you can do for another is not just share your riches but reveal to them their own.

Benjamin Disraeli

THE LESSON ★ We all gain from a guide. At the heart of this is a spiritual mentor. The Hierophant acts as this teacher. If you encounter The Hierophant, it may be an indication that you need to examine your spiritual beliefs, spiritual practices or spiritual life, particularly in terms of the communal expression of that spirituality. The Hierophant is the male counterpart of The High Priestess. But whereas she is concerned with intuitive wisdom, The Hierophant is more connected with the concept of moral law. If he appears on your journey, perhaps there is a need to return to your spiritual roots, make a confession or explore forgotten traditions. We consult The Hierophant about the great questions of the soul which sometimes torture the mind; we ask for his benediction. The Hierophant can be regarded as the spiritual master representing the higher powers and forces, who through his role and his presence, reminds us that we are mortal, fallible, and that we must put our trust in him as much as in ourselves. The Hierophant has three stages of grace - faith, hope and charity - of which he is a symbol. He is a man to whom you can confide, and a good advisor, who will offer enlightened support, help and backing. But The Hierophant insists that if you seek his guidance, that you follow his example and adhere to the rules, thereby setting a good example for others. He also encourages you to walk the Path that you choose for yourself, because he knows that learning through experience - after being taught by example - is the best way.

There are only two ways of spreading light; to be the candle or the mirror that reflects it.

Edith Wharton

SYMBOLISM ★ In simple terms, The Hierophant represents a teacher. He represents the teaching of, and adherence to, a set of beliefs that act as a spiritual guide in life. In most Tarot decks this card is titled 'The Pope', connecting it to the Christian faith. In other decks, it is called The Hierophant, which implies any form of esoteric teaching that holds a personal value or meaning for you. This card ultimately symbolises the advice given from a perpetrator of wisdom of understanding, and your role is to respect this advice, but also to listen to your inner core of wisdom and access the knowledge you already hold which enables you to govern your own life. Therefore, this card also symbolises your higher self.

In most decks The Hierophant is seated on a throne between two pillars, raising his hand to bless his priests. At his feet are two crossed keys, both made out of gold (sometimes gold and silver), which symbolise the expression of both insight and logic. The triple cross and three-tiered crown featured in the card represent the Divine, intellectual and physical worlds. In Christian terms, bearing in mind this card is often titled 'The High Priest' or 'The Pope', they relate to the trinity of Father, Son and Holy Spirit.

In some decks, there is a bird at The Hierophant's feet, symbolising the spirit, flapping its wings, denoting the god's rulership over spiritual *and* temporal matters.

OVERALL ★ CONNECTING IT ALL UP ★

The best teachers are those who tell you where to look, but don't tell you what to see.

Alexandra K. Trenfor

The Hierophant, or High Priest, is a man of great knowledge, a medicine man, the one who finds and prescribes a remedy, a mediator. This word also derives from medium; the intermediary, the messenger. And this is very much the role played by The Hierophant, high priest of knowledge, whose wisdom relieves, liberates and fortifies our minds, bodies and souls.

The Hierophant is often shown as a pope. His triple-layered crown stands for unity in mind, body and spirit, which in many decks is also represented by his three-pronged staff. Crossed keys, one silver and one gold, appear frequently to symbolise masculine and feminine principles, and also demonstrate The Hierophant's ability to unlock the gates to heaven and hell, hinting at both good and evil. He holds a book or scroll, suggesting his wish to learn and gain knowledge. Usually seated between two pillars which symbolise the opposites of day and night, good and evil, and life and death, The Hierophant acts as the balancing force between them.

At its best The Hierophant is a benevolent teacher, kind and understanding. This card symbolises a wise and capable advisor, forgiveness and comfort, the influence of established faith and the power of the conscious mind. It represents a teacher and rules to get along by, being concerned with the concept of moral laws. Its divinatory meanings are ritualism, kindness, mercy, inspiration, forgiveness, compassion, servitude, timidity, overt reserve, captivity to one's own ideas, conformity, a religious or spiritual leader, tendency to cling to ideas and principles, long after they are outdated.

The Hierophant essentially stands for spiritual enlightenment. As a priest or holy man, he represents those who wish to expand their understanding of the meaning of life. Unlike The Emperor whose interests lie primarily in material matters, The Hierophant's interests are planted firmly in spirituality. He is attracted by the search for truth, philosophical and spiritual, and is not bound by any particular religion or dogma.

The Hierophant often represents an older man who has knowledge and wisdom and great experience of life. He is a man you could confide in, a sound advisor, and wise and enlightened supporter. He is a man from whom you could ask a recommendation, a right or an authorisation. He may be a judge, a barrister, a doctor or a knowledgeable, respected and cultured man in a high-powered position who is perhaps responsible for some important mission.

The word "Hierophant" shares the same origin as the word "hierarchy," which refers to a structure of varying levels of authority; and a Hierophant is indeed a high-up authority on matters of faith. As such, he has the power to speak on behalf of God (whatever or however you perceive Him to be), to impart the teachings of Divine wisdom, and to serve as a bridge between one world and another.

When he shows up in a reading, he is telling you that this might be an optimal time to make friends with a supportive network of people who have integrity and a strong moral compass, who could in turn become a spiritual mentor to you. It also describes that this is a time to question and review any rules, restrictions or limiting beliefs that have been placed around your current situation, either by yourself or by others. This can help to lift any blocks to the manifestation of your goals and dreams.

★ HOW THIS CARD RELATES TO TAURUS ★

The Hierophant, the keeper of tradition, is assigned to Taurus,
the sign of stability, luxury and pleasure.

Corrine Kenner

Much like Taurus in the zodiacal context, The Hierophant is the quiet but all-powerful force of the Tarot experience, and deeply rooted in tradition, while adhering to imposed, consistent rules. Like the Bull, The Hierophant is unmoveable and unmoved, like a solid mountain or rock, and his consistency and sound counsel is both comforting and enlightening. A guardian of time-honoured and long-standing values, beliefs, rituals and practices, The Hierophant holds true and faithful to his spiritual principles, providing a stellar example of stability and convention. Loyal, dedicated and enduring, both Taurus and The Hierophant can be rocks of solidarity, assurance and comfort during difficult times. Taurus is never a rebel, and will rarely seek to overthrow the establishment or even something with which she does not agree, much like the character in her special card, The Hierophant, for her Path is one of peace, reliability, balance, harmony and security. Her - like The Hierophant's - advice is simple: "Live life peacefully, stay on your rightful Path, give guidance when asked, do the right thing at all times, practice kindness, acceptance and compassion, and always practice proven traditional methods which will keep you grounded, stable and loving towards all." And indeed, on some deep primal and spiritual level, we all need the safety, shelter and sanctity both Taurus and The Hierophant can provide.

✭ DIVINE MANIFESTATION USING THE HIEROPHANT ✭

You can Divinely manifest things in your experience through tapping into your inner Spiritual Guide.

The Hierophant indicates there is a search for meaning underway in your life. Seek out mentors, experts and like-minded friends. The Hierophant is a conservative, patient man who appreciates stability and tradition. He is wise, compassionate and kind. He is quietly persevering, and offers a chance to examine spirituality as a means for understanding life's changes. To be mentored is both a privilege and an enriching experience. The Hierophant imparts the message that we should not only seek out a mentor, but also develop our own wisdom and insights so that we might then be able to act as a Hierophant to others.

✭ EXERCISES TO TAP INTO YOUR INNER HIEROPHANT ✭

✭ If you had free, unlimited access to a spiritual guide, practitioner or course, who would you choose? Some ideas are a priest, a mentor, a reiki healer, a crystal healer, a spiritual leader, a Zen master, a life coach, a monk, an astrologer, a general counsellor, a spiritual retreat, or any number of other helpful guides you can think of. Now, imagine that you *do* have the money allocated for your spiritual development, progress and health, and research different sources to find someone or something who specialises in the field you'd like to seek guidance from. Make initial contact and begin your journey now.

✭ Have you ever benefited from a mentor or spiritual guide? It could've just been a one-off event, like a Tarot-reading by a travelling reader, or a sessional basis, such as trauma counselling, or even ongoing, such as having a special mentor in a close relative or business advisor. We regard some people as our mentors without them even knowing it sometimes, so consider these people too, such as someone you greatly admired and wished to emulate, or a friend who was always there when you were feeling down with comfort and great advice. Reflect on some thoughts around how you benefited from this very special relationship, whether it was professional or incidental, formal or informal, structured or loose, paid or unpaid.

★ THE LOVERS ★

Ruled by Gemini

Number ★ 6
Astrological Sign ★ Gemini

The figures (The Lovers) suggest youth, virginity, innocence and
love before it is contaminated by gross material desire.

A.E. Waite, *The Pictorial Key to the Tarot*

Keywords ★ Choices, Options, Complementary Opposites, Decisions

Magical Title ★ Oracles of the Mighty Gods, Children of the Voice Divine
Divinity ★ Apollo
Spiritual Value ★ This Arcanum turns up when you need to do some tidying up in your mind, to sort what is best among all the ideas you have stored there. It can help you make balanced choices that promote harmony in your life, and also helps in developing acute intelligence and quick thinking when it comes to making serious 'crossroads' decisions that may affect the rest of your life.

★ KEY THEMES ★

"Making the Best Choices For My Higher Good"

★ Choice ★ Desire ★ Decision ★ Temptations ★ Union ★ Reconciliation ★ Harmony ★ Sacrifice ★ Indecision ★ Trials and Options that May be Linked to Relationships ★ Relationship Decisions Resulting in Stability ★ A Return to Good Health ★ Carefully Weighing Options ★ Need for Balance ★ Marriage and Weddings ★ Complementary Opposites

Meditation ★ "I have the right and the power to make my own decisions as I stand at the many forks in the roads of life, and I know all these choices will be correct and for my higher good."

★ *When Working with this Card* ★

MAIN ENERGIES ★ Love, Discernment
MAIN GOD OR GODDESS TO INVOKE ★ Venus / Aphrodite
CANDLE COLOUR ★ Pink
MAGICAL TOOLS OR SYMBOLS ★ Heart, Yin/Yang
CRYSTALS ★ Rose Quartz, Rhodochrosite, Diamond, Emerald, Bloodstone, Jade

ASSOCIATED BEINGS, GODS, GODDESSES & ARCHETYPES ★ The Divine Couple, Angels, the Solar Archangel, Innerworld Masters and Saints, Apollo, Venus, Astarte, Erzulie, Branwen, the Lord and Lady of Harmony and Light, Freya, Kamadeva, Aphrodite, Krishna, Radha, Eros, Cupid.

ARCHETYPES ★ The Lovers embody the twin principles of opposition and attraction, as well as choices to be made between two often equally strong desires. They are the Divine Couple, who encapsulate the pull of this force between the ever-present yearnings and conflicts of our inner decision-making mechanisms.

CHAKRAS ★ Use this card to balance and meditate upon the Solar Plexus, Heart and Throat chakras.

Solar Plexus ★ Behind the Navel ★ Yellow ★ Fire ★ Personal Power, Confidence & Control

Heart ★ Heart Region ★ Green ★ Air ★ Love & Compassion

Throat ★ Throat Region ★ Light Blue ★ Sound/Ether ★ Communication & Self-Expression

TREE OF LIFE ★ In western magic, which combines the Tarot paths of the Major Arcana with the ten sephiroth on the Tree of Life, the path of The Lovers connects Tiphareth and Binah, spheres which represent the Divine son and the Great Mother.

NUMERIC SIGNIFICANCE ★ Six is the principle of reconciliation. In alchemy, it represents the union of fire and water, brought into a harmonious relationship. Six is shown as a hexagon, or a six-pointed star made up of two interlaced triangles, which point above and below, symbolising unity between heaven and Earth. A perfect number because it is the sum of its factors (1, 2, 3), six is balanced, and is associated with family love and domesticity. Ruled by Venus, the number six is a loving, stable and harmonious vibration. Venus is the planet of love, beauty and harmony, which encapsulates the essence of what The Lovers are trying to achieve.

THE FOOL'S JOURNEY ★ It's time for The Fool to learn about sex, relationships and choices. The Lovers card represents yin and yang, attraction, desire and romance. A variety of archetypal equivalents exists for this card, including Romeo and Juliet. Mythological lovers are often fated to heartache because love is not without difficulties.

> The Lovers is the vision of unity that the heart carries, bridging the spheres of matter and Spirit.
>
> **Paul Hougham**

THE STORY ★ The Lovers can represent both virtue and vice - the basic alternatives. This card obviously refers to strong emotions, and choices of the heart which cannot be made by logic alone. In older decks this card shows a young man who has to make a decision between two women while the Cupid hovers above, aiming his arrow. Later versions of The Lovers replaced Cupid with the fiery archangel St Michael, and the group below by figures of Adam and Eve alongside the Trees of Knowledge and Life. However, hidden in one of them is the serpent of temptation - again, indicating the choice: to eat the forbidden fruit, or to not eat it?

> Two roads diverged in the wood and I took the one less
> travelled and that has made all the difference.

Robert Frost

THE MESSAGE ★ Traditionally an image of duality and choice, The Lovers represent the yin and yang forces of the Universe and their natural attraction to each other. Love, or the coming together of these complementary forces, can occur on many levels. In its deeper, more esoteric form, the image refers to the merging of these opposite qualities within a being, which leads to wholeness. In Tarot The Lovers usually signifies a sexual union is in process. Tantra teaches that the union of humans through the sexual act causes a dissolution of ego boundaries and the experience of ecstasy. When The Lovers appears in a reading, it signals that a significant decision or relationship is on your mind; you are either working on a partnership in which you are already involved, or preparing for a liaison with a new partner. It may be intimate or romantic in nature, or it may be a close but platonic friendship. In any case, being a lover is on your mind. Feeling the pull of this magnetic force, you face a choice. If the question is something to the tune of, "Are we going to be lovers or not?" and you feel passionate excitement about this query, then you can be assured you will soon be taking a journey to a deeper place, but to do so, you are asked to trust, to risk and to face the unknown. The yielding required of you as you leap into space together is a surrender to the Divine force of love itself, and the resultant energy is transpersonal - that is, it transcends both your own and the other person's characters. Either way, trust is of the essence in this partnership and communication is key; you can share yourself safely with that person.

> Free will means that you can choose to abide by the laws that speak within your deepest intuition, or you can let impulses, fears, and habits run the show. If you sometimes resist or ignore higher wisdom in favour of immediate gratification, the consequences of your choices eventually guide you back towards alignment with the laws of Spirit; one choice leads to a sunlit path and another to hurdles and tests that instruct and strengthen you, so all things serve in their own ways.

Dan Millman

THE AWAKENING ★ You come to understand that your relationships with others are an outer expression of the desire for inner connection, and that loving another person helps you to discover new aspects of yourself, and so to grow. If you fall passionately in love, it will teach you the difference between co-dependency and genuine caring and sharing. With The Lovers, you learn more about yourself through another. Your relationships reflect your own inner balance. Though this card usually indicates a love affair is or is about to be in progress, the choice is not always romantic or sexual in nature but may be between any two allurements.

> Real poetry doesn't say anything; it just ticks off the possibilities.
> Opens all doors. You can walk through any one that suits you.

Jim Morrison

THE LESSON ★ The Lovers are telling you to be happy and enjoy your relationship. However, you must be prepared to make compromises and sacrifices if it is to work successfully. A sense of humour, and shared interests and aspirations are important. They warn you not to fall in love with love itself: it is the other person who matters, and it is important that you know the others' true character. If you are not in a relationship, this card could indicate imminent union, a loving impulse or an irrepressible attraction. If you have recently fallen out with your lover, this card suggests you will be reconciled. The second meaning of The Lovers concerns choice: the querant will have to make a difficult decision and usually this will involve certain amount of sacrifice. You may be torn between what you think you should do and what you really want to do. The Lovers card can also be interpreted as representing a choice between two aspects of femininity - that of the chaste maiden (symbolising the inner Path of The High Priestess) or that of the fertile seductress (symbolising the outer Path of The Empress). However, because this card is about unity as well as choice, the inner and outer Paths must be brought together in harmony and integrated into the self. The Winged God of Love, Cupid, who is aiming his arrow at the male figure in the card, indicates through wearing a blindfold that he cannot help the man make the decision; rather, that the man must face the task of reconciling the opposites alone. How he does this will have a significant impact on his future Path and a ripple effect on those around him, therefore the needs of others will need to be considered. Knowing all this, The Lovers represents a person's deep motivations, desires, wishes, and their ability to select one Path.

SYMBOLISM ★ The young man in The Lovers image holds the woman's hand to make his feelings known. She looks away uncertainly, seemingly contemplating whether or not to accept his offer of love, symbolising the choices this card indicates need to be made. They are watched by an elderly figure, a wise old man, who symbolises the knowledge of lifelong experience. He is armed with this wisdom, well aware of the decisions that lie before the young lovers, even if they are not.

The Cupid is a character from classical mythology, and is pictured in this card peeking out from the clouds, preparing to fire his arrows of love at the woman, as if imploring her to make the right decision, one that is based on sound consideration of all the available facts.

OVERALL ★ CONNECTING IT ALL UP ★

May your choices reflect your hopes, not your fears.

Nelson Mandela

The Lovers is the card of romantic choices, passion and temptation. The image shows two lovers who are close but, in the gap between them, is the snake of temptation. The face looking down represents the power of love, but it is linked with the Gemini star sign, so there are two ways to use this love - wisely or recklessly. As such, this is both an exciting and an intriguing card.

Although the symbolism of the two people who depict The Lovers implies that this card is about romantic relationships alone, it encompasses all relationships, but particularly close ones, and indeed the decisions that one makes around those relationships that impact one's life Path.

In a general life reading, both your working life and your home-life will involve choices. As for your love happiness, The Lovers indicates that it is important that you make clear, sincere choices. Trying to run two intense relationships (romantic or otherwise intimate) could lead to losing both of them.

It points to the fact that you will soon be facing an important relationship decision, because this card holds two very different people for you. One person is kind and loving, and offers you nourishment and security in both heart and home. This person is already close to you and you have only to reach out. But there is still a small gap between you. The second person seems to have a direct link to your passion and dreams and the relationship would be propelled by a most powerful choice; this relationship would demand a great deal from you, and you would need to be very independent and emotionally secure to deal with this person. So, you do need to think very carefully about this option.

This card refers to strong emotions, a choice of the heart that cannot be made by logic alone. Its divinatory meanings are love, beauty, harmony, perfection, trust, deep feelings, freedom of emotion, optimism, the necessity of trial, struggle between sacred and profane love, and a meaningful affair, perhaps one that already exists being enhanced in some way.

It shows a young man standing between two women, as if making a choice between them. The women may symbolise the paths of vice and virtue, as one woman appears young and seductive while the other one looks older and wiser. It could also signify the choice between mother or lover, and the dilemma of separation. Sometimes a winged Cupid flies above, pointing an arrow at the young man's heart as if to influence his decision. In some decks this Cupid is blindfolded, representing that love can be blind. In the Universal Waite deck, the image shows Adam and Eve making the decision of whether to disobey God and eat the forbidden fruit of knowledge, or to obey Him and remain in ignorant bliss.

The Lovers card represents the power of the human heart, the power of attraction, a deep emotional nature, and the need to listen to one's desires. It also symbolises love, reconciliation, physical pleasures and that a dramatic change of attitudes will lead to happier times. The Lovers card encourages you to consider your options and prepare to make a decision. The blind Cupid can indicate that our method for making choices may not always be well informed, and is heavily weighted in favour of what we desire rather than what is actually good for us. The wisest approach here is to consider the consequences of the options and what will accompany the outcome. The choices indicated by this card aren't always restricted to love affairs or relationships, but the decision in question *will* be of a personal nature and relevance. The Lovers also represent our innocent selves before we become sullied by life, and bring in their wake unification and problems solved. It can suggest that a happy personal or business relationship is just ahead, if we only take the path of being true to ourselves, making the choice that *feels* right rather than what is *considered* right, and following our heart's desires, which result in our emanating of pure radiance and therefore attracting that which we have asked for.

As this card is connected with the astrological sign of Gemini, The Lovers can suggest you need to be aware of your arms, hands, shoulders and lungs, and that depletion of nervous energy may be a danger for you.

Spiritually, this card represents the chance to pursue a fulfilling opportunity. Life is now presenting to you a Path which may lead to happiness, but this is only potential until you decide to take that first step. It is time to commit yourself to that next part of your journey, usually with a partner, and this relationship can be an opportunity for creative growth. This particular relationship offers you a chance to reveal yourself to someone else who recognises your unique qualities, and to share part of life's journey with another. It is time to ask yourself: How can I detect the underlying unity between apparent opposites such as sacred and profane, male and female, spiritual and material?

This card is not always about choice, but can be strongly about unity: the inner and outer Paths - both expressions of the Divine must be brought together in unity. The Lovers show that our task is to recognise the underlying unity between these apparent opposites and to integrate them into our self. It illustrates the dangers and pitfalls that attend all choices, particularly those made in the name of love, and that affairs of the heart are neither easy nor straightforward. You must understand that any choice related to love (of any nature) will inevitably bring about repercussions and possible complications, like the ripples caused by a stone being thrown into a pond. However, this card is not only about decisions in love, it denotes *all* choices. And choices always bring about changes, having far-reaching consequences, which is why they must be looked upon and considered from all angles before that ultimate decision is reached.

Ultimately, The Lovers represent an outcome between past and present circumstances and the Path ahead. It indicates there is currently, or will be, a relationship in your life which has forced you into experiencing some kind of trial or choice. If not about love, then it suggests a choice must be made that has heartfelt consequences. It offers temporary respite from existential loneliness. It is wise to move forward to the new opportunities awaiting you. The challenge first is to unify opposing forces within yourself to create a new, harmonious whole.

★ HOW THIS CARD RELATES TO GEMINI ★

The Lovers, who think and speak as one, are assigned to Gemini, the sign of thought and communication. The Lovers themselves are twin souls, with their arms and hearts entwined. The sign (Gemini) represents the duality of two separate individuals working in tandem ... Both the Gemini Twins and the two Lovers in the Tarot card represent a diversity of thoughts and experiences, and the versatility and expanded point of view that a partnership can bring to any situation.

Corrine Kenner

Geminis are insatiably curious, youthful, flirtatious and playful, and the same thing could be said about the essence of The Lovers. Together, the combination of Gemini and The Lovers suggests that two heads are better than one, and that two intersecting points of view can indeed coexist harmoniously.

The Lovers usually represents a choice, and any choice usually presents us with a dilemma or a duality of sorts. Gemini's dualistic nature resonates with The Lovers card, and the decisions that this card implies, are something which the Gemini soul grapples with on an almost constant basis. The Lovers also signifies a temptation that may be present in our experience, and asks us to choose between things like clinging to our youth or ageing gracefully, taking a bite out of the forbidden apple or being resolutely disciplined, and the pervading allurements of vice or virtue. Gemini, being the sign of the youthful, charming Twins, will usually choose to remain the Peter Pan by clinging to his innocence and freedom from care, and will take the fateful bite rather than exercise self-restraint. He is, after all, the cunning trickster of the zodiac and will push his luck and his limits at every opportunity possible. But Gemini would do well to grasp this card's symbolism, particularly when it relates to the all-important choices we are confronted with on our life's Path at some point - for the outcome of these significant decisions will have a profound impact on his future Path and a ripple effect on those around him. Knowing all this, The Lovers represents a person's deep motivations, desires, wishes, and ability to select one path - something which doesn't come naturally and is therefore an acquired skill and taste for most Geminis. It may be a bitter pill to swallow, but The Lovers tells Gemini that he will be forgiven if that pill is balanced out with a little virtue from time to time.

✶ DIVINE MANIFESTATION USING THE LOVERS ✶

You can Divinely manifest things in your experience through tapping into your inner Decision-maker.

The Lovers is largely about choice. It is telling you that if you have a difficult decision to make about something, you are literally standing at the crossroads. But you can't stand at this intersection forever; you know you have to make a choice, make a leap, sooner or later, as life will not wait for you to catch up. What to do? Firstly, you are asked to trust, to risk and to face the unknown. This is similar to the first 'challenge' you faced with the Eager Fool, the Divine Child. But at this stage on the Tarot Journey, you are a fully-fledged adult and have a lingering sense of, "If I choose this path then I will gain this but lose that, and if I choose that path then I will gain that but lose this." Decisions, especially potentially life-altering ones, are rarely easy to make, as each important choice we make about our Path, is fraught with risks - mostly those of loss, gain, compromise, surrender and sacrifice. The yielding required of you as you leap into space is a surrender to the Divine force of love itself, and the resultant energy is transformational. Whatever choice you make at the many crossroads of life, trust is of the essence. The Lovers indicates a time to make an important decision about your life. Decisions take courage, leaps take boldness, and trust takes deep wisdom. Have you cultivated these traits to their fullest in your-self yet? Any decisions you reach now will significantly influence your future, making it all the more important to weigh up your options carefully and thoroughly consider all angles. A decisive point has been reached, and this important choice must be made with reference to true desires rather than duty. A dramatic change of attitudes will indeed lead to happier times. Learn how to make effective decisions about your life, and the Path may well appear at your feet as you walk.

★ EXERCISES TO TAP INTO YOUR INNER LOVERS ★

★ Decisive people get ahead in life! I read a book once, about a man who was wanting to hire someone who would undertake a very lucrative project for him (of course the candidates didn't know that the project was lucrative and would make them over a million dollars in a short time). He interviewed many people, and dismissed them all, even though they were extremely learned, qualified, and well-presented. Upon interviewing one person, however, he gave them the job on the spot. Why? Because that person passed the interviewer's 'test' - you see, the interviewer gave each of them a very succinct overview of the project, then asked, quite simply, "Are you willing to take it on?" Each time, as soon as this question was asked, he watched the clock for thirty seconds, and if the thoughtful respondent hasn't given him a response by then, he told them they didn't have the job and bid them farewell. For his one and only criteria for the right person for the job, was *decisiveness*. He figured that if someone isn't decisive in life, they are not going to be very effective in work. One man he interviewed answered within twenty-eight seconds, just making the time, and he was hired. The book this winning candidate researched and ultimately wrote, became a classic and sold millions of copies, and still continues to sell to this day. For his decisiveness, this man swiftly went on to become a millionaire - no mean feat in the 1930s! And the book, for your information, is called *Think and Grow Rich*, by Napoleon Hill. Why not try saying yes or no very quickly to everything (within reason) asked of you (at least within 30 seconds). Imagine that you are this man in the interview, with the boss watching the clock. Time is ticking away. Yes or no. Say it with heart, say it with feeling and say it with meaning. What will you say yes to *today*? The clock is ticking …

★ Have you ever seen the movie Sliding Doors? I would suggest that you watch it, and reflect upon the impact different decisions and split-second events can have on our destiny. After watching the film, ask yourself about a decision, big or small, you've made in your past, and consider the two very different roads your life would've taken with each one. This movie itself, and the concept that one seemingly tiny moment can alter the whole course of our life, teaches that we are perpetually standing at a crossroads with every turn we make, every delay we encounter, and every thought we entertain and then act or not act upon. The tragedy - or perhaps the blessing - of life, is that we never know where the alternative choice, the Path we could've chosen but didn't - could've led us.

★ Are you at a crossroads or do you have an important decision to make about something in your life at this time? What will you lose if you take the path your heart is telling you to? Is it this fear of potential loss that is stopping you? What will you gain? Ponder these questions, and work out which side scores the most points for you. Then take one step along that path and see how it feels.

★ THE CHARIOT ★

Ruled by Cancer

Number ★ 7
Astrological Signs ★ Cancer & Sagittarius

Keywords ★ Victory, Willpower, Control, Progress

Magical Title ★ Child of the Powers of the Waters, Lord of the Triumph of Light
Divinity ★ Poseidon
Spiritual Value ★ The Chariot is the sublimation of the Psyche, and may be used to master periods of delusions or uncontrolled fantasies. This Arcanum helps you to find a more balanced, centered path, so that you may discover a personal expression for your spirituality. As well as fostering gentleness and benevolence, The Chariot can help you work on every aspect of your unconscious, by bringing to light those elements that have been buried deep inside. It is a useful card for resolving rampant fantasies that have no grounding in reality, and for assisting the Magus who wants to cast spells.

The Chariot is the speed and wildness of the journey across the abyss, the discipline to be able to go the distance without distraction.

Paul Hougham

★ KEY THEMES ★

"Riding to Victory"

Triumph Over Difficulties, Struggles and Battles ★ The Arrival of Help At the Hour of Need ★ Positive and Fruitful Efforts ★ A Journey ★ Good News ★ Expansion ★ Control Regained ★ Progress ★ Success ★ Audacity ★ Faith ★ Fighting Spirit ★ Positive Outcome ★ Beneficial Change ★ An Important Achievement ★ Self Discipline ★ A Great Leap Forward ★ Positive Challenges ★ Willpower ★ Public Recognition ★ Perseverance ★ A Promotion or Award ★ Travel ★ Modes of Transportation ★ Willpower

Meditation ★ "I practice self-restraint, control and gentle influence to obtain any desire or goal I wish to. I understand intuitively that I must exercise balance, discretion, discipline and sound management in my life's journey if I am to arrive at my destination victoriously."

★ *When Working with this Card* ★

MAIN ENERGIES ★ Courage of Convictions, Drive, Progress, Empowerment
MAIN GOD OR GODDESS TO INVOKE ★ Bel
CANDLE COLOUR ★ Red
MAGICAL TOOL OR SYMBOL ★ Two Sphinxes, Yin/Yang

CRYSTALS ★ Carnelian, Ruby, Topaz, Garnet, Yellow Sapphire

ASSOCIATED BEINGS, GODS, GODDESSES & ARCHETYPES ★ Transpersonal or Catalytic Beings, Minerva, Briggidda, Bel the Lord of Light, Hermes, Apollo, Horus, Pagan Goddesses of Cultural Development, Patronesses of Solar Heroes, the Prince, the Son, the Rescuer.

ARCHETYPES ★ The Chariot is a metaphorical vehicle for forward progress, travel, change and motion. The young charioteer is in command of his physical, emotional and spiritual drives, even when they seem to conflict each other. The Chariot is the Herald, the Hero, the Messenger, the Outlaw, the Warrior.

CHAKRAS ★ Use this card to balance and meditate upon the Sacral, Throat and Crown chakras.

Sacral ★ Below the Navel ★ Orange ★ Water ★ Physical, Sexual, Creative & Material Desires

Throat ★ Throat Region ★ Light Blue ★ Sound/Ether ★ Communication & Self-Expression

Crown ★ Top of Head ★ Purple ★ Thought/Knowing ★ Spiritual Wisdom & Enlightenment

TREE OF LIFE ★ In western magic, which combines the Tarot paths of the Major Arcana with the ten sephiroth on the Tree of Life, the path of The Chariot connects Geburah and Binah.

NUMERIC SIGNIFICANCE ★ A mystical number which is associated with philosophy, spiritual insights and wisdom, seven is the number of mysticism and illusion, meditation and contemplation, profundity and depth, vision and perception. The Septenary or the Heptad as it is sometimes known, is the most interesting and mysterious of the primary numbers. To the Greeks and Romans, it was the symbol of good fortune, being connected with periodical changes of the Moon; and the seven notes in music gave rise to the philosophy of the 'harmony of the spheres' and the depiction of the Universe as one vast musical scale. Often linked to the world of dreams, seven governs the imagination and the study of magic. Number seven is a deep-thinking, spiritual vibration; symbolically it is the number for perfection. It signifies fine powers of sympathy, intuition and insight, and has long been regarded as symbolising spirituality, mystery, magic and the occult. Seven is the number of wisdom and relates to the completion of cycles. There are seven personal planets in astrology, seven days of the week, seven pillars of wisdom, seven chakras, seven wonders of the world, seven musical notes, seven Gothic gods, seven earths and seven hells and seven heavens in Islamic tradition, seven worlds believed in by the Chaldeans, seven degrees of initiation in various eastern orders, seven colours in a rainbow, seven crystalline systems, seven seas, seven continents, seven virtues, seven vices and seven deadly sins. Seven is a sacred number to the Native American

Cherokee nation; it represents seven directions: north, south, east, west, above, below, centre. Seven signifies a full range of differences. It contains diversity within a recognisable order, like the spectrum of colours in the rainbow. In some schools of alchemy, the power of seven has been described as the *Power of Fusion*. The power of seven is connected with oneness, community and Cosmic consciousness, and describes a poetic, mystic ability to tune in and to be at one with all life and All That Is, the point to which the charioteer is ever steering towards.

THE FOOL'S JOURNEY ★ Here's where The Fool encounters the two sides of any issue and learns about compromise and balancing conflicting forces. In Jungian terms, the Chariot represents the struggle between light and shadow.

THE STORY ★ Here a victorious young man, standing upright in a chariot that has four columns and a luxuriant canopy, sets out on an adventure, or returns triumphant from battle. His chariot is drawn by two horses or sphinxes, who offer him wisdom, but may also represent his sexual drive and spirituality. He is powerful, demonstrated by his crown, and he is positive in outlook. The Chariot is representative of achievement, popularity, control and celebration. You may feel that your particular chariot is being drawn by two very different horses because doubt, uncertainty, struggles and conflicts plague your journey. However, the outcome will be worthwhile. The Chariot is also a card of movement, travel and transport.

> Water at 211 degrees makes hot coffee. Water at 212 degrees becomes steam and can move a ship around the world. Move out of the hot water of mediocrity and into the steam of outstanding success.
>
> **Zig Ziglar**

THE MESSAGE ★ The Chariot card is saying congratulations, as you have successfully balanced a challenging situation and it is now time to bask in the joy of this accomplishment. It is important to exercise determination, kind but firm self-control, and the willingness to go the distance. The Chariot represents the perseverance not to give up when emotional issues threaten your stability. You have garnered approval, respect and admiration from those around you for your ability to see both sides, make decisions and take action.

> You have enemies? Good. That means you've stood up for something, some time in your life.
>
> **Winston Churchill**

THE AWAKENING ★ The ability to relate to another increases your sense of inner strength and guidance, allowing you to make decisions to consciously initiate changes in your life. In order to triumph, you must take the reins of control and not let go. Enlist the help of outside forces in your quest, and know that right now there is no time or place for emotions, just single-minded concentration on your goal. This need for control shifts into the knowledge that by being focused and true to your objectives, you can shape the course of your life rather than drift along aimlessly. You are quite right to feel strong and optimistic, and should accept any challenge that is offered. The Chariot encourages you to expand your horizons through study and adventure, for whatever your age you are young at heart! You can now focus your will and work towards your goals. The time is ripe for travel, intellectual journeys and fulfilling your potential. The qualities that have enabled the Chariot steerer to succeed, however, carry a word of warning: you must enjoy this moment of glory with the knowledge that it, like other such moments and heroes, will pass. It is vital not to become so flushed with success that you become arrogant.

> It is the soul's duty to be loyal to its own desires. It must abandon itself to its master passion.
>
> **Rebecca West**

THE LESSON ★ The Chariot announces a situation to come, in which one has to move forward, show courage, willpower and determination, and feel confident in order to attain one's goal. It represents conflict, but a necessary one - one that encourages change and growth - for it is this force of destiny which drives one to achieve great things. The Chariot indicates overcoming snares and obstacles, with the help and protection of Providence. The Chariot is an encouragement to go forward with the choices that have been made, and the objectives that have been set. It is also a strong sign that you will gain victory, and sometimes foretells a move, travel, movement in general, a journey or a piece of unexpected good news that you are about to receive. Be self-reliant and you will gain success.

SYMBOLISM ★ The Chariot represents the power of the will over the body, emotions and mind. In essence, it signifies one's ability to exercise control when deciding on a new course or direction, as the mind and emotions can be fickle and easily influenced. The Chariot symbolises success and marks a new stage or change in circumstances. It denotes a certain degree of detachment, as it illustrates how we can be affected by the senses and yet still manage to conquer them and forge ahead.

The Chariot shows three-fold imagery - the Chariot steerer, detached and powerful, and the dual forces of the two horses that he drives and controls. The steerer appears confident, using the force of his will to guide the Chariot's movement.

The two horses or sphinxes drawing the vehicle represent the opposing tides of the mind and emotions that would gallop out of control and cause confusion if not ruled by a greater force - the indomitable will.

OVERALL ★ CONNECTING IT ALL UP ★

> To understand the heart and mind of a person, look not at what he has already achieved, but at what he aspires to do.
>
> **Kahlil Gibran**

The chariot depicted on the card is sometimes drawn by two sphinxes, symbolising the mystery of the future as well as the positive and negative forces that persist through our lives. The sphinx also represents enigmas. Another image that appears frequently is that of two horses pulling or looking in opposite directions. Both images symbolise a struggle between two forces, both of which are strong and valid, but opposite in their desires. Usually, one of the horses is black and the other is white, further suggesting this apparent conflict and their opposing natures, and it is the task of the charioteer to keep those forces under control. In some cards where the chariot is being driven by two horses, one horse is aiming right, with its head turned slightly in that direction, while the other horse is going straight ahead, as if it were wearing blinkers or refusing any change of direction.

The number of the Chariot, seven, is usually considered a sacred, mystical number, embodying a sense of spirituality, accomplishment, magic, music and enchantment. And indeed, perhaps it is these which the Charioteer has achieved mastery over. It almost always symbolic of a victory of self-discipline, or the mind having achieved control over opposing forces, the theme of The Chariot being the balancing of opposites. Indeed, the balancing and integrating of differing forces is a common issue that appears in many cards of the Major Arcana.

The Charioteer is not necessarily cut off from his emotions, but he is not focused on them at this time; they may even be seen as 'entanglement'. He tells you that if you don't distract yourself with feelings but keep control of your reins and your eyes on the prize, whatever your goal, this focus will pay off. This should be a time when you are maintaining a strong division between your professional life and your feelings, but you have the ability to bridge the gap and connect the two if the task calls for it. In any case, you can harness the energies you need to accomplish your goal, just as the horses or sphinxes are harnessed and moving ahead.

Although The Chariot suggests a state of inner conflict, it also indicates unexpected good news is on its way. Its other divinatory meanings are adversity, possibly already overcome, conflicting influences, turmoil, success, vengeance, the possibility of a voyage or journey, escape, rushing into a decision, the need to pay attention to details, and urgency to gain control of one's emotions. This card is about victory and conquest over difficult odds, the force of destiny which drives one to achieve great things, renewed optimism and motivation; by being self reliant one can attain high levels of success.

When The Chariot appears in a reading, it could also mean that there are conflicts between yourself and those around you, and an element of compromise might be necessary, whether the dispute is internal or external.

Overall, the Chariot is a passionate card, suggesting that your feelings of desire are inflamed and stirred up, and that a sense of calm and balance is needed to create a state of stability.

★ HOW THIS CARD RELATES TO CANCER ★

The Chariot, the protected home on wheels, is assigned to Cancer, the sign of motherhood, home, and family life. Cancer's Crab carries his home on his back.

Corrine Kenner

At first consideration, Cancer doesn't seem to have much in common with the victorious, adventurous spirit of The Chariot card. If we search a little deeper however, we will find that the charioteer never leaves his family or home for too long, and only for necessary expeditions, that benefit both his domestic life and his community. Additionally, both are unquestionably resourceful, tenacious, intuitive and protective - just as a seeking traveller might be. In any case, charioteers are usually on a quest for the betterment of their business, trade, communities, or family life, concerns they have in common with Cancer. The Chariot itself also offers a home away from home for the Cancerian charioteer wishing to bring a little piece of home and familiarity along for the ride.

The Chariot ultimately suggests an inner conflict, and the fact that the charioteer is clearly having trouble keeping his horses in control is an indication that his feelings are in opposition; he knows he needs to steer the middle course, but that isn't an easy task. This may translate into something simple, for instance one part of you wants to remain idle while the other half wants to undertake and complete a task. This leads to an internal battle which sometimes has the outcome that neither side achieves a satisfactory result. Cancer lives out the internal battle that the Chariot represents every day. A great paradox inherent in the Crab's character is that although she is tenacious and persevering, she is also easily defeated and withdrawing if the stakes become too high (or, in a metaphorical sense, if the horses' strength overwhelms her); far from weak, but deeply vulnerable, this is Cancer's troubling conflict - to control the horses using her innate might, or let them win and take her where she doesn't particularly wish to go, because she has surrendered to outside forces. The Chariot is a tough lesson for the Cancerian soul to learn, for she wavers and she flinches at even slight conflicts or obstacles. But the inner war she is fighting needs to be resolved before the horses completely throw her off balance. If she fails to restore her sense of control over that or those which seek to steer her, instead of the other way around, she will fall off and has every chance of staying there until she is ready to re-emerge from the safety of her shell - which we all know can sometimes take a very long time. All in all, the Chariot relates to Cancer in sharing with her the eternal paradox of vulnerability which leads to defeat, versus careful control which leads to personal triumph.

★ DIVINE MANIFESTATION USING THE CHARIOT ★

You can Divinely manifest things in your experience through tapping into your inner Power.

Carrying the spoils of war, a princely warrior triumphantly reaches the finish line. With a robust physique and stern resolve, the Chariot steerer has harnessed not only his considerable energies, but also those of nature. Self-assurance and bravado have held him in good stead in the headlong race against formidable opposition. By suppressing feeling and emotion, the Chariot steerer has held onto the reins and moved from barren fields into green and flowering ones. The same it is with you, and if you can find ways to access these inner treasures and resources, you are well on your way to achieving your goals, aims or ideals. The Chariot indicates a man who combines imagination with mental discipline and tenacity, displaying natural leadership abilities, and his Tarot essence embodies these qualities. Try to cultivate them in yourself for the sake of your own progress. Leaders are not born, they are made, many of them self-made. And one way to become a leader, an authority, a director of yourself, is to master and practise the fine art of sound decision-making. This card is telling you that if you wish to accomplish your goals or create the life of your desires, that you need to stop dilly-dallying and start calling the shots; discipline your horses to gallop in the direction of your dreams and never allow them to be blinkered by distractions or what lies behind them. Stay grounded and calm and above all, be clear about what you're ultimately trying to achieve.

★ EXERCISES TO TAP INTO YOUR INNER CHARIOTEER ★

★ Write down one area in your life where you are making considerable progress at the moment ~ be it in the form of your child, your marriage, mind development, a health issue that is finally dissolving, or a restored friendship. How has this boosted your feelings about yourself in general? Reflect on your thoughts around this.

★ If there is an area in your life in which you are not making progress and feel pulled back, are you able to examine it to see if the horses pulling your chariot are actually moving in different directions, i.e. you are feeling conflicted or indecisive about something that has the power to influence the course of your life? If so, look at ways that you can bring them back into alignment so that they are both steering the same course. Is there a way you can possibly find a middle ground, a happy medium with this situation that is pulling you in different directions?

★ STRENGTH ★

Ruled by Leo

Number ★ 8 (or 11 in some decks)
Astrological Sign ★ Leo

Keywords ★ Gentle Force, Courage, Inner Fortitude, Power

Magical Title ★ Daughter of the Flaming Sword, Leader of the Lion
Divinity ★ Ares (second aspect)
Spiritual Value ★ Strength represents the mastery of the lower by the higher. It is the soul which holds our wildest passions in check, even though her feet are planted on Earth. This Arcanum may be used to eliminate any psychic blockages that you hold onto from any past experiences so you can move forward with increased vitality, willpower, purpose, fighting spirit and overall capacity.

★ KEY THEMES ★

"The Inner Warrior"

Courage ★ Fortitude ★ Moral Fibre ★ Firmness ★ Power ★ Confidence ★ Great Inner Strength ★ Forgiveness ★ Compassion ★ Patience ★ Willpower ★ The Courage of Your Convictions ★ Belief in Own Strength ★ Gentle Force ★ Determination ★ Domination of Instincts ★ Tranquil Strength ★ Dauntlessness ★ Triumph ★ Control of a Situation ★ Victory Achieved Through a Gentle, Measured Approach

Meditation ★ "I have the courage, resolve and spiritual fortitude to overcome all."

★ *When Working with this Card* ★

MAIN ENERGIES ★ Courage, Acceptance, Love, Trust, Empowerment
MAIN GOD OR GODDESS TO INVOKE ★ Apollo
CANDLE COLOUR ★ Red
MAGICAL TOOLS OR SYMBOLS ★ Sword, Eye of Horus
CRYSTALS ★ Ruby, Red Jasper, Garnet, Bloodstone, Tiger's Eye

ASSOCIATED BEINGS, GODS, GODDESSES & ARCHETYPES ★ Angels of Building or Blessings, Solar Archangels, Belenos, Apollo, Sekhmet, Bast/Bastet, Jupiter, Sirius, Athene, Hathor *, Anubis, Son of Light, the Heroine, the Amazon.

* Like most warrior goddesses, Hathor tended only to fight in defence, or to right a wrong on behalf of someone she loved, which is also typical of the Greek goddess Athene (wisdom), the most powerful of all warriors; this is another way of saying that wisdom ultimately conquers force. This suggests that energy can either heal or nourish, when used constructively, or break and destroy if used destructively.

ARCHETYPES ★ Strength is the powerful lady with the heart of a lion. Gently holding the jaws of a wild cat, she calmly controls a force that would otherwise overcome and conquer her. Strength is the Heroine, the Anima, the Maiden, the Amazon.

CHAKRAS ★ Use this card to balance and meditate upon the Solar Plexus, Heart and Crown chakras.

Solar Plexus ★ Behind the Navel ★ Yellow ★ Fire ★ Personal Power, Confidence & Control

Heart ★ Heart Region ★ Green ★ Air ★ Love & Compassion

Crown ★ Top of Head ★ Purple ★ Thought/Knowing ★ Spiritual Wisdom & Enlightenment

TREE OF LIFE ★ In western magic, which combines the Tarot paths of the Major Arcana with the ten sephiroth on the Tree of Life, the path of Strength connects Geburah and Chesed.

NUMERIC SIGNIFICANCE ★ Universally, eight is the number of cosmic balance. Eight is the most balanced of numbers - a fact that, whether by accident or design, is perfectly reflected in the symmetrical Arabic symbol or numeral '8' that we use to represent it. The symbol '8' also demonstrates indestructibility in that no matter at which point we start to draw it, we always end up where we started. Like the zero symbol or the circle, it has no end and no beginning, and therefore stands as a symbol of eternity; in fact, when placed on its side, the figure 8 is a symbol for everlasting life. It is also the number of Divine law, so some sort of karmic situation may manifest which will teach you an important lesson or lessons, such as wrestling with a fierce lion, a metaphor for your inner demons. Eight stands for the octave. It is also the number of architecture and structure, where two sets of four can be combined elegantly together. The steps of the octave, which we associate mostly with notes in music and also possessing a vibrationally-connected connotation, are said to represent a cosmic order, in which you find a similar note at the top to that at the bottom, but at a different pitch or level. The octave is generally seen as a 'vertical' structure. Eight can be found in the octagon, or can be seen as two interlaced squares, or an eight-fold star. Ancient numerologists sometimes interpreted the potential of eight as an Energy which networks, connects, circuits and organises the Worlds. It represents the point at which the infinite and finite merge, where the spiritual materialises and matter spiritualises, where the unconscious becomes conscious and conscious becomes unconscious, and also where life follows death and death follows life. It is through the power of eight that Spirit dissolves into matter and matter can be transmuted into Spirit, a concept that the Strength card encapsulates.

THE FOOL'S JOURNEY ★ After encountering his dark side, The Fool needs to learn to trust himself and develop self-confidence. This card is equated with the Jungian hero or heroine.

> Strength is the place of self-dominion where we know the defining discipline of the warrior.
>
> **Paul Hougham**

THE STORY ★ Strength is a situation which is well in-hand, controlled, and of which one is in charge. It signifies a courageous person, endowed with a tranquil strength, a resolute temperament and sound self-control. The lady depicted in most decks has tamed the animal's wild nature with her spiritual touch. She has no need of physical strength, for by love she has conquered. The crown the lion wears in common symbolism signifies that he is King of the Beasts, while the brave young woman on the Strength Tarot card, with the sign for 'infinity' crowning her highest energy centre, renders her the Queen of Strength. By conquering the natural fears of her own bestial nature, she has harnessed the infinite power of her Spirit.

> The bravest thing you can do when you are not brave is to profess courage and act accordingly.
>
> **Corra May White Harris**

THE MESSAGE ★ Sometimes called Fortitude, this is one of the three virtues that appear in the Tarot deck - the others are Justice and Temperance. The Strength card will appear when you need to know that you're stronger than you realise and that you can definitely handle your current challenges. Look upon your current situations as opportunities from which to learn and grow so that you can apply the knowledge gained with a superbly magical touch.

> Courage is resistance to fear, mastery of fear, not absence of fear.
>
> **Mark Twain**

THE AWAKENING ★ In the face of fear, act calmly and with love and you will gain the true strength of an integrated body and spirit. Through gentleness you will accomplish what force cannot. Strength promises victory to those who know how to direct their natural gifts and willpower into the right channels, and who persevere in their efforts with unflagging energy and focus. It is through the power of inner peace and love that the character featured on this card is able to tame the ferocious beast and can open his mouth with sheer will but little physical effort. Indeed, the strength of her soul and the force of her love will tame the lion more effectively than any violence, aggression or savagery. She represents the overcoming of difficulties and weaknesses of character through steady persistence. The lion symbolises power and positive energy, and the human figure harnesses that power. Drawing this card will always make you the master of yourself and/or the situation in which you find yourself. It tells you that, if you handle circumstances in a positive, concentrated and gentle manner, you will achieve your aim.

> I am not afraid; I was born to do this.
>
> **Joan of Arc**

THE LESSON ★ Strength indicates that personal courage and discipline are required in order to reach a goal. The struggle between human and lion is a reflection of bravery, and although the portrayal of a person fighting this beast is depicted as a physical one, it also relates to inner struggles. The message is to keep going through a difficult situation instead of running away from it. This does not suggest that you should put up with being bullied, but on the contrary, its wise counsel is that you should quietly and courageously stand up to tyranny. Truth, light, tact and diplomacy are far more effective, and will win you respect and admiration.

> Archetypal heroes are always snatching defeat from the jaws of victory. When the going gets tough, the tough get going - but the enlightened? They surrender.

Martha Beck

SYMBOLISM ★ Strength's symbolism lies in the reconciling of your base instincts, the taming of your wild stirrings, bestial urges and primal desires, with your higher levels of will and consciousness. Its message is in keeping with the evolutionary process of the Self depicted in the Major Arcana: the development of self-knowledge that raises your awareness to a high understanding and fuller integration of your whole self. It represents passion for life that provides the energy to overcome even tough challenges. A symbol of the ultimate the life force expression, Strength gives you the knowing that you are grounded and strong, stronger indeed than you think.

The Strength card features a powerful human figure (the conscious mind), sometimes male and sometimes female, fighting to prise open the jaws of a lion (the untamed instincts), conquering the beast without the use of his club (or force). The club, which is lying on the ground, is apparently redundant, revealing that physical weapons are not necessary when the force of pure will is available and utilised.

Where the figure is female, she represents the feminine aspect of Strength. It is not by aggression or forceful coercion that she shuts the lion's jaws; it is by her inner peace, assurance and fortitude. This lady, clothed in a white robe symbolising purity, could be seen as a maiden, of following sign Virgo's ilk.

The lion struggles feebly against the person, but has evidently already accepted his defeat. This symbolises the conscious mind having supremacy over the primal animal nature.

OVERALL ★ CONNECTING IT ALL UP ★

> Nothing is so strong as gentleness; nothing so gentle as real strength.

St Francis De Sales

This card indicates courage, fortitude and accomplishing feats with gentle firmness and determination. As this card is ruled by Leo, it also signifies honour, reliability, honesty and a fixed sense of purpose. It depicts a beautiful young woman wrestling with a powerful lion, attempting to 'tame' the beast by holding his jaws open, a symbol of control rather than destruction. The lion is a representation of strength and potent energy that must be controlled or regulated if its damaging impulses are to be curbed. The fact that it's (usually) a female who is subduing the creature suggests that the strength required to wrestle with potentially negative forces is not about physical prowess, but rather emotional fortitude. It represents a woman who has discovered her strength and who is prepared to expand her life with quiet courage and self-confidence. Her gentle firmness is representative of the higher, immortal spiritual self, which means this card is telling us not to allow our rational, objective mind (the lion) to overrule our spiritual wisdom (the woman). The brim of the lady's hat is in the shape of a figure of eight, the symbol of infinity, which is also worn by The Magician, further emphasising her connection with inner wisdom and the spiritual realm.

Divinatory meanings of the Strength card are firstly, strength, and also courage, power, conviction, resolution, energy, defiance, action, confidence, zeal, mind over matter or matter over mind, and accomplishment. It symbolises resolute action and a willingness to boldly stand up for what is right, regardless of the consequences. Other themes are physical strength, a fight for fair play, courage in defeating mean attitudes and hatred, and rapid health improvement if illness has been recently experienced. Furthermore, you will triumph over enemies and setbacks.

When working with this card, ask yourself how you can strengthen your own sense of purpose to succeed on your journey, and remember that progress on the Path to self-discovery is made through gentle strength, not severity. Its message is that there is no need to worry or lose sight of your goals, for even though the road you are on may seem difficult, you will get there in the end. Patience, perseverance and self-awareness are needed to keep you on track. You also need to nurture your spirit, fortify your morals and foster self-discipline.

This card is a good indication of recovery from illness or other difficulties and may describe a situation that must be confronted bravely even though you are fearful. The Strength card represents the power of healing by the bringing forth of the 'feminine force', into a place where wild animals are tamed and the world of unseen forces is explored through it.

When the Strength card appears in a reading, it means you are experiencing yourself as ready and able to get what you want in life. Grounded and centred in your experiences of powerful energy, you know from deep within your heart what you need, and since your own needs are connected with the needs of others, you are able to provide this power and share its energy with others. You are able to reach out and heal or touch another life, and you do this with passion and a sense of deep caring. You have the ability to move others through your expression of your convictions and powerful feelings.

The Strength card indicates that there is magic afoot in your life at this time, so now is an opportune time to ask for what you have always wished for, for it is now ripe for manifestation. The time may also be right for a 'shaman journey', in which you could find yourself an animal spirit-helper. Your psychic powers are ready to open up, your visions are vivid, and you may even hear your own oracular voice.

Overall, the image in Strength signifies that if the inner animal urges within each of us can be used positively and without overuse of force, great things can be achieved, and any adversities can be easily overcome through the use of your vast inner resources.

★ HOW THIS CARD RELATES TO LEO ★

Strength, the master of gentle force and control, is assigned to Leo,
the sign of lionesque courage and heart.

Corrine Kenner

The fact that there is a lion in the Strength card suggests strong links to the sign of Leo, whose symbol is this majestic, mighty beast. 'Gentle force' is a term to describe the essence of this card, and provides another connection with Leo, who himself uses an all-powerful and solid manner to achieve the desired effect. Leo, although prone to being overbearing and boisterous, also has a subtle side, a side that he will bring out when the situation or need calls for it. He has the uncanny ability to discern the amount of Strength something requires, and will apply his energy accordingly, wilfully and with a self-assured air of authority. Somehow, the mighty Lion always seems to strike just the right balance to obtain his goals. Unyielding, fixed and sturdy, he instinctively knows when to lay down and surrender, and when to stand up and fight - and does both with an unmatched nobility, valour, willpower, daring, self-confidence and unflinching inner power. The Lion, like the character in the Strength card, rightly deserves his birth-given right to show it all off after he has successfully conquered the beast.

★ DIVINE MANIFESTATION USING STRENGTH ★

You can Divinely manifest things in your experience through tapping into your inner Fortitude.

The Strength card tells you that you need to know you're stronger than you realise and that you can definitely handle your current challenges. However, instead of using force and barging through obstacles, you're better off with an approach of compassion, gentleness and firm kindness, as the strength that your setbacks call for can only come from the softness of a spiritual core. You need to release harsh judgements and practice forgiveness and patience, and your strength and effectiveness will increase. You need to believe in yourself and your ability to grow from your trials. Strength can conversely mean that you are experiencing yourself as ready and able to get what you want in life. Grounded and centered in your experience of energy, you know from your *heart* what you need. There is indeed magic afoot in your life at this time, and if you haven't already accessed it, it is available to you. When working with this card, try wishing for what you have always wanted - now is the time it may manifest; in any case, the energy is there for you to harness and utilise to your great advantage. Look upon your current adversities as opportunities for Divine learning and the infinite potential to grow in direct proportion to the size of your dreams.

★ EXERCISE TO TAP INTO YOUR INNER STRENGTH ★

★ Do you have something in your life that you are needing to cultivate courage or spiritual fortitude around? Write down some thoughts about it, and list small steps you can take towards confronting your fears or lack of courage ~ by examining and confronting those parts of yourself that are fearful of standing firm in your convictions about something that is important to you, you may find your courage will find the passage to the light easier. If you make inner confrontations with your shadow self an important part of your spiritual growth, your fortitude will come to the fore to help you fight your battles.

★ THE HERMIT ★

Ruled by Virgo

Number ★ 9
Astrological Sign ★ Virgo

Keywords ★ Withdrawal, Retreat, Solitude, Contemplation, Inner Journeying

Magical Title ★ The Prophet of the Gods, The Magus of the Voices of Light
Divinity ★ Eros
Spiritual Value ★ The Hermit is the eternal seeker, the Pilgrim soul, and represents wisdom sought for and obtained from above. In the mystical titles, this card combines with the Magician and the Hierophant as the three Magi. The Hermit can be used when you are needing Divine inspiration, or the need to re-establish connection with the inner and uppermost parts of your being. It can awaken you by being an expanding force that supports the realisation of your deepest desires.

★ KEY THEMES ★

"The Spiritual Illuminator & Enlightened One"

Introspection ★ Awareness ★ Quiet Contemplation ★ Reflection ★ Solitude ★ Withdrawal ★ Spiritual Learning ★ Self-discovery ★ Soul-searching ★ Good Advice ★ Wisdom ★ Embarking on a Spiritual Quest ★ Re-evaluation of Plans ★ Slow and Profound Evolution ★ Search ★ Discovery ★ Knowledge ★ Discernment ★ Patience

Meditation ★ "I embrace my inner self through solitude. I will find the answers I seek through quiet, gentle retreat and thoughtful introspection, and endeavour to share the insights with others when I re-emerge restored, enlightened and transformed."

★ *When Working with this Card* ★

MAIN ENERGIES ★ Inner Knowing, Wisdom, Gentle Flow, Enlightenment
MAIN GOD OR GODDESS TO INVOKE ★ Athena
CANDLE COLOUR ★ Black
MAGICAL TOOL OR SYMBOL ★ Lantern
CRYSTALS ★ Amethyst, Purple Fluorite, Moonstone, Opal, Blue Lace Agate

ASSOCIATED BEINGS, GODS, GODDESSES & ARCHETYPES ★ Supernal, the Holy Spirit, Saturn, Erlang Shen, Minerva, Athene, Mimir, Asi, Saraswati, Emer, Omoikane, Breath of Spirit within the Great Mother, the Guide, the Magical Helper, the Wise Old Man, the Wounded Healer.

We hear the call of our wild. We play games to end their games … The play is part of our work of unweaving and of our weaving work. It whirls us into another frame of reference. We use the visitation of demons to come more deeply into touch with our own powers/virtues. Unweaving their deceptions, we name our Truth.

Vicky Noble

ARCHETYPES ★ The Hermit is a recluse, far removed from the noise and chaos of everyday civilisation. Looking inwardly, he reflects on spiritual concerns, and carries the light of wisdom as a beacon for others to follow. He is the Mystic, the Scribe, Magus, the Self, the Miser, the Shaman, the Mentor, the Messenger, the Teacher, the Visionary, the Wanderer, the Wizard.

CHAKRAS ★ Use this card to balance and meditate upon the Third Eye and Crown chakras.

Third Eye ★ Between the Eyes ★ Dark Blue ★ Light ★ Clairvoyance, Wisdom, Intuition & Vision

Crown ★ Top of Head ★ Purple ★ Thought/Knowing ★ Spiritual Wisdom & Enlightenment

TREE OF LIFE ★ In western magic, which combines the Tarot paths of the Major Arcana with the ten sephiroth on the Tree of Life, the path of The Hermit connects Tiphareth and Chesed.

I love to be alone. I never found a companion that was so companionable as solitude.

Henry David Thoreau

NUMERIC SIGNIFICANCE ★ Nine is a significant and magical number. The number nine is usually regarded as second in significance only to number three among the odd numbers, primarily because it is the product of three by three. It is almost the most indestructible of the odd numbers in the sense that all its multiples reduce to nine if we add together the digits of which they are composed. It is sometimes considered the ultimate number, with special and sacred significance. The Nonagon or the Ennead as it is otherwise known, was regarded in many ancient cultures as Perfection and Concord, and as being unbounded. Magicians of former times would draw a magic circle nine feet in diameter, in which to practice their magic. The power and potential of the number nine is linked to the powers of Law, balance and completion. Nine, being the number of imagination, intuition and holistic perception, liberates the inner artist in you. It also stirs your natural, innate healing potential and your deepest psychic self. It is the number of the Universe and of vision, representing spiritual ideals and philosophy, concepts which the Tarot's Hermit heartily embraces.

> This is the hermit of the Tarot; the number which refers to initiates and to prophets.
> The prophets are solitaries, for it is their fate that none should ever hear them.
> They see differently from others; they forefeel misfortunes.

Eliphas Levi

THE FOOL'S JOURNEY ★ This is The Fool, but instead of looking skyward while he walks towards a cliff, he's looking inward, where he'll learn about the benefits of meditation and reflection. The archetypal equivalent here is the Wise Old Man or solitary wizard.

> The Hermit is the witness of our internal solitude, the intimacy of
> our own signature before we expand into the Universal.

Paul Hougham

THE STORY ★ Carrying his luminous but strangely lit lantern, The Hermit walks the enlightened Path of wisdom. He walks alone and at night, where both his robe and the dark conceal him, for his teachings are only for those who seek him out. The Hermit's symbolism shows you how to attune to your inner wisdom. He represents a turning away from the external world to focus inwardly. In spite of his reclusiveness, he carries a lantern to light the Path ahead, which may be symbolic of his quest for knowledge, and also that introspection is not all about darkness - in fact, one requires the darker recesses of the soul to be illuminated during the 'search'. Sometimes he is accompanied by a serpent, which represents the cycle of death and rebirth.

> I went to the woods because I wished to live deliberately, to front only the essential facts of
> life, and see if I could not learn what it had to teach, and not, when I came to die, discover
> that I had not lived.

Henry David Thoreau

THE MESSAGE ★ The Hermit is the wise, Solitary One, a seeker who knows how to call down the power of the Moon, to converse with spirits and work magical spells. The Hermit is telling you that you need to spend some quiet time in meditation. This is a time to reflect, in order to reassess your direction and your commitments. You would benefit from some time alone, listening to your inner voice. This card is compelling you to learn to feel comfortable in your own company. It indicates a time of spiritual awakening, enlightenment, wisdom-seeking, and journeying to the inner depths. This card's essence also suggests that perhaps it is time for you to seek out a spiritual guide, teacher, healer or mentor for yourself before undertaking the arduous task of probing the inner workings of your soul.

> The cyclone derives its power from a calm centre. So does a person.

Norman Vincent Peale

THE AWAKENING ★ The Hermit is not looking for his way, but rather is showing and lighting the way. He is the master of light, the illuminator, whose lantern represents wakeful consciousness, the eternal soul, vigilance, foresight, perceptiveness and inner light. He is the interpreter of oracles, the bearer of revelations, the inner voice which has been silenced for so long. If this solitary provider of wisdom is followed with reverence, he will shed much light upon any problem. Through his urging, you to take some time out, he can help you to become more aware of your motivations, your aspirations, your desires, and to give a greater meaning to your life, confronting you with your true Path. The Hermit represents the inward self, troubled by deep but enriching and fruitful thoughts, or he could represent the presence of another person in your life, an older one, who has acquired some wisdom or specific knowledge you could benefit from, or perhaps The Hermit simply stands for a solitary, isolated person - which could be you or someone in your close experience. He can also signify a time in your life when you will be on your own, a kind of journey through your own inner 'desert' * landscape.

* Did the creators of the Major Arcana make a glaring spelling error when they wrote 'Hermit' instead of 'Ermit'? No, but it is interesting to note that 'Ermit' is a Latin word of Greek origin whose first meaning was 'desert'; then it came to mean 'he who lives in the desert', in solitude.

THE LESSON ★ You have a desire for quiet introspection, to assimilate the changes taking place within. Through this, you understand that by listening to your inner spirit you can acquire wisdom. Others recognise this and seek out your advice, after which you find yourself drawn out into the world again. The Hermit encourages you to increase your knowledge of the world through study and experience. He suggests that sometimes you need to withdraw and re-consider your true self. Like the accomplished shamans and wise women everywhere, The Hermit contains both the male and the female, the active and the receptive, and the Sun and Moon within. He has learned the power of energy retention and transmutation, and can now choose how to spend or store those energies. He knows that plunging down into the unconscious is a vital part of the soul's search for meaning. The time out he embarks upon is both healing and rejuvenating. Like a caterpillar, he seeks transformation. And like the caterpillar, he spins fibres around himself and later emerges as something new and different. But the awakening can evoke pain: indeed, turning away from the world to discover whether you are really alive is undoubtedly painful, but it is in this conscious acceptance of loneliness that a natural process of healing occurs. And through this inner listening, The Hermit often becomes a teacher, a way-shower to others.

I study myself more than any other subject. That is my physics. That is my metaphysics.

Michel de Montaigne

SYMBOLISM ★ Nine, The Hermit's number, always symbolises wisdom and a sense of sacred magic. Nine multiplied by any number reduces to nine, making it essentially indestructible. The Hermit is a man whole within himself, an example to all of us of what it means to be *ourselves*. His active inner light shines out to touch others with the knowledge he has gained on his journey.

The Hermit's monk's robe is brown, which is symbolic of the renunciation of worldly pursuits and pleasures in order to disassociate from the world and retreat into the self. It also indicates that he intends to use his spiritual insights in a practical manner. The lantern he carries is symbolic of the guiding light of inner knowing and insight.

The card depicts an old man whose head is bowed down, with a long grey beard and a hunched back who is shrouded in a hooded dark robe of a monk, with only his hands and a tiny portion of his face visible. In one hand, he holds a staff to support himself and in his other hand he holds a lit lantern which he shines upon the Path before him. His lantern denotes the light he uses to light up his inner world, which, as he grows older, he learns to appreciate. He has an aura of mystery about him, standing alone against a grey horizon; even the Earth's natural richness seems to elude him.

The Hermit is a reflection of age, and represents the wisdom of age, using his lantern to illuminate the Path towards self-enlightenment. He is sometimes said to be The Fool midway through his journey, a little wiser, more restrained and less impatient. He warns you to bring all the elements of your life together - action, emotions, finances and morality - to enable you to handle the changes ahead wisely. The Hermit represents re-evaluation, for The Hermit is an old man who looks back on his past and realises that there must be more than this. He knows next to nothing of the 'greater reality' and fears even his own ignorance about wider realms. However, The Hermit *does* show a willingness to remedy that ignorance and offers the patience and discipline required to utilise past experiences and old lessons to make the most out of the future.

OVERALL ★ CONNECTING IT ALL UP ★

Solitude is the cure for loneliness; like cures like ... The spiritual traditions of many cultures require a time of arduous solitude as a necessary prerequisite to self-knowledge.

Caroline W. Casey

Along the Tarot journey, this is where The Fool comes across a mood of grey stillness. The lacklustre energy of the image does not mean it is dull or symbolic of stagnation, however. Rather, it is symbolic of wisdom; The Hermit looks down carefully to see where he is going, suggesting wisdom, caution and experience. The Hermit alludes to the solitary nature of the 'life traveller' in all of us, trudging intently onwards with a solemn and silent determination. He walks alone through the night, with only the glow of his intuition (the lantern) to guide him.

This card can be interpreted as standing for caution, old age and experience. The Hermit is not a pessimist, but he has become wary through age and experience; he has learned to be a realist. A prudent attitude is recommended, so sudden courses of action are not the wisest at this time. It is a time for withdrawal from action, towards inner meditation.

The Hermit also signifies the realisation that there is always something new to learn, and serves as a warning against thoughtless actions. The time is ripe for withdrawal from the chaotic outside world in order to enter the peaceful inner one. This is a time for soul-searching and seclusion that is consciously chosen rather than imposed from without; it implies time spent alone for meditation and reflection rather than out of any sense of isolation. This means gently freeing our minds of the external chatter and noise, to allow time and space for our thoughts to clear, and denotes the need for patience and an opportunity to work things out quietly. A degree of solitude is often required and temporary disengagement is allowed. The Hermit enjoys being alone - which isn't the same as being lonely; rather he teaches the lessons of solitude, which is often one of people's great fears. He also teaches us to accept, rather than fight, the passage of time, so the rewards he brings lie in the fostering of patience, tolerance and serenity.

This period of withdrawal is an opportune time to ask oneself if one listens too much to the opinions and advice of others, because often the wisest counsellor of all is the voice of one's inner self. The Hermit teaches the lesson of time, and the inevitability of old age. The truth is, we are always essentially alone, but to face this fact involves wisdom and acceptance, and once we accept it, it becomes far less frightening or threatening. Acceptance, endurance and inner quiet to obtain self-understanding, and timeless wisdom, are the messages learned through our encounter with the wise Hermit. Other divinatory meanings are counsel, knowledge, servitude, solicitude, prudence, discretion, caution, circumspection, vigilance, self-denial, regression, fear of discovery, a tendency to withhold emotions, and annulment.

Although there is a substantial emphasis on solitude and withdrawal in this card, it is also strongly suggesting that you need to share the wisdom of your journey with someone, perhaps through finding or even becoming a spiritual mentor. The Hermit signifies sacred teaching in a broad sense, so it could mean that you have a special brand of understanding to impart to others, or that perhaps it's time for you to find a spiritual guide.

The Hermit also represents the steadfast courage and determination needed to continue on the 'journey', as he trudges intently onward. Overall, he can be equated with timeless knowledge, making the card a potent reminder that the truth of existence is to be found within ourselves, since we are each part of that Universal truth.

★ HOW THIS CARD RELATES TO VIRGO ★

> The Hermit, the quiet leader, is assigned to Virgo, the sign of responsibility and dedicated service to others ... At their core, Virgos are somewhat isolated ... They are also extremely helpful, (so) once you seek them out, they are more than willing to share the wisdom they have accumulated on their own journeys ... The combination of the wise old Hermit and the brash young Magician (Mercury) relates directly to Virgo's desire to teach and help other people.
>
> **Corrine Kenner**

Virgo and The Hermit have much in common. Both are wise beyond measure, years and even themselves; both need regular time out to replenish their stores; both carry with them an inner wealth of knowledge, sometimes shared, at others kept to themselves; both are on an eternal quest of self-knowledge and self-improvement; and both are essentially content to keep their own counsel and their own company. The Hermit possesses a gentle wisdom that lights his Path ahead, and he uses this lantern of insight to illuminate the road ahead for other travellers of the Path. Virgo contains the same brand of inner knowing, and, ruled by the intellectual planet of

Mercury, imparts her sagacity to others through her sound advice, analytical understandings and sharp perceptions - but only after much contemplative and sometimes confronting introspection.

✶ DIVINE MANIFESTATION USING THE HERMIT ✶

You can Divinely manifest things in your experience through tapping into your inner Self.

The Hermit tells you that you need to spend some quiet time in meditation. Take some time out to reflect and undertake an inner quest of discovery, in order to reassess your direction, your priorities, your commitments, your dreams, and those things you hold most dearly close. It is a paradox that we often only really fully realise the importance of our relationships with others upon experiencing genuine and substantial periods of solitude. To Divinely manifest your heart's desires, you would benefit from some time alone, listening to your inner voice. The Hermit's meaning compels you to learn to feel comfortable in your own company, to allow insecurities or fears about being truly alone, dissolve. Be silent and experience the joy that comes from seeking the truth and Path of your own heart. After this period of silence, introspection, journeying to your inner depths, and time out from everyday life and noise, you may experience a spiritual awakening, wisdom, even enlightenment. And once you have emerged from your otherworld, use your newfound awareness to light the way for others using your Lantern of Wisdom. Through the powerful lessons that can be gleaned by self-exploration, you can become the lightworker, the way-shower that assists others on their own quests. You have become, after these times of solitude, the sage, the teacher and the student all at the same time.

✶ EXERCISES TO TAP INTO YOUR INNER HERMIT ✶

✶ Do you enjoy solitude or do you find it lonely? Regardless of your true nature, take at least one pre-planned hour out to yourself on a regular basis, for the sole purpose of meditation, introspection, thought regulation, or the experience of simple solitude. Afterwards, reflect on what you discovered about yourself. Expect some negative emotions to have arisen and deal with them gently, particularly if you are not used to periods of seclusion, isolation or alone time. This is a sign that you have been courageous enough to confront your fears by stepping out of your comfort zone. Reward yourself for your bravery if you have found it difficult to 'sit' with yourself. With practice, it will get easier - and ever more satisfying.

✶ Are you an introvert or extrovert by nature? A simple way you can determine this is to answer this question: does being around people revitalise and restore you, or does being on your own revitalise and restore you? If you answered yes to the former, you are likely to tend towards extroversion. If you answered yes to the latter, you are likely to tend towards introversion. It is important to know this about your core self, as it will give you important clues that are the keys to unlocking your psyche and your highest potentials.

★ WHEEL OF FORTUNE ★

Ruled by Jupiter

Number ★ 10

Astrological Signs ★ Pisces, Sagittarius & the Fixed Signs: Aquarius, Taurus, Leo and Scorpio

Keywords ★ Change, Acceptance, Fate

Magical Title ★ Lord of the Forces of Life
Divinity ★ Hermes (second aspect)
Spiritual Value ★ The Wheel of Fortune can help you to develop better self-control and a deeper understanding of yourself and your role in the Divine occurrences, ups and downs, and synchronicities in your life.

★ KEY THEMES ★

"What Goes Down Must Come Up"

A Miracle ★ Adjustment in Circumstances ★ A New Chapter ★ Changes in Fortune ★ Unexpected Turn of Events ★ Fate and Free Will ★ A Twist of Fate ★ Continual Movement ★ Responsibility for One's Own Destiny ★ Good luck ★ A Happy Accident ★ Balanced Karma ★ Destiny ★ Acceptance ★ Progress ★ Possibility to Intervene or Act

Fortuna, the Goddess of good luck's energy is strongly embedded in the Wheel of Fortune card, and when this card appears in a reading, it means that:

Fortune is indeed smiling on you and you may as well surrender to the flow, because something remarkable - a big event - is taking place. ... Although fate does not in any sense control our lives, when something has been wished for and worked towards, it is the Goddess Fortuna who decides on the timing of the event. The Wheel of Fortune signifies a high point, a wish coming true, the manifestation of something anticipated.

Vicky Noble

Meditation ★ "I accept that life has its inevitable ups and downs, some over which I have control, others which I don't. At the heart of this is providence, and in providence I trust."

★ When Working with this Card ★

MAIN ENERGIES ★ Discernment, Trust, Acceptance
MAIN GOD OR GODDESS TO INVOKE ★ Fortuna
CANDLE COLOUR ★ Rainbow
MAGICAL TOOLS OR SYMBOLS ★ Wheel, Circle, Pentacle
CRYSTALS ★ Green Aventurine, Labradorite, Yellow Sapphire, Lapis Lazuli

ASSOCIATED BEINGS, GODS, GODDESSES & ARCHETYPES ★ Lunar Spirits, Thrones, Taranis, Daimones, Angels, the Universe, Elementals, Faeries, Fortuna, the Dagda, the Morrigan, Arianrhod, Minerva, Lakshmi, Brigid, Flower Maiden (Celtic), Hernes, Jupiter, Venus, Mercury, the Trickster.

ARCHETYPES ★ The Wheel of Fortune is the spinning wheel of destiny and fate, and because nothing is certain but change itself, the Wheel of Fortune reminds us that always trying to exert control over our destiny and fate is futile. It is the Creator, the Destroyer, the Ferris Wheel, the Fates, the Teacher.

CHAKRAS ★ Use this card to balance and meditate upon the Solar Plexus, Third Eye and Crown chakras.

Solar Plexus ★ Behind the Navel ★ Yellow ★ Fire ★ Personal Power, Confidence & Control

Third Eye ★ Between the Eyes ★ Dark Blue ★ Light ★ Clairvoyance, Wisdom, Intuition & Vision

Crown ★ Top of Head ★ Purple ★ Thought/Knowing ★ Spiritual Wisdom & Enlightenment

TREE OF LIFE ★ In western magic, which combines the Tarot paths of the Major Arcana with the ten sephiroth on the Tree of Life, the path of The Wheel of Fortune connects Netzach and Chesed, the first of these being a feminine sphere, the latter masculine.

NUMERIC SIGNIFICANCE ★ The sum of the first four numbers, 1 + 2 + 3 + 4, 10 is considered by Pythagoreans as the great number of all things, the archetype of the Universe. According to ancient mathematicians and philosophers, ten is the most supreme number, since it encompasses all arithmetic and harmonious proportions. Pythagoras said that ten is the nature of the numbers because all numbers come to her, and when they do, they return to the Monad (number one), the beginning. It represents Divine power. Ten is the number of the Sun, symbolising the cosmos, the paradigms of creation, completion and perfection. A very fortunate and 'holy' number, it leads you to victory in situations where others fear to tread. It suggests vibrant and creative originality. If number one signifies the origin, beginning or initialisation, number ten indicates an outcome, end or fulfilment. This principle of conclusion, if represented on a wheel, would come right before a re-birth, i.e. the beginning of a new cycle. Therefore, ten represents the culmination and potential inherent in all achievement. The power of ten sends us back to the starting point, that is to number one and the figure zero (which signifies untapped potential and innocence), because it heralds the end of a cycle, it makes continual regeneration and rebirth possible. According to Cornelius Agrippa, "The number 10 ... is the total number, the full path of life." The divine aspect of the number ten means sky, the highest integrity, absolute fullness, and an ultimate return to unity on a new, transformed level. The Wheel of Fortune embraces these very concepts and principles at its core.

> Ten is the number for Pure Intellect and Measure. Creation gave humans the power of Reason and Self Choice. Ten is also the number of the humans' Higher Self, their Sacred Twin. What can give better measure than this Spirit-Knowing? Come, children, have you met your Self?
>
> **Lightning Bolt (Hyemeyohsts Storm), Metis Medicine Man**

THE FOOL'S JOURNEY ★ Having completed the personal aspects of his journey, The Fool now encounters the outside forces associated with it. The Wheel of Fortune is all about destiny, the things of life that are beyond his control, but it also teaches The Fool that through wise discrimination, he can also exercise his free will. This is exemplified by the *Serenity Prayer*.

> God grant me the serenity to accept the things I cannot change, the courage to change the things I can, and the wisdom to know the difference.
>
> **Reinhold Niebuhr**

THE STORY ★ Tarot historians believe the word Tarot itself derives from the Latin word *rota*, as in 'rotation', and reflects the ancient sense of life as a moving wheel. The 'wheels within wheels' that make up the Wheel of Fortune, rotate and turn like the ever-spinning rhythms and cycles of life. The traditionally shaped wheel holds the symbolism of the Sun and the cosmos, and is an enduring symbol of human endeavour and advancement. A spin of the wheel may bring unexpected luck, opportunity and good fortune, or it may cause the reverse, and present obstacles to our desires. A confrontation with some 'demon' from the past may occur with a turn of the wheel. These could be fate, part of a Divine plan, or karma, but what seem to be beginnings and endings are in fact just part of the never-ending circle of life. Rising up from the horizon are two puffs of smoke that symbolise the form of spirit, signifying that in spite of all the changes, nothing remains but the elusive essence. Animals of varying characters and powers are depicted around the circle, and ultimately atop the wheel reigns a Sphinx, with flowing eyes that oversee all the cycles, evolutions, revolutions and recurring patterns. The Sphinx, in her quiet wisdom, knows that no one stays on top forever.

> Wheel of Fortune is the flamboyant abundance of our roller-coaster ride into the realm of soul, aware of the cyclical return to places of home.
>
> **Paul Hougham**

THE MESSAGE ★ The Wheel of Fortune frequently appears as a motif in medieval art and was an attribute of Fortuna, the Roman goddess of fate (Tyche was the Greek equivalent). Fortuna represents each moment's potential for luck or ill, with the turning of her wheel bringing happiness and success to some, and misery and misfortune to others. She is often depicted blindfolded, because fate is morally blind. The Wheel of Fortune signifies an important turning point for good or bad, and tells us that life is not a merry-go-round, but rather a roller coaster, encouraging us to realise that there is ultimately purpose and equilibrium in everything that happens to us. This card usually denotes a time of positive change, or a situation that suddenly moves forward. Fortune is on your side! This card also offers a chance to step back from circumstances in order to notice life's seasons, or the natural 'turning of the wheel'. In doing this, you will know when to plant seeds and when to harvest.

THE AWAKENING ★ It is not the Wheel of Fate but the Wheel of Fortune; this nuance is important. Indeed, the very fact that the wheel is activated by a handle, suggests the notion of free will at play. In other words, you have the choice to act or not to act, to use or not to use the handle in order to activate the wheel of your destiny. In any case, this card must prompt you to become aware of your share of active, conscious or unconscious responsibilities in the situations, circumstances or events you inevitably have to confront. Sometimes it indicates that we have to remain committed in order to progress; other times it means that for the moment, we can do nothing else but allow events to take their natural course.

> The truth of course is that there is no journey. We are arriving and departing all at the same time.
>
> **David Bowie**

THE LESSON ★ Ask your own spiritual guides or gods or goddesses to deliver to you your desires and just fortunes. Meditate on the Wheel of Fortune as you ask, and finally, take the chance and turn the wheel, for you never know where it may come to rest. The Wheel of Fortune represents the ability to understand and accept things, encouraging you to embrace changes in life wholeheartedly.

SYMBOLISM ★ In Buddhist thought, the Wheel of Life is *Samsara*, the never-ending, going-nowhere spinning circle of illusion that represents the physical and emotional world of the senses. Buddhists believe the solution is to get off the Wheel by transcending these physical and emotional worlds. Some other religions and thoughts, suggest a coming to terms with the Wheel by understanding the laws of cause and effect, and by directing one's life accordingly.

The Wheel of Fortune symbolises the constant cycles that run through life. We may experience high and low points, yet the Wheel continues to turn. Therefore, the fundamental message of the Wheel is that you need to be attuned to the still centre within yourself, whatever the outer circumstances may be.

The Wheel of Fortune is turned by a blindfolded figure, looking in the opposite direction, symbolising that the ways of fate are a mystery and that you can only accept change, and work with it. The other figures, sitting on the Wheel and falling off as it turns, represent the varying experiences of life, and emphasise that resistance to change is completely futile.

The Rider-Waite Wheel of Fortune card depicts a serpent descending and a devil-like creature - Anubis, a jackal, perhaps - ascending. Some Tarot scholars claim that the devil at the bottom of the wheel is there to keep up alert, to help make us aware that all things are subject to change. Anubis is regarded by others still, as a more positive force: although he is a dark, ominous figure, he is rising *with* the wheel upwards, suggesting the hope of new life for those who understand the natural cycles of the wheel.

The eight spokes stand for the eight points of the compass, reminding us that no matter where we are and no matter what happens, providential care is always with us. On the vertical spoke, there are two astrological glyphs: one is Taurus and one is Aquarius, signifying perhaps that the Wheel deals with the material (Taurus) and the ethereal (Aquarius) aspects of life, in other words things that can be grasped and others that can't - much the same as the changing tides of fortune and fate. The Taurus glyph could alternatively be the symbol for the planet Mercury, which stands for knowledge, travel and communication.

Some Tarot decks depict the Wheel of Fortune as the Zodiac Wheel. This symbolism is quite apt, for just as we can do nothing about the turning of the stars in the sky, so we cannot avoid the turning of fate. This symbolism also suggests that we don't always have Earthly control over our fate and destiny. It further shows that there are higher laws set by a cosmic order.

OVERALL ★ CONNECTING IT ALL UP ★

In the mundane world, the Wheel of Fortune points to the laws that govern life and death - the principle of change within which nothing is constant, nothing can be grasped and held with certainty. The only freedom from the wheel possible while on Earth comes through accepting its motion and living in harmony with it.

Alfred Douglas

Throughout history, the Wheel has been a potent image. In medieval times, when the Tarot first appeared, the Wheel represented not only the zodiac but also the cycle of birth and death, and the spinning wheel of the Fates. In this sense, the Wheel of Fortune denotes the uncertain nature of existence, as well as movement and change. Tarot historians believe the word Tarot itself derives from the Latin word *rota*, as in 'rotation', and reflects the ancient sense of life as a moving wheel.

This card signifies that a new chapter is beginning, a decision of importance is to be made, or that a new run of luck is commencing. The depiction of the turning Wheel of Fortune dates back to medieval times and, as a familiar Tarot image, it reveals four men who are attached to the wheel's rim. The goddess turning the wheel is blind, symbolising the element of chance that exists as fortunes of men rise and fall. The man at the top rules, the man descending has ruled, the man at the base of the wheel is without rule, while the man ascending will rule one day. Traditionally the card is said to be concerned with the beasts it portrays in some decks, and with the wheel itself; the Sphinx or Angel at the top says, "I rule," the serpent, "I have ruled," and the dog, "I will rule." (Other cards may have other animals aside from these, such as a monkey-like creature or jackal-headed man, and a hare. Each of the four corner figures has an open book in front of them, as if declaring their knowledge or mastery. Some older decks still show two people celebrating together at the top of the wheel while a third man is hurled off the edge of a precipice. At the corners of some cards are figures: a bird, a lion, a bull and a human). These various depictions and meanings clearly reflect the ongoing peaks and troughs of life, and suggests that no one is exempt from a sudden change of fortune, be it for better or worse.

The Wheel of Fortune signifies that a new chapter is about to commence or an important decision must be made. The angels sent you this card because of positive changes occurring in your life, so expect and enjoy new beneficial opportunities as they present themselves. It is equally important that you always expect the unexpected. You must not worry or be afraid of the unexpected, because it opens up new perspectives for you.

The Wheel of Fortune's association with the planet Jupiter links it with the transcendence of time, ruling the higher mind of Sagittarius and the devotion to intangibles of Pisces. Its divinatory meanings are destiny, fortune, fate, outcome, culmination, approaching the end of a problem, good or bad luck (depending on the influences of nearby cards), inevitability, a turn for the better, the end result of past actions and the workings of destiny, which no one can ever completely understand.

This is an optimal time to make big *and* small changes, major *and* minor adjustments. Take the next leap with the knowledge and faith that everything will work out well for you. Old blocks are lifting, and everything now moves forward swiftly. If recent events have shaken your faith, you will soon see how they were actually positive for you. In essence, rapid and necessary advancement is possible and highly likely now.

This card suggests the course of events from beginning to end, advancement for better or worse. It also signifies the end to current problems and some marked strokes of luck. But the Wheel of Fortune is a curious mix of fate and free will, as suggested by the wheel itself. The Wheel in some cards is kept in balance by a figure who sits at its top and aims to keep the equilibrium; she may or may not be successful. Two creatures are pictured trying to unbalance the wheel. They represent both positive progress and possible difficulties, denoting uncertainty - the Wheel could turn in either direction.

This card is the symbol of the paradox of stability and change. The true self of man, which is hidden from his conscious mind, very often remains at the still hub of the wheel, like the blindfolded goddess pictured in the centre of the wheel. The hub remains stable and represents the true self, although the external or conscious situations around it change, as reflected by the moving outer rim. Fate is the circumference of the wheel, and this true self is at the centre. The hub enables the rim to turn and therefore controls all that comes its way. It indicates that each man turns his own wheel to whichever point his true self dictates.

Taking responsibility for your life's Path, rather than blaming fate for things you don't like, is a powerful course to take, and the Wheel of Fortune suggests that it's time to take this responsibility upon yourself. So, when joy or sorrow comes into your life, it isn't happiness or misfortune has befallen you, but rather you have turned to face it. You need to ask yourself the questions: Why is it that I remain on the wheel with my destiny left to fate? Am I ready for changes to occur in my life? Do I need to develop more flexibility in my outlook? Have I been keeping to my safe lifestyle for too long and is this making me out-dated in my viewpoints? Do I need to move with the times and control the Wheel of destiny myself? Once you start examining and questioning the meaning of your life, perhaps one day you will be able to step off the wheel and take the reins of your own destiny through the discovery of your true nature.

Overall, this card alludes to the mystic idea of karma, individual inner growth towards wholeness and harmony, symbolised by the circular mandala, and is a fortunate card, implying that your rightful destiny will unfold positively. Fortune is indeed smiling on you, and you may as well surrender to the flow, because something remarkable - a big event - is taking place. The Wheel of Fortune signifies a high point, a wish coming true, the manifestation of something anticipated. Ultimately, this card carries the message that the more aware you are of your own power over your destiny, the clearer things will appear - and also, perhaps the most poignant message of this card, that the wheel will turn in your favour eventually.

★ HOW THIS CARD RELATES TO JUPITER ★

The Wheel of Fortune is assigned to Jupiter, the expansive planet of luck and burgeoning growth.

Corrine Kenner

Astrologers call Jupiter the Greater Benefic, the bringer of luck, opportunities, adventure, new horizons, and good fortune. This planet of increase and expansion is the perfect ruler for the Wheel of Fortune. Jupiter, bestower of luck, wisdom and success, that which we make ourselves, and that which we attract through the laws of attraction and sheer chance (if indeed you believe there is such a thing), shares many qualities with the essence of the Wheel of Fortune card. As such, both the planet and the card symbolise luck and opportunity, twists of destiny and turns of chance, and fate and riches in all their forms. Jupiter's very nature is to fulfil - he delivers the goods at the end of the lesson. At his best, he can be the happy ending, and the strength that allows us to endure trials. But Jupiter's blind enthusiasm can just as easily lead to fanaticism as his enjoyment of pleasures often lead to perilous excesses. Such is the Wheel of Fortune's nature, for as the Wheel of Life turns, so too do our circumstances, emotions and fortunes. If we ascend too high, while the ride to the top is fun, we have further to fall (excesses, indulgences, addictions), and if we ascend too low, we can hit rock bottom with an unpleasant thud. But the wisest among us know that what goes up must come down, and ultimately, that if we hit rock bottom, the only way to go is up. The Wheel of Fortune, like Jupiter, advises that change is inevitable in the continuous turning of Life's Wheel, and that fate and free will can be used interchangeably to powerful effect. One thing is certain, if never predictable - our fortunes will always encounter periods of highs and lows, ups and downs, and climbs and falls. But the ever-benevolent Jupiter will always smile upon us through it all, and help us find our feet if we fall.

★ DIVINE MANIFESTATION USING THE WHEEL OF FORTUNE ★

You can Divinely manifest things in your experience through tapping into your inner Opportunist.

The turning of the Wheel of Fortune carries the message that what goes around, comes around, or what goes up, must come down. You will reap what you have sown, therefore you must think ahead and consider your actions today, wherever you find yourself on the wheel. To avoid being ruled by fate, take responsibility for your life and what happens in it. Be open to new and unexpected opportunities, allow for receiving, and above all, take risks. It is vitally important to always expect the unexpected. You must not worry about or fear the unexpected because it opens new perspectives for you. You need to understand that there will always be highs and lows. Good or bad, trust that all is happening for your higher good. Accepting this brings a calmer, more holistic perspective, and your dreams into clearer, more vivid focus.

★ EXERCISE TO TAP INTO YOUR INNER WHEEL OF FORTUNE ★

★ Examine your beliefs about fate versus free will. Do you believe we are born with a predestined Path, and that everything that happens to us keeps us on that rightful Path, or do you believe that we are born as blank slate canvasses, on which we can paint the pictures and write the script of our own lives as we go? Perhaps you take the middle ground, which combines a bit of both of these concepts. Maybe you are unsure altogether, or you might not have ever thought about it before. Do you live life by default, going with the flow, drifting rather aimlessly, thinking that things will just happen as they will but at the same time reacting to circumstances as though you have no control over them? The Wheel of Fortune's meaning helps you really know yourself better through pondering these very important concepts, for what you believe about fate, free will, and the overall Wheel of Life plays an immense role in how your journey ultimately unfolds.

★ JUSTICE ★

Ruled by Libra

Number ★ 11 (or 8 in some decks)
Astrological Sign ★ Libra

Keywords ★ Fairness, Morality, Balance, Karma

Magical Title ★ The Holder of Balances, The Daughter of the Lord of Truth
Divinity ★ Athena
Spiritual Value ★ The Sword that Justice holds prods us ever forward by keeping the field level through Truth and Justice. This Arcanum can help you to find practical solutions to restore balance and harmony after conflicts, and adds energy to your life by helping you develop courage, combativeness, ambition, and a fighting spirit when and where they are needed most.

★ KEY THEMES ★

"Divine Karma"

Karma ★ Rational Thought ★ Impartial Judgement ★ Fairness ★ Equilibrium of Mind ★ Fair And Just Decisions ★ Standing up for Beliefs ★ Doing What is Right ★ Resisting Injustice ★ Issuing or Accepting an Apology ★ Righteousness ★ Morality ★ Legal Decision or Intervention ★ Resolution ★ Balance

Meditation ★ "I rely upon the Divine unseen force of Justice to prevail in all situations. I seek not to control but to balance. I hold true and deep to the belief that what goes around comes around; I trust that Karma will serve the natural justice that I, in my human Earthly form, cannot."

★ *When Working with this Card* ★

MAIN ENERGIES ★ Fairness, Discernment, Wisdom, Karma, Trust
MAIN GOD OR GODDESS TO INVOKE ★ Themis
CANDLE COLOUR ★ Blue
MAGICAL TOOL OR SYMBOL ★ Scales
CRYSTALS ★ Emerald, Agate, Turquoise, Yellow Calcite, Jade, Clear Quartz, Hematite, Sapphire

ASSOCIATED BEINGS, GODS, GODDESSES & ARCHETYPES ★ Angels, Archangels, Inner Saints and Masters, Ma'at, Varuna, Justitia, Nemesis, Anubis, Forseti, Themis *, Osiris, Jupiter, Aino, Belet Seri, Akonadi, the Morrigan (Severity), and Daghda (Mercy), the Judge and the Jury.

* Themis was the most important of the Lesser Gods in the Greek pantheon. She was the goddess of Justice and her province included the Earth. Themis was also called Euboulos, the good counsellor, and she was always at the side of Zeus as his advisor. Her mission was to maintain order and regulate all ceremonies. Themis was protectress of the just and punisher

of the guilty, and as Goddess of Wisdom she advised the judges in their verdicts. She possessed the gift of prophecy and it is said that she once owned Delphi. Temples in honour of Themis were erected throughout Greece in such places as Athens and Olympia, and she was portrayed as a woman of austere appearance, carrying a pair of scales.

ARCHETYPES ★ Justice is the enforcer of karmic and spiritual laws in our life's experiences. As the ultimate arbiter, she holds a two-edged sword, reminding us that fairness often cuts both ways. She is the Ruler, the Guardian, the Gatekeeper, the Teacher, the Judge.

CHAKRAS ★ Use this card to balance and meditate upon the Heart, Throat and Crown chakras.

Heart ★ Heart Region ★ Green ★ Air ★ Love & Compassion

Throat ★ Throat Region ★ Light Blue ★ Sound/Ether ★ Communication & Self-Expression

Crown ★ Top of Head ★ Purple ★ Thought/Knowing ★ Spiritual Wisdom & Enlightenment

TREE OF LIFE ★ In western magic, which combines the Tarot paths of the Major Arcana with the ten sephiroth on the Tree of Life, the path of Justice connects Tiphareth and Geburah.

NUMERIC SIGNIFICANCE ★ Eleven is the first master number that does not reduce to a single digit. It expresses a high level of humanitarianism, intuition, inspiration, prophetic ability, and illumination, as does its Tarot card Justice. It amplifies the power of the number one and is regarded by some as the 'resurrected lightbody'. Eleven brings the merger of the individual with the Universal and the transmutation of Earthly urges into the spiritual light of unification, compassion, universality, and brotherhood. The number eleven character has the intensified aspects of an enhanced 1, and is doubly charged with inspiration, leadership and charisma. The first of two master numbers (the other being 22), this is the number of special mystical awareness, possibly balanced between good and evil, concepts that the Tarot's Justice grapples with. The Minor Arcana of the Tarot have 56 cards. If we add 5 + 6 we get to the master number eleven. It symbolises illumination and intuitive understanding, especially of spiritual truths or principles. The number eleven symbolises truth found in faith, not in logic. Number eleven characters are the teachers, the visionaries and peacemakers, embodying the principles of Justice.

Eleven is the number of force; it is that of strife and martyrdom. Every man who dies for an idea is a martyr, for in him the aspirations of the spirit have triumphed over the fears of the animal.

Eliphas Levi

THE FOOL'S JOURNEY ★ Some aspects of life might seem beyond The Fool's control, but at the same time, justice *does* prevail. The Justice card is about learning our lessons, being rewarded for the good we do, and likewise, being punished for any evil we do. Justice teaches the Tarot's Fool to discriminate, to make impersonal decisions and dispassionate evaluations, to weigh up, to balance, and then ultimately to make rational choices. Although the laws of nature are difficult, if not impossible, to tame and manipulate for all the human striving of fairness, justice is nevertheless one of the noblest conceptions of the human spirit.

> Charity begins at home, and justice begins next door.
>
> **Charles Dickens**

THE STORY ★ Justice is one of the three virtues in the Tarot's Major Arcana - the others are Strength and Temperance. A very favourable card, it indicates that the outcome of the situation in question will be good, and that the querent is in a strong position to reach the correct decision over a current challenge. Justice is a detached, but fair, mediator who helps to resolve inner and outer conflicts through the courage of her convictions. The crowned figure of Justice is often seated between pillars representing mercy and punishment. In her hands, she holds the balance and sword. Her face is resolute and firm in conviction and in most images, she wears no blindfold, so she sees all the facts.

THE MESSAGE ★ The Justice card evokes in us the Universal understanding of virtue that can be traced to Philo's four cardinal traits: wisdom, temperance, courage and justice. Justice represents the laws of nature, as well as the relentless workings of fate - through the slow, regular turning of the Wheel of Karma. Modern Hopi Indians believe that, in both the natural and the supernatural worlds, there is a fixed order and life is cyclical. Like the ancient Egyptians, they understand that we must remain in harmony with this Universal order and maintain our connection with it through blessings and rituals. If harmony does not prevail, then life will not progress smoothly and humanity will not prosper. Errors must be recognised and order must be restored in order for karmic forces to adjust to and overcome any adverse conditions. This is Justice's task - to maintain and restore order and equilibrium, therefore ensuring karmic balance. Justice guides you towards wise and carefully considered decisions, ones made with fairness and objectivity.

THE AWAKENING ★ Behind Justice's throne there are sometimes depicted two upright columns representing moral strength and integrity, mercy and punishment, and she has the power to differentiate between right and wrong. She always implies the need to find or recover a balance between opposing forces or contradictory elements. She advises that although the *human* judicial system may be fooled, Divine justice can never be escaped. When Justice appears in a reading, you are coming to consciousness about your place in the Universal scheme of things. There is some way you can feel karma working in your life. Maybe you are winning a custody or law suit case, or perhaps you have a newfound sense of yourself as powerful and moving through life with purpose. Maybe some conflict in your life has come to a resolution, or things have worked out after a period of disharmony. Whatever the case, things are setting themselves right again and you can feel your own peace returning.

THE LESSON ★ Justice is implacable; in the search for truth, Justice will always prevail. Have faith that Justice will triumph, and leave the punishment of those you think have done the wrong thing in her wise and capable hands. Justice encourages you to be firm and decisive, and advises to think through the situation carefully. Nemesis, goddess of Divine vengeance, who turns the wheel of retribution and makes whatever adjustments are necessary to set things right again, is aligned with the concept of the Justice card. We experience fate in our lives when it seems to step in and cause certain events to occur that 'punish' us for our wrongdoings, but whatever Path you choose to take, the future is in your hands. An option that seems a difficult and uphill Path is likely to turn out well for you in the long-term, so do not be afraid of obstacles that appear to be in your way, for you have an inner well of strength and a harmonious approach that will overcome them. The Justice card belongs to Libra, the cardinal Air sign of social fairness and equality, symbolised by the Scales. Libra, being ruled by Venus (goddess of love) considers everything in terms of others. Libra loves beauty and harmony, and wants to bring her surroundings to a state of peaceful co-existence. In this way, Libra is Nemesis, the cords of retribution and just rewards, that draw the human race together, and urges to connect each of us with the All - after all, a blessing on one of Earth's children blesses all, just as a curse on one hurts all. Justice advises to be practical, rigorous, stern but fair, kind, patient, objective, honest, and sympathetic to those weaker than yourself. Of course, it is always possible to appeal against what has been judged. But, once the sword has fallen, a page has been turned.

SYMBOLISM ★ In the Tarot, Justice is always shown as a woman, following the tradition of the ancient Greeks for whom Themis was the goddess of justice. She wears the red robe of worldly power, her sword ready to cut through any ignorance that might impede her from reaching spiritual enlightenment, while her scales help her to weigh up the value of all things and maintain a fair balance.

The Justice card counsels us to be aware of the consequences of our actions, that we control our own destiny, and to behave responsibly and with dignity. It signifies the wisdom to take responsibility for the way we live our lives and brings the understanding that there are underlying cosmic laws by which we are all affected; it therefore symbolises the realisation that whatever events occur in your life, you have a choice in how you respond to them, which will then determine your attitudes, perceptions and directions thereafter.

At the heart of the Justice card are the notions of self-understanding and the idea that you control your own fate and are thus accountable for all your actions.

The goddess on the Justice card holds the scales to weigh up right against wrong, and the sword to enforce her judgement. She stands as if ready for action and wears items of armour, symbolising a determination to fight for what she knows is right. Sometimes the scales may be gold and silver, symbolising the integration of feeling and logic.

OVERALL ★ CONNECTING IT ALL UP ★

I say that justice is truth in action.

Benjamin Disraeli

The crowned figure of Justice is often depicted as a blindfolded lady, seated between pillars representing mercy and punishment, holding in her hands the scales and the double-edged sword, her face resolute and firm with conviction. The scales represent balance and equilibrium, while the sword stands for truth and justice. On one of the throne's shorter pillars often sits an owl, the ancient bird of wisdom, known for its clear vision and ability to see in the dark. Colour is an important element of this card. Red, the colour of passion and desire, and green, healing and love, work together to create harmony. The colour purple, which symbolises wisdom, is also often used, as wise insights are necessary in order to make sound judgements. The imagery in this card suggests the theme of mental clarity, and the need for the mind to seek logical solutions to difficult problems.

The Justice card does not deal with the justice of humankind, with its codes, laws and rules, for this is a uniquely human conception which sets us apart from the animal kingdom and creates a framework, by which we must all abide, to preserve social order. What the Justice card deals with is more primitive, primary and primordial, dictated by the survival instinct or the vital need for the absolute, rather than from a moral code or stance.

This card indicates fairness and balance, the need to be logical and diplomatic and to argue in a balanced way. It is a very favourable card in a karmic sense, indicating that justice will be served in the settling of an issue, and that whatever the outcome of a particular situation, it will be a fair and just one. The appearance of Justice means that matters must be viewed through an impartial lens. This is a time to use the rational mind and judicious thought processes to weigh up a problem or situation. Justice is a thinking card which needs to be approached from a logical standpoint, and emphasises that all considerations must be carefully weighed up.

It also impels you to do what you know is right, take responsibility for your actions, stand up for your beliefs and offer or accept an apology where it is needed.

Its divinatory meanings are reason, justice, proper balance, harmony, equity, virtue, honour, righteousness, virginity, just rewards, equilibrium, impartiality, poise, and the eventual outcome, whether favourable or unfavourable, will be truly fair for the person concerned.

When the Justice card appears, it indicates firstly that events have turned out the way they were 'meant' to work out; that is, situations happening to you now have been shaped by your past actions and decisions. In other words, you have what you justly deserve. Secondly, it indicates a possibility and a need for seeing the truth of this outcome, signifying absolute honesty - with your past and yourself. At the same time, it shows the possibility that your actions in the future can be changed by a lesson learned in your present situation. Look for the seed of truth in your current situation, and it can guide you to make the most accordant decisions leading to your optimal future self. This card represents seeing all the facts, without succumbing to temptation or envy to misguide you. The Justice card suggests the ignorance of the law is no more excuse in the courts of life than in the courts of people. It tells us that laws must be studied and obeyed if the penalties and punishment for rebelling are to be avoided. However, being too harsh is also not ideal and the balance must not be tipped. Ultimately, Justice carries the message that, although the human judicial system can be fooled and flawed, Divine 'higher' justice can never be escaped.

★ HOW THIS CARD RELATES TO LIBRA ★

Justice, the model of fairness and equanimity, is assigned to Libra,
the sign of equality and social grace.

Corrine Kenner

Since perception (in Libra) is razor-sharp, this sign of justice will bring equity and balance to all areas of human relationships. And with the harmonious vibrations from Venus, the high ideals of cosmic reciprocity incorporated here will find a perfect channel for expression. The advanced soul will strive for equality and fairness in all decisions and matters which come under its jurisdiction. Law and liberty are its very life-blood, and where it sees injustice it will fight on a mental level, with all the eloquence at its command, in order to remedy the position ... As diplomat and arbitrator, it is poised, like the Ape of Thoth, in the centre of the scales. It follows the middle way, holds the balance between all opposites, and upholds the light of spiritual truth and justice.

Patricia Crowther

Libra is the sign of the Scales, an instrument that keeps its harmony and equilibrium only when in balance. The Tarot Justice card depicts the scales of balance, the emblem of Libra, and its iconographic imagery connects the card to the Libran concepts of equanimity, compromise, order, fairness, honesty, truth, and just rewards and penalties. The symbol of the Scales further emphasises that the main function of this sign - as is the function of the Tarot's Justice - is to establish equilibrium and to maintain a balance between the conflicting forces of good and evil. The higher nature of Libra is primarily influenced by the higher powers of the intellect and an objective state of mind, which is impartial and not attached to form or matter but is solely interested in the flow of ideas and unbiased fairness. Symbolically, Libra's scales - like the lady in Justice - are constantly weighing and measuring the quality, impartiality, or justice of his social interactions and all-important relationships. The Libran scales are constantly used to weigh up whether or not a situation or person is being fair, and to decide if justice is being served. If not, Librans see it as their noble duty to rectify any imbalance, and that is why, far from being compliant and indecisive, they can sometimes be outspoken and strident. Determined to put right injustices and restore balance and harmony, Libra and Justice alike, will somehow always make exactly the just and proper decisions for all involved.

★ DIVINE MANIFESTATION USING JUSTICE ★

You can Divinely manifest things in your experience through tapping into your inner Karmic Compass.

Justice's task is to maintain and restore order and equilibrium, therefore ensuring karmic balance. Justice guides you towards wise and carefully considered decisions, ones made with fairness, just consideration, and objectivity. It suggests that when you have a decision to make, you need to trust that order and fairness will be of paramount consideration when Divine Justice ultimately makes its decision. More often than not, unless you have incurred major karmic debts, the decision will be made in your favour; and all will turn out positively for you. The Justice card also solemnly reminds you to thoroughly review any legal documents or contracts before signing them. Justice holds the scales. You need to understand that whatever happens over the course of your life is a result of your past actions, current thinking, or is simply what you are attracting to yourself on a subconscious level. You also need to realise that even if things aren't working out so well at any stage of your life's Path, it is usually an indication that something is off-balance in your mind, body or spirit, and that nature will restore equilibrium when it is the right time to do so, by working in calm, quiet ways, sometimes giving us what we *need* rather than what we *want*. In every situation, including those in which you have done the wrong thing, trust that Karma works in mysterious ways, but it always has your back.

★ EXERCISE TO TAP INTO YOUR INNER JUSTICE ★

★ Is there a situation in your life where you feel you had / have no control over but that the person involved has wronged you in some way (a past or present situation)? Imagine that that person, at some stage in the cycle of the Universe's ever-unfolding karmic cycles, will receive their due karma. Meditate on this knowing, and gently forgive and release that person from your grip, trusting that higher powers and laws will perform justice for you. And if you don't believe in karma, why or why not? Does it mean that you hold onto resentments, hurts, anger, and unforgiveness for long periods of time, sometimes for your whole life after the event, or simply that you don't believe in such ethereal, unseen forces? If it is the former, examine how burdening yourself with the weight of resentment, hurt, anger or unforgiveness might impact on your own life and progress?

★ THE HANGED MAN ★

Ruled by Neptune & the Element of Water

Number ★ 12
Astrological Sign ★ Pisces

Keywords ★ Suspension, Sacrifice, New Perspectives, Faith, Surrender

Magical Title ★ The Spirit of the Mighty Waters
Divinity ★ Artemis
Spiritual Value ★ The Hanged Man is the self-sacrifice that leads to rebirth, the shamanic trance that leads to renewal, death the leads to resurrection. This Arcanum carries an elusive and profoundly significant symbol and meaning. It is sacrifice; it is the descent of the Spirit into Matter, the incarnation of the Great Spirit into human, the submission to the bonds of matter so that the material may be transcended. The Hanged Man can be used when you seek Divine Guidance and inspiration for some aspect of your experience. It can sustain you in your efforts, and bestows a feeling of balance, opening you up to higher aspiration by increasing your receptivity to the Divine energies.

★ KEY THEMES ★

"Self-Imposed Time Out"

★ Sacrifice ★ Period of Inactivity, Respite or Transition ★ Forfeiting One Thing to Gain Something More Valuable or Desired ★ Trust ★ Faith ★ Letting Go ★ Surrender ★ Introspection ★ Suspension ★ Stepping Back ★
★ Inner Journeying ★ Transformation ★ Progression ★ Renewal ★ Rebirth ★
★ Epiphanies ★ Unexpected Life Changes ★ Unusual Solutions ★ The Need for Patience ★ New Perspectives

Meditation ★ "I am willing to be patient and accepting as I await the next chapter of my ever-unfolding life experience, and to sacrifice things to make way for other, improved things."

★ *When Working with this Card* ★

MAIN ENERGIES ★ Surrender, Flow, Acceptance, Spiritual Love, Enlightenment
MAIN GOD OR GODDESS TO INVOKE ★ Odin
CANDLE COLOUR ★ Purple / Violet
MAGICAL TOOLS OR SYMBOLS ★ The World Tree, Runes
CRYSTALS ★ Apophyllite, Amethyst, Purple Fluorite, Lavender Jadeite, Rose Quartz

ASSOCIATED BEINGS, GODS, GODDESSES & ARCHETYPES ★ The Martyr, Sons of Light, Saviours and Redeemers, Archangels, Sacrificed Kings and Heroes, Odin, Christ, the Great Mother and her Son, Saturn, Apollo, the Rebel, the Seeker, the Wounded Healer.

ARCHETYPES ★ The Hanged Man is the visionary who sacrifices his comforts and passions for a time, knowing that he will be rewarded with better things as a result. He is the Martyr, the Messiah, the Poet, the Mystic, the Scribe, the Shaman.

CHAKRAS ★ Use this card to balance and meditate upon the Third Eye and Crown chakras.

Third Eye ★ Between the Eyes ★ Dark Blue ★ Light ★ Clairvoyance, Wisdom, Intuition & Vision

Crown ★ Top of Head ★ Purple ★ Thought/Knowing ★ Spiritual Wisdom & Enlightenment

TREE OF LIFE ★ In western magic, which combines the Tarot paths of the Major Arcana with the ten sephiroth on the Tree of Life, the path of The Hanged Man connects Hod and Geburah.

NUMERIC SIGNIFICANCE ★ Twelve is the cyclic number; it is that of the Universal Creed. A powerful sign of completeness. The 'Tree of Life' bore twelve fruits, and in many other traditions, it relates to the space-time continuum - for example the months of the year, a clock face, the twelve hours each of day and night, the divisions of the houses and zodiac signs of the horoscope - and represents a completed cycle. Twelve turns the wheel of the heavens and represents this cosmic order of things. It concerns extension, expansion and elevation, and liberation from the bondage of time and space. In the metaphysical science of numbers, twelve signals completeness, totality. It rounds off all the basic variations, combining them in one harmonious, comprehensive whole.

THE FOOL'S JOURNEY ★ Here is where The Fool must learn when a period of suspension is needed, in order to take time out for spiritual restoration. This could be a self-imposed standstill, or necessitated by circumstances that are beyond The Fool's control. Either way, he must sacrifice activity for a time and surrender to the flow, so that he may become more self-aware in the long run. Hanging by a thread, the Hanged Man is learning the lessons of letting go and of not being ruled by the material or the mundane. This is The Fool searching for spiritual enlightenment and psychic revelation.

> Life is like a landscape. You live in the midst of it but can describe it only from the vantage point of distance.
>
> **Charles Lindbergh**

THE STORY ★ Under a calm, blue sky and above a radiant, flourishing earth, a man hangs upside down, suspended by one foot from a wooden beam. This scene is not one of torture or punishment, but part of a natural and even necessary, process. The young man's life appears to be in limbo, but his expression shows only acceptance and absolute faith at this moment of total surrender to a higher force. He may be listening to an inner voice, speaking to him the truths that are completely the opposite of all that he has previously believed. He may also have deliberately sacrificed himself to attain some desired goal. He seems to be in a trance and a state of illumination. It does appear, however, that the pattern of his everyday life has been reversed to provide a new outlook. The water flowing beneath him symbolises that the young man has risen above emotional turmoil and upheavals to accept the suspension of his usual, or old, way of life. The enforced period of waiting may be viewed as a way of gaining new eyes and a fresh standpoint.

You cannot teach a man anything; you can only teach him to discover it within himself.

Galileo Galilei

THE MESSAGE ★ The Hanged Man represents change, but it is usually an alternation in mental attitudes rather than physical circumstances. Look at things from a different perspective. The Hanged Man indicates a temporary standstill. When the Hanged Man shows up, it means that you are temporarily out of the game of life, either because you have chosen to do so, or you have been forced to take some time in suspension. This is necessary, as it will allow to draw important lessons from what has occurred in your past.

THE AWAKENING ★ The Hanged Man cuts across all our ideas of materialism, hedonism and selfishness, and tells us that new perspectives are required to conquer these potentially ravaging vices and states of being. These new viewpoints can be acquired through sacrifice and self-imposed suspension, and you are reluctantly forced to accept that it is necessary to adopt an attitude of surrender while you wait for the tide to turn. The Hanged Man signifies the ability to accept delays, and to recognise that correct timing is essential.

To attain knowledge, add things every day. To attain wisdom, remove things every day.

Lao Tzu

THE LESSON ★ Do not be disconcerted by the appearance of the Hanged Man. He is not in distress; he is simply, literally 'in suspension', in limbo, waiting for something to happen. He signifies that you are between two phases in your life, perhaps waiting for news before you can move forward. Patience and self-control are key during this period of self-suspension. For it is often only in the stillness of suspension, that you can hear the answers you are seeking.

SYMBOLISM ★ This card depicts a young man hanging from a tree or suspended from the gallows by the ankle. His other leg is folded behind him, forming the shape of the number 4 or an inverted triangle, symbolising the descent from higher to lower, or conscious into unconscious. This suggests a sacrifice, giving up one thing for something more desired. The Hanged Man, in this act of sacrificial surrender, is declaring: "I cannot have a risen, powerful life without first of all dying to self." His arms are folded behind his back. The man's face does not look tortured or fearful, but rather it is serene and calm. He wears a green shirt, and one of his stockings is red and the other one white. A pool lies beneath him, and despite his perilous position, a halo glows around his head and his expression is not unhappy. The twelve branch stumps on the two wooden pillars supporting the scaffold from which he hangs, represent the twelve signs of the zodiac, suggesting that the Sun has run its course through the signs and seasons of the year and is ready to enter the final phase. Pisces represents a death or a letting go, once a person has thoroughly experienced an entire cycle of life, and symbolises the subsequent turning toward the soul or higher self.

The man hangs from his foot, the part of the body attributed to Pisces, and the sign of purification and sacrifice.

The Hanged Man symbolises the patience involved in waiting to see what unfolds naturally, and gives you acceptance that everything happens in its own good time. He symbolises a state of inner peace and a spiritual surrender to the natural order. The upside-down man's pensive and resigned facial expression symbolises the need to go inward to find a new perspective on the situation. The plank of woods from which he is suspended has been cut to fit between the two trees, indicating that this state of suspension in life is deliberately engineered. In some decks, a halo of light surrounds the man's head, symbolising that he is attuned to - or becoming attuned to - his spiritual nature.

OVERALL ★ CONNECTING IT ALL UP ★

He who would accomplish little must sacrifice little. He who would accomplish much must sacrifice much.

James Allen

The Hanged Man's ruler, Neptune, is a planet associated with self-sacrifice, dreams, mysticism and inspiration. Its watery nature suggests that time is fluid and dissolves all undesirable circumstances eventually. This card's divinatory meanings are transition, change, reversal of the mind in one's way of life, renunciation, abandonment, the changing of life's forces, the approach of new life forces, a period of respite between significant events, sacrifice, repentance, regeneration, readjustment, and that life is in suspension.

The Hanged Man card represents a sacrifice of some kind which results in transformation, and is identified with the Norse God Odin **, who hanged himself voluntarily from the World Tree, Yggdrasil ^, for nine days and nights in order to gain spiritual insight and wisdom, and was reborn anew. Like Odin, none of us can know the full meaning of being alive until we have ourselves on the World Tree and allow its roots to extend far beyond our deep wells of worldly experience, and its branches pointing upwards towards the endless stars. Another interpretation is that the traditional values of society are turned upside down and that things can then be looked at from a different angle.

This card bears the message of independence and feeling life through an inner awareness rather than doing what others expect or demand from us. Interestingly, reversed, the Hanged Man symbolises fighting your inner self in some way, denying your inner voice a hearing, and battling uphill against life. The essential meaning of this card is sacrifice: the voluntary surrendering or shedding of something in order to gain something of far greater value. It can signify that one's life is at a standstill, however, although circumstances may not be to one's liking, it is not as bad as one thinks it is. It tells us to take life patiently until we see that the time is right to make the necessary improvements to the situation. It represents the turning point in psychological development, the point at which we must come to grips with the unconscious forces within and surrendering the conscious ego in order to delve into the oft unknown territory of our inner world. The conscious mind is volunteering to 'die' in order to bear a new and fruitful life in the unconscious, despite the inevitable fears we hold. This involves faith, hope and trust.

The Hanged Man indicates a time of greater self-understanding, and perhaps a decision to abandon worldly values. Here, The Fool must take a risk and dare to take that inner journey, to plunge into the depths of the self, to seek the inner reality needed to become whole. And from that sacrifice come things of infinitely greater value: enlightenment and renewal. Overall, this means it is time to review your plans, and look at things from a new perspective.

The Hanged Man encourages you not to take premature or hasty action, but rather you should wait, for even though waiting is trying, you need to control your restlessness and be philosophical in outlook. Accept the fact that you have already achieved a great deal, and trust that your experience will stand you in good stead for what is to come. Be forgiving of those who have harmed you, and aim to balance materialistic progress with spiritual development. The task it sets is to explore the mysterious gift of life and ultimately, experience rebirth.

When this card appears in a reading or your life, it does not mean you are going to die, but that you are going to lose yourself; this does not imply crucifixion or pain, but rather a sense of ecstasy and surrender to love. You may want to do something to literally turn yourself upside down temporarily, to change your perspective; in doing so, try to channel your pure inner child, and envision how they would laugh and squeal with delight if turned upside down by an adult.

The Hanged Man card prompts you to ask questions of yourself such as: What is the best way to spend my time during this period of waiting? Is it possible that a different approach would work better? What preparations can I make for the future, considering the options that are open to me? Am I avoiding reality or making a decision? Am I only deceiving myself about my concern for the future when my inaction is really caused by cowardliness or laziness? The Hanged Man signifies a temporary pause in life, and tells us to cultivate patience, go with the flow and accept the changes that are occurring. Ultimately, the symbolic descent from the conscious mind into the unconscious enables you to discover what is truly important to you. You may even need to step outside of the norm and the mainstream right now and embrace your unique and eclectic beliefs or attitudes. It's also an opportune chance to be generous with your time, attention and gifts - this tithing will be returned to you manyfold by the Universe.

** One of the mystical of the various Tree of Life legends is that of the Tree of Yggdrasil in Norse mythology. The main character of the story, Odin (sometimes called Woden), the Father/God of the Nordic pantheon. He is the invisible Soul of the World that animates all things and travels through the nine Nordic worlds like a breeze. He rides upon a magical steed named Sleipnir, as his deep azure cloak reaches into infinite space. A white serpent (wisdom), skilled in magic, lies at his feet at all times, and he has two familiars, ravens called Muninn, meaning 'memory', and Huginn, meaning 'thought', who represent his soul. Each day the birds fly around the world and then report back to him, telling him everything that has occurred. Not only does he stand for the mind of God, he also has many other talents, including writing, shape shifting, intellect, communication, inspiration, magic and seership. The story goes that this legendary hero wanted above all to find wisdom and acquire the gift of prophecy. To do this he was required to hang upside down on the world tree, Yggdrasil, for nine days and nights, each day and night representing one of the nine sacred worlds in Nordic lore. At the dawn of the tenth day, Odin reached down into the roots of Yggdrasil and drew out the runes, the magical alphabet of the Nordic peoples. Hanging there wasn't all he had to endure; he also had to make a sacrifice and exchange one of his human eyes for 'the sight'. This tale teaches us a lesson, not dissimilar to that contained in the meaning of The Hanged Man - that sometimes we must sacrifice those attitudes that we have outgrown to expand spiritually. Odin could not truly see until he looked within; and neither can we.

^ In Scandanavian mythology, Yggdrasil is the World Tree, an eternal green sacred ash which stood at the centre of the Norse spiritual cosmos and which overshadowed the entire Universe. Its branches, roots and trunk united heaven, Earth and the nether regions. The roots of Yggdrasil lay in Hel, while the trunk ascended through Midgard, the Earth. Rising through the mountain known as Asgard, it branched into the sky - its leaves were the clouds, its fruit the stars. The most satisfactory explanation for the translation of the name Yggdrasil, is 'Odin's Horse' (Ygg is another name for Odin, and drasill means 'horse'. However, drasill can also mean 'pioneer' or 'walker', translating the word Yggdrasil literally into 'Odinwalker'.)

★ HOW THIS CARD RELATES TO NEPTUNE & THE ELEMENT OF WATER ★

> The Hanged Man, suspended in an alternate reality, is assigned to Neptune,
> the planet of mysticism and illusion. The glyph, King Neptune's trident,
> symbolises a watery world that exits alongside our own earthly reality.

Corrine Kenner

Key themes of the Hanged Man card are sacrifice, spirituality and ultimate enlightenment, all of which relate to both Neptune and the Water element. Neptune and the Waters over which it rules, dance on the mystical side of life, prone to fantasising, daydreaming and idealising. Seeing the world through rose-coloured glasses much of the time, Neptune and Water compel their subjects to believe in magic, dreams, fairytales and happy endings. But the Hanged Man serves as a reminder that a new perspective is needed, and in order to gain new insights, one needs to experience a temporary standstill or suspension. Neptune and Water's energies exude the urge to dissolve boundaries, to experience oneness, to merge, to flow, to undertake the spiritual, divinatory or occult arts, and the needs for unity, mysticism, transcendence, utopia, sacrifice and devotion. The Hanged Man spends a period of time - even days - suspended in a trancelike alternate reality, a concept which seems in perfect sync with Neptune, the planet of nebulous spiritual and psychic enlightenment. The planet Neptune, composed mostly of ethereal mist and gasses, seems to escape the bounds of ordinary physics, just as the Hanged Man does in his state of dreamlike illusion. And just as Neptune does in a birth chart, the Hanged Man represents a period of willing self-sacrifice and suspension of everyday worries and concerns. He seeks - and succeeds - to transcend Earthly limitations, through fantasy, imagination, meditation and dreaming. Eternally tuned in to a higher consciousness and representative of collective feelings and Universal love, both of their primary functions is to remove barriers, not by tearing them down, but by gently dissolving them; in fact, Neptune would like everything rendered to a state of liquid suspension, to be formless, to be returned to the state of nebulousness that existed in the *beginning*. These are the lessons of the Hanged Man, and demonstrate its links with the mystical Neptune and the purifying, transformative powers of Water.

✶ DIVINE MANIFESTATION USING THE HANGED MAN ✶

You can Divinely manifest things in your experience through tapping into your inner Perspective.

Sometimes we need to look at things from a different perspective. It may seem that time is frozen, that we are stuck, that the unfolding of events and circumstances has come to a standstill, or, more precisely that we find ourselves at a time in our life when we are unable to take action but have to undergo the consequences of our actions, good or bad, and draw lessons from them. This period may seem restrictive, but you are being forced to step back from the situation and become introspective in order to listen to your higher, stiller mind. Waiting has its place in any plan. Waiting, not knowing what to do next, is trying, but you must control restlessness and be patient and philosophical in outlook. As you 'wait', be forgiving of those who have harmed you and aim to balance materialistic progress with spiritual development. The word 'yoga', a Hindu spiritual and ascetic discipline, means 'to unite'. To create a unified, integrated psyche, try the yoga posture called The Bow. The flow of energy it helps circulate through your body will direct and focus your mind on the lessons you need to be learning. Importantly, you need to know that sometimes you need to hang yourself up by the feet and suspend yourself. This needn't remove you from the circle of life, in fact the opposite is true: it keeps you Divinely flowing through the cycle, yet you are calmly unaffected by its goings on. This trust in the flow and discernment for when you really need to suspend yourself, will only draw towards you greater and greater things - in time.

✶ EXERCISE TO TAP INTO YOUR INNER HANGED MAN ✶

★ Is there anything in your life you need to take a step back from to see it in a clearer perspective? If so, think of ways that you can take that step back, and then discover any new thoughts you have around it from this new outlook. Give yourself a period of deliberate suspension, e.g. allow yourself one worry-free day, during which any time a negative thought or concern enters your mind, you allow it to dissolve, postponing it until tomorrow, or next week, or until a time of your own nomination. Give yourself a break, a self-imposed standstill, free from worry or care about worldly concerns.

★ DEATH ★

Ruled by Scorpio

Number ★ 13
Astrological Sign ★ Scorpio

Know ye the gateway to life is through death.

Thoth the Atlantean

Keywords ★ Change, Renewal, Transformation, Endings, New Beginnings

Magical Title ★ The Final Equaliser
Divinity ★ Kronos
Spiritual Value ★ This Arcanum is the initiation in which the character willingly undergoes 'death' to attain the knowledge of the Higher Self. The character is dismembered, reassembled, and absorbed into the Greater Self. It symbolises all the aspects of disintegration, transmutation, time, and age, and sometimes - but rarely - destruction. Its destructive side may only play out for the purposes of subsequent purification and renewal. The Death card can assist you in eliminating old, outmoded habits and patterns that have become obstacles to your progress.

★ KEY THEMES ★

"A Change for the Better"

Endings ★ Transitions ★ New Beginnings ★ Death of That Which has Outlived its Usefulness ★ Regeneration and Rebirth ★ Severance ★ Change ★ A New Outlook on Life ★ Crossroads ★ Necessary Conclusion ★ Beneficial Turning Point ★ Inevitability ★ Transformation ★ Completion

Meditation ★ "All that has gone before, including my mistakes, is preparation for a better Path ahead. This new life or way of being, will be exactly the right one for me. Death will show me the way. I surrender to it with the enlightened knowledge that it is for my higher good, and am letting go of all that is no longer needed."

★ *When Working with this Card* ★

MAIN ENERGIES ★ Transcendence, Release, Empowerment, Renewal, Transformation, Purification
MAIN GOD OR GODDESS TO INVOKE ★ Anubis
CANDLE COLOUR ★ Black
MAGICAL TOOL OR SYMBOL ★ Egg
CRYSTALS ★ Jet, Black Tourmaline, Smoky Quartz, Black Obsidian, Malachite

ASSOCIATED BEINGS, GODS, GODDESSES & ARCHETYPES ★ Transhuman Beings, the Grim Reaper, Don, Anubis ^, Mars, Kali, Anu, Pluto,

Astarte, Ereshkigal, Mithra, Asar, the Morrigan, Osiris, Minerva, Hades, White Lady, Macha, Thoth, Persephone, Santisima Muerte, Baal, Ammit, Hecate, Hel, Ceridwen, Selket, Adonis, Megaera, Melqart, the Great Mother, all Ancient Goddesses of Death, the Afterlife and Resurrection, the Gatekeeper, the Judge, the Guide, the Psychopomp.

^ Anubis is one of the most iconic gods of ancient Egypt, and was associated with mummification, embalming, protection of tombs, and the afterlife. He is usually depicted as a jackal-headed god with a human body, who was revered as a helping the deads' paths through the underworld. Anubis was regarded as the psychopomp (conductor of souls) in the afterlife and his totem of the jackal is probably due to the fact that real jackals would hunt on the outskirts of the desert, near the necropolis and cemeteries throughout Egypt. He is also associated with Scales; in the *Book of the Dead,* Anubis weighs the heart of the deceased against the weight of a feather in a balance, the feather emblematic of "Ma'at" or truth, the heart representing the deceased's conscience. If the scale of justice tipped toward the heart, the dead person would be devoured by Ammit, a female demon the Egyptian people labelled 'devourer of the dead'. If the scales of justice tipped towards the feather, Anubis would lead the decedent to Osiris so that his or her soul could ascend to heaven. In Egypt, there is a beautiful statue of Anubis as a full jackal in the tomb of Tutankhamun.

ARCHETYPES ★ Death is the card of transition. Like the Grim Reaper, who clears away all outworn debris, situations and experience, the card depicts the turning of a page, the completion of one chapter of life, and the exciting beginning of a different story. Death is the Destroyer, the Guardian Angel, the Shaman, the Fates, the Shadow, the Sorcerer.

CHAKRAS ★ Use this card to balance and meditate upon the Crown chakra.

Crown ★ Top of Head ★ Purple ★ Thought/Knowing ★ Spiritual Wisdom & Enlightenment

TREE OF LIFE ★ In western magic, which combines the Tarot paths of the Major Arcana with the ten sephiroth on the Tree of Life, the path of Death connects Netzach and Tiphareth.

> It is truly a great cosmic paradox that one of the best teachers in all of life turns out to be death …
> The question is, are you going to wait until that last moment to let death be your teacher?
>
> **Michael A. Singer**

NUMERIC SIGNIFICANCE ★ One more than 'perfect' twelve, this number is usually associated with ill fortune and the black arts, but it can also be a positive force. Thirteen is a number that is associated with witches because there are thirteen Full Moons and lunar months in a year, and the date Friday the 13th was once considered to belong to the Moon Goddess. It is considered unlucky for some, but for those who practise Moon magic, it is extremely auspicious. If we examine the meaning of the concept 'superstitious', it helps us understand why the number 13 has such a sinister reputation. Originally, *superstitio* meant 'to stand above, to dominate, to surmount, or to survive'. Superstition was therefore an idea that gave humans the means of standing above the hazards and unpredictable events of life, of controlling their destiny and their instincts, of surmounting their trials and shortcomings, and of surviving whatever might befall them. Today, the part of superstition which survives is the belief, most often groundless, in certain signs, gestures or rituals to which are attributed a particular value, influence or power. In Tarot, the Death card's number is thirteen, the magical lunar number of witchcraft and the ancient religion of the Goddess. A typical year is composed of thirteen lunar months - it was patriarchal culture that deleted the thirteenth month, contrived the solar calendar we use today, and put an aura of bad luck around the number thirteen. Once the most sacred of numbers, signifying the end and the beginning, the number thirteen has fearful connotations borne out of myth and superstition. This could be linked with the fact that when death comes too soon, as it does so often in our world, the natural cycle of life seems to have no satisfying or discernible 'ending', it leaves the soul somehow 'unfinished', the task undone, the full life unlived, and we may feel intense fear, guilt, frustration and deep grief. If we can understand that nothing ever really dies, it only transforms, then our fears may slightly or even fully dissolve. And in every process of Death, here is simultaneously a rebirth - the central message being that Life and Death are ever shifting poles of the same phenomenon. The ominous reputation of Friday the 13th, for example, may essentially derive from the legend of the Last Supper, the day when the 12 Apostles gathered around Jesus to share his last meal with him. From what historians tell us, the Last Supper was on a Friday, and when one knows what happened to Jesus - the thirteenth guest - after his meal, one can easily see why some came to consider Friday marked with the number 13 as an unlucky day. However, further back in time, the Chaldeans, who lived by the rhythm of twelve lunar months, added a thirteenth every six years. During this thirteenth month, all activity had to cease, since it was considered particularly unlucky - and this was 1,500 years before Christ.

> For life and death are one, even as the river and the sea are one.
>
> **Kahlil Gibran**

THE FOOL'S JOURNEY ★ This is one of the harder lessons The Fool must face: the knowledge and confronting of inevitable endings and necessary but painful change. But this is also where he will learn that death is not always the ending it appears to be, but rather a potential beginning and that new things cannot be started without old things coming to an end.

> A mind that is free of fear and sharp of thought is ready to understand the secret and silent language of Death. Discovering the power of your undying spirit - the most crucial - will connect you to the very essence of the dead, who are creatures of spirit themselves. We are kith and kin to the denizens of the underworld. The key to this spirit connection is magic, (and) as one evolves, he becomes more attuned to the guiding presence of the spirit forces around him. Our spirits yearn to fly across time and space and to travel as dignitaries to the kingdoms of the dead.
> For this to happen, we must set our souls free ...
>
> **Christian Day**

THE STORY ★ Here we have two symbols which both have a sinister reputation: death and the number thirteen ^. On no account should this card be regarded as a portent of literal, physical death. Like all the other Major Arcana cards, it is merely a *symbol* of death - essentially, that of an ending or a change.

> ^ The number 13 is not a fatal one, as many people believe. In ancient times, they claimed that 'somebody who knows how to use the number 13 will obtain force and power'.

Linda Goodman

THE MESSAGE ★ The skeletal form of the figure in the Death card is a reminder that death exists within life. In the skeleton, we see that the superficial has been pared away; all the desires of the flesh have been banished. He wishes not to be feared, for he symbolises the ultimate rebirth or regeneration that occurs with any death or ending; when transition occurs, new growth arises. An act of release can make it possible to move forward again. Though death can involve profound change, it can also be seen as a form of purging, of liberation. You must destroy old patterns to reveal a new, uncluttered, rewarding Path. Endings are usually painful, but ultimately, your fear of Death must be recognised and faced before it is allowed to interfere further with your enjoyment of life. The Death card signifies the end of a phase or situation. This will be a time for spiritual transformation, a time to move on! Shake off the old and welcome in the new! The Death card signifies relief or sadness, but there is no benefit in remaining in this situation or feeling. It is a card pointing to inevitable positive changes, confronting your fears, relationship transitions and eventual spiritual evolution.

> Quantum field theory tells us that we are like charged particles. We are 'excitations of energy' on the quantum vacuum that emerge from nothingness, travel for a while in this world, and then merge back into the vacuum from which we came - only to re-emerge as another pattern of energy at another time. Death is a journey through life: it is a path at the centre of every path, an essential part of the spiral of existence.

Danah Zorah and Ian Marshall

THE AWAKENING ★ You are beginning to realise how much you have been weighed down by past mental and emotional baggage. Unhealthy relationships and old habits need to be consciously discarded and this is usually an uncomfortable and unpleasant process, but leaves you feeling free to be more truly and fully yourself.

> 'Die and become', that is, 'Die to this existence and be reborn on a higher level.'

Johann Wolfgang von Goethe

THE LESSON ★ Although change is a necessary part of life, few of us welcome it with an open heart. For most, letting go of the unfamiliar can be sad and harrowing. If you are having trouble dealing with change, be assured that a sense of liberation will swiftly follow and replace any sorrow or pain - in essence, you will undergo a spiritual rebirth and awakening once you allow for this very necessary release.

> Every moment of one's existence is growing into more or retreating into less.
> One is always living a little more or dying a little bit.

Norman Mailer

SYMBOLISM ★ The Death card quite simply symbolises rebirth and transformation - new life emerging from old - and warns you that you need to let go of something. It can be seen as the snake that sheds its skin, or the caterpillar morphing into a butterfly upon coming out of the cocoon. The scythe the skeleton is using to clear the Path ahead is symbolic of sweeping away the old in order to make space for the new. The river running through the centre of some cards shows a new beginning for the emotions, and the need to move on and go willingly with the flow of change.

OVERALL ★ CONNECTING IT ALL UP ★

> After my death, the molecules of my being will return to the Earth and sky.
> They came from the stars. I am of the stars.

Charles Lindbergh

In the Tarot tradition, there is nothing alarming about Death - on the contrary, its message is a positive and optimistic one. Following the transformation of the Hanged Man, this card further emphasises that it is by 'dying' or shedding the old, that the Tarot traveller is reborn. Spiritual 'death' and 'rebirth' were essential rites in all the ancient mystery traditions. At this stage of the Tarot journey, the traveller knows that life is eternal, and even physical expiration is not the end of existence but simply the spiritual revelation of our true natures.

This card, depicting a skeletal figure, most recognised as the Grim Reaper, who wears an unthreatening grin and who rides a white horse while reaping, with a scythe, a harvest of heads, hands and feet, can represent the sudden collapse of events when least expected. The skeleton can symbolise separation and liberation of the spiritual self from the body and the material plane, while the corpses and other human parts on the ground represent obstacles to attaining this revelation, such as misdirected ambition and egotism. The skeleton is indeed busy with his scythe, clearing a Path for you on which he encourages you to walk towards the future, uncluttered by past mistakes. Two human heads are sometimes depicted on the Death card; one wears a crown, the other is a lesser mortal, emphasising that we all, in whatever area of life, experience periods of change that lead to new beginnings. In some decks, Death is depicted wearing a full suit of armour. The skeleton image in most decks, is symbolic of the inner self (the skeleton) is the most durable part of the physical self and it is indeed what holds us up.

The figure of Death is commonly depicted as a skeleton who is cutting down Kings, bishops, maidens and children - no one is except - demonstrating that power, status, beauty and youth don't provide protection against the inevitable change that Death insists upon when usefulness has outworn its welcome. Around his skull, death sometimes wears a white funeral shroud, which was once the swaddling cloth of birth. Therefore, the shroud represents the close connection between birth and death. This need not necessarily be a bad thing, and can indeed signal new growth, or the death and subsequent rebirth that is characteristic of Scorpio, the astrological sign with which this card is linked. Its divinatory meanings are transformation, clearing the old to make way for the new, unexpected changes, loss, alteration, the ending of a familiar situation or friendship, abrupt change of the old self through a symbolic 'death', financial loss, illness, or the beginning of a new era. It could also signify inevitability and the futility of trying to change plans or avoid a situation.

The Death card could frighten those who don't fully understand its meaning. It isn't about physical death, but rather, necessary changes, and endings that lead to beginnings, as can be so clearly seen in the seasons. It tells you that you are at a crossroads in your life. It can mean that a change you are facing is actually a blessing in disguise, a clearing out which will make way for something better, but it can be regarded as harsh fate which does not consider personal feelings; it can be an enforced change, such as the removal of something that should have been given up, for it is no longer serving you. Only rarely will the card signify death in its literal sense; mostly it simply means a major change in life.

The time is right for you to cast aside that which you know is finished and make a fresh start, by putting past longings and regrets behind you. It advises you to look forward, be brave and open-minded, never think "If only," be hopeful and be positive in outlook. This change in your life may be either self-initiated or thrust upon you. In whatever way change arises, the outcome will be successful and rewarding. And always remember that time flies - so make the most of it!

Death is change. In shamanistic terms, Death is the period of time when the body is still and without a heartbeat, the door opens, and the soul crosses the threshold between this world and the beyond. In one sense the shaman lies in a trance, as an accident victim might lie in a coma; if the soul does not return to the body, then death is complete. Like the night, Death is dark, quiet, lacking sunlight and the warmth of the life force. But night is paired with day, and the Sun *will* rise again. From the point of view of the physical body, Death is an ending, signifying that one's time on Earth has expired. But from the soul's viewpoint, physical Death is the beginning of a new journey, an expanded state of being, in the formless realms.

The Death card being connected with Scorpio, its force is also attributed to Pluto, named for the Greek god of the underworld. A planet of regeneration, Pluto changes us from that deepest place inside of us. Through the process of facing death, through meditation or dying, one comes to know the soul more deeply. Scorpio rules mysticism, the occult, death, transformation, the sex organs, the deep unconscious, and the ability to channel healing energies.

When the snake sheds its skin, it acts as if with instinctual consciousness of the rebirth that is occurring, with a calm acceptance of the process. In contrast to the snake, humans often fear losing the old skin, even when it has begun to constrict our growth. We fear the unknown, and are naturally always more comfortable with the old. If we could just become more like the shedding snake, we would allow our outworn ways to fall away and for our inner, renewed skin to emerge. Similarly, this card is a metaphor for that shedding of our old, worn skin so that we can free our spirit to move on to fresh starts.

The Death card should not fill you with fear or dread, but alert you to the fact that something is approaching its natural ending. This may come with sadness or relief, and very often a mixture of the two. However, you feel, take your time in adjusting to this new change in your life; it's not necessary to rush ahead. Be kind to yourself during this period of transition, and seek the support you need.

So many different situations and symbols are connected with the Death card, and many of them are potentially happy events. For example, marriage is the death of single life, but it can be hoped it is the happy transition to a shared life. There is always a sense of nostalgia about any ending, so other examples could be linked with leaving a job, home, or school - they are all healthy, necessary changes, yet each one evokes the emotions portrayed by Death; that is, they all involve saying goodbye to an old, comfortable way of life.

When connected with relationships, this card highlights what you fear losing in a relationship - even if you know that a coming change is inevitable, you may struggle against it. You need to realise however, that love can shift into a whole new dimension, however changed or transformed it becomes in the process.

Ultimately, Death comes to all, bringing with it new life. The emphasis here is on the transformation from one state to another; the end of one phase brings the birth of a new. Quite simply, without Death there is no new life, only stagnation. As the ultimate symbol of transformation, this card shows that, by accepting the loss of old love, old links and old ideas, life opens up to great new gains and possibilities. And once you have mastered the powerful lessons and heeded the profound messages of Death, you will fear it no longer.

★ HOW THIS CARD RELATES TO SCORPIO ★

Death, the ruler of the Underworld, is assigned to Scorpio, the sign of sex, death, (and) transformation.

Corrine Kenner

The essence of Scorpio is self-mastery, the understanding of its own transformative powers. This profound understanding embraces the idea that without death, there is no life. Scorpio contains things on a deep level, is psychologically penetrative, and usually awakens to consciousness through endings - essentially, they must go through the 'death' of something to re-emerge transformed. Indeed, deaths and rebirths are what bring out Scorpio's best. Scorpio acknowledges this concept on a deep-seated level and indeed at *all* levels - physically, mentally, emotionally, psychically and spiritually - and as such most true Scorpios experience many deaths in many forms every single day - for this is the zodiac sign that instinctively knows that to die is to be reborn anew, converted into a different state, another life, a higher stage, or an entirely new plane of existence. Scorpios, more than most, also know that matter and energy can never essentially be created or destroyed, but merely *transformed*. This is the essence of the Death card, and is what links it so strongly with the sign of the Scorpion - as well as to Scorpio's other potent symbol, the legendary Phoenix, who is born anew, improved and brilliant, from its own ashes.

★ DIVINE MANIFESTATION USING DEATH ★

You can Divinely manifest things in your experience through tapping into your inner Resilience.

Though death can involve profound change, it can also be seen as a form of purging, of liberation. You must destroy old patterns to reveal a new, uncluttered, rewarding Path. Endings are usually painful, but ultimately, your fear of Death must be recognised and faced before it is allowed to interfere further with your enjoyment of life. The Death card signifies the end of a phase or situation. This will be a time for spiritual transformation, a time to move on! Shake off the old and welcome in the new! The Death card signifies relief or sadness, but there is no benefit in remaining in this situation or feeling. It is a card pointing to inevitable positive changes, confronting your fears, relationship transitions and eventual spiritual evolution. Unhealthy relationships and old habits need to be consciously discarded and this is usually an uncomfortable and unpleasant process, but leaves you feeling free to be more truly and fully yourself.

★ EXERCISES TO TAP INTO YOUR INNER GRIM REAPER ★

★ Think of one situation, feeling or relationship which is no longer serving you and that you need to set free in order to create a new space in your life for something else to come into your experience. Write this situation, feeling or relationship down in a symbol or a word, and burn it by the flame of a black candle. Visualise yourself being reborn and renewed from this act of purging and release, even if it is only symbolic. Then, think about how you can banish the situation from your experience in a way that is for the highest good of all concerned. You don't have to act on this thought, but certainly ponder it. See the positives of letting go, relinquishing those things that you know are not good for your soul, and of that part of you dying, then of later being reborn.

★ De-clutter. Give yourself a spiritual enema! A good clean-out can do absolute wonders for your spirit. It's interesting to know that one of the first things that happens if you are admitted to a hospital in some parts of the world, is that you are given an enema. This is because most medical professionals understand that the body's natural ability to heal itself is greatly enhanced if the eliminatory channels are clear. So the medical staff apply an enema in order to flush waste out of the patient's system. This makes a sound analogy for clutter of the mind, spirit or physical space in which you dwell - *clear the channels to facilitate healing, flow and an easier opening for which good can come pouring into your life.* It's a funny thing about humans, we are always sending out flaring flames of desire: "I want this," "I wish for that," "I desire this in my life," "I want that thing to come to me" ... but so often we fail to realise that to draw our desire towards us, we must clear a space for it. Where will it 'fit' in your life if you haven't created spiritual or literal room for it? How can you expect a new lover to come into your life when you sleep across the whole bed? How can money be drawn to you if your purse needs a major clean-out or its stitching is falling apart (symbolically money will slip right through it)? How can you attract new curtains if you haven't taken the old ones down already? This process of clearing out, of purging, of cleansing, of eliminating, can sometimes feel like loss or even a small death. But it is through this little death that something better can come into your experience. De-cluttering, throwing things out, and coming to the acceptance that there is a time and place for things in your life to fall away and die, allows for manifestation to occur effortlessly. So, clear the channels, unblock your Path, and prepare to receive! Have you given yourself a spiritual enema lately?

★ TEMPERANCE ★

Ruled by Sagittarius

Number ★ 14
Astrological Signs ★ Cancer & Sagittarius

Keywords ★ Moderation, Balance, Blending

Magical Title ★ The Bringer Forth of Life, The Daughter of the Reconcilers
Divinity ★ Hestia

Spiritual Value ★ The path of Temperance has been called 'the Dark Night of the Soul', because it leads from the core of the Lower Self to the centre of the Higher Self in on the Middle Pillar of the Tree of Life. This Arcanum may be used to free you from your rampant passions and impulses, while simultaneously helping you to understand their true origins. Because it is a moderating energy, it is beneficial to use Temperance in conjunction with another Major Arcana card (of an opposite nature) in order to stabilise the corresponding trait. It fosters concentration, patience, seriousness, willpower, and perseverance.

★ KEY THEMES ★

"Walking the Tightrope"

Moderation ★ Successful Blend ★ Balance ★ Union of Opposites ★ Successful Partnerships ★ Blended Ideas ★ Pleasant Relationships ★ Cooperation ★ Self-restraint ★ Waiting for Perfect Timing ★ Revelation ★ Message ★ Regeneration ★ Advantageous Transactions and Negotiations ★ Mutual Understanding ★ Opportunities

Meditation ★ "I walk the Path of moderation, temperance and gentleness, and trust that when working from my pure heart and soul, successful blendings and unions will take place and unfold naturally."

★ *When Working with this Card* ★

MAIN ENERGIES ★ Moderation, Balance, Discernment, Integrity
MAIN GOD OR GODDESS TO INVOKE ★ Sol
CANDLE COLOUR ★ Blue
MAGICAL TOOLS OR SYMBOLS ★ Cauldron, Scales
CRYSTALS ★ Apophyllite, Blue Lace Agate, Green Aventurine, Chrysocolla

ASSOCIATED BEINGS, GODS, GODDESSES & ARCHETYPES ★ Sons of Light, Archangels, Saviours, the Zodiac, Sol, Neptune, Nephthys, Apollo, Holy Grail, the Alchemist, the Guardian Angel, the Magician.
ARCHETYPES ★ Temperance is the archangel of balance, dexterity and grace, demonstrating that moderation can serve as a bridge to wholeness and integrity. She

is the Creator, the Enchantress, the Magical Helper, the Sorcerer, the Magus, the Witch, the Wizard.

CHAKRAS ★ Use this card to balance and meditate upon the Solar Plexus and Heart chakras.

Solar Plexus ★ Behind the Navel ★ Yellow ★ Fire ★ Personal Power, Confidence & Control

Heart ★ Heart Region ★ Green ★ Air ★ Love & Compassion

TREE OF LIFE ★ In western magic, which combines the Tarot paths of the Major Arcana with the ten sephiroth on the Tree of Life, the path of Temperance connects Yesod and Tiphareth, and is an integral part of the mystic journey up the Middle Pillar.

> The being who has attained harmony - and every being may attain it - has found his place in the order of the Universe and represents the Divine thought as clearly as a flower or a solar system. Harmony seeks nothing outside itself. It is what is ought to be; it is the expression of right, order, law, and truth; it is greater than time and represents eternity.
>
> **Henri Amiel**

THE FOOL'S JOURNEY ★ With transformation comes the lessons of moderation and perspective. In Temperance, The Fool learns all about tolerating differences, learning patience, measuring and combining the correct amounts of anything, and waiting rather than rushing in head-first.

> I think there's some connection between absolute discipline and absolute freedom.
>
> **Alan Rickman**

THE STORY ★ Temperance is one of three virtues to appear in the Tarot - the other two are Justice and Strength. Temperance indicates you are in fine balance, or about to become so. The natural movements of energy around and within you are in harmony and integrated; you are not fragmented or disconnected from yourself. You may even feel in a heightened state of consciousness, able to absorb much more than usual and to assimilate it naturally within your being. You may be experiencing a new sense of courage and wellbeing. This card carries with it an enormous power. If it is a gift managed with clarity and love, its message has been received. Use your powers wisely.

> Alchemy itself does not deal too much with the first half of the creative cycle; our starting point in alchemy is to find that seed of gold, release its potential, and transmute it back to gold, therefore creating the second half of the Cosmic cycle. We then gain wings to fly, spiritually, and may become witnesses to some of those secrets of creation.
>
> **Cherry Gilchrist**

THE MESSAGE ★ In Tarot tradition, the Temperance card represents the empowerment of alchemy, that mystical process of blending the parts of the self until fusion is achieved and the 'philosopher's stone' is created. Alchemy is a philosophy and practice that spans both science and mysticism. First conceived as a process similar to fermentation, in which common base metals might be transmuted into gold or silver, over time the alchemical process became an analogy for psychological and physical transformation also. In ancient times, as alchemy became ever more spiritual and concerned with more abstract and philosophical concepts, eventually it was considered that the transmutation of base metals into gold was simply a metaphor for the transformation of the prime matter, in this case the human soul, into a much purer and higher state of wisdom and being. Jung spoke of a synthesis of the contrasts inherent within the human spirit, in terms of inner healing via the individuation (integration) process. However, we use our personal magic, there are times in everyone's life when things work out well and when everything runs smoothly. Temperance suggests that such a time is on its way to you, perhaps after a considerable period of inner conflict. This card shows a young woman pouring liquid from one container to another, suggesting the mixture of ingredients to formulate just the right potion. The success of the experiment will depend not only upon how well the various ingredients of circumstance are blended but, on the attention and patience shown to ensure that everything is mixed at the right time. Temperance is all about balance and moderation. It also signifies cooperation and compromise, keeping a moderate pace and striking equilibrium between contemplation and action. It suggests that you need to be cautious about making impulsive decisions or moves, and instead choose the 'Middle Way' *, the Path of moderation and balance.

* Buddhist thought describes the 'Middle Way' as a path of moderation that sits between extremes. This, according to its doctrine, is the path of wisdom.

> If gravity is the glue that holds the Universe together, balance is the key that unlocks its secrets. Balance applies to our body, mind and emotions, to all levels of our being. It reminds us that anything we do, we can overdo or underdo, and that if the pendulum of our lives or habits swings too far to one side, it will inevitable swing to the other.
>
> **Dan Millman**

THE AWAKENING ★ An angel is featured on the Temperance card. This is the ancient depiction of a messenger. But she is not just a simple conveyor of a message; she advises and moderates while she passes on the information. Without the circulation of information and the transmission of energetic currents, no life would be possible. In the same way as water - which, because it follows the rotational movement of the Earth, flows ceaselessly and continuously, fertilising and regenerating the Earth - so flow the currents of life and of thoughts. They circulate within and through us, renewing themselves as well as us. These energies are like a source of nourishment, and this nourishing cord is pictured on the Temperance card, as the continuous flow of water being decanted between the two vessels by the angel. They ultimately stand for fruitfulness, action, flow, life and vitality, but always tempered with wisdom, discernment and restraint.

Be moderate in order to taste the joys of life in abundance.

Epicurus

THE LESSON ★ Temperance is all about the process of refining something to make it more balanced and thereby making it work more effectively. A good example of the concept of the word temperate is the temperate zone on Earth, which is situated between the vast frozen landscapes of the poles and the burning heat of the equator. It takes from both these areas and moderates the temperature and conditions between the two, making parts of the world that are not too hot and not too cold, where people can live more comfortably and plant and animal life can flourish. The Temperance card brings you tidings, a message, revealing that information will be given, that a revelation will be made or received. The dialogue is always open with Temperance, its presence reassuring because it tells you simply that, with time, everything becomes transformed and ultimately sorted out. Of course, it also pledges moderation, understanding, and tolerance, and it frequently appears when a transaction or negotiation is underway. Finally, by allowing this free flow of energies and currents, it presents you with new opportunities and possibilities that you may seize.

The choicest pleasures of life lie within the ring of moderation.

Benjamin Disraeli

SYMBOLISM ★ Temperance is a symbol for moderation and balance, indicating the need for an attitude of staying centered and avoiding extremes. The angel depicted on the card is representative of the spiritual aspect of ourselves. She rests her feet on both the land and the water, symbolising the harmony of the physical body and the emotions, and the grounding of ideas received from the waters of the subconscious so that they may be put to practical use. This depiction can also be linked to the book of Revelation. In that book, we experience the cosmic contrasts of good versus evil, and can be taken as a lesson that some things cannot be reconciled and must be excised if we are to be healed.

Water flows back and forth between the two cups, symbolising the combining of energies to create a union of opposites. The cups represent our ability to receive and exchange information.

The pool shown in the picture represents the subconscious, from which flows ideas, dreams, inspiration and creativity. The water is moving, showing that the energy is mobile but always accessible.

OVERALL ★ CONNECTING IT ALL UP ★

Thank God every morning when you get up that you have something to do that day which must be done ... Being forced to work and forced to do your best will breed temperance and self-control, diligence and strength of will, cheerfulness and content, and a hundred virtues which the idle never know.

Charles Kingsley

The word 'temperance' means moderation and a lack of extremes. It is one of the cardinal virtues. The angel of Temperance strives for a sense of emotional calm and serenity, and offers the qualities of compassion and forgiveness.

The card depicts a winged angelic figure is pouring liquid from one container into another, representing the flow of the unseen and mysterious into the seen and known, or from the unconscious mind to the conscious, showing the need for the constant flow between the two. It is also said to symbolise the past merging with the future.

She is a kindly, thoughtful, caring, motherly, comforting and beautiful woman, who is bringing you the message of encouragement. She says you should take a practical outlook, through controlling your emotions but not suppressing them. You should make certain that you enjoy and believe in what you are doing, and this will lead to a peaceful and harmonious existence. She warns that short cuts to success will not pay off, and that a slow, steady way leads to a fulfilled life. Always be realistic and while you should partake of Earthly delights and pleasures, you must guard against overindulgence and thoughtlessness where food and sex are concerned.

Some decks show the cups as gold and silver, symbolising the conscious and the unconscious mind and the need for movement between them. She represents the balance between the conscious and the subconscious mind, and echoes the teachings of the ancient Greek oracle at Delphi, which advocated "moderation in all things," as well as the doctrines of the Buddha, which encourage us to always seek the middle way over and above extremes.

This card relates to mixture and combination. Its meaning is to exercise careful control of volatile factors so that they result in a successful conclusion. Temperance is a card of healing and harmony indicated by the figure pouring water from one vessel to another, thereby encouraging us to let our life force flow freely. It counsels us that compromise is the answer to any problem and suggests the need for cooperation. It is now time to work with others in a collaborative way, sharing and pooling resources rather than hoarding them. It denotes a time to seek others to support your endeavours and find ways of working as a team rather than in opposition. After all, prosperous relationships are those in which both parties work together keeping the other's best interests at heart for the good of the whole. The liquid being poured from one vessel to the other also suggests that relationships are positively enhanced by the sharing of feelings, for after all, if water doesn't flow it's in danger of stagnating.

Its divinatory meanings are temperance, moderation, patience, accommodation, harmony, combining to make a perfect union, management, fusion, adjustment, consolidation, successful combination, beneficial influence, and accomplishment through self-control and frugality. It signifies a harmonious partnership, the healing effects of time, self-control, adaptability, and the assurance that peace will be restored after a troubled time. It teaches that we must first test the waters and never dive into a situation without thinking, to be patient and take things slowly, and to go carefully "where angels fear to tread."

Magically, Temperance symbolises that wishes will be fulfilled if the power of the imagination is expressed with balance and in harmony with our inner selves.

★ HOW THIS CARD RELATES TO SAGITTARIUS ★

Temperance, who straddles the divide between two worlds, is assigned to Sagittarius, the sign of long-distance travel, philosophy, and higher education. The Sagittarian archer - half horse, half man - also combines two widely different experiences, while his arrow soars across long distances on its way to new horizons.

Corrine Kenner

Although extravagant, anything but subtle and adventurous rather than moderate, Temperance is linked to the sign of the Archer through its ability to tame the wild beast and rein in the rampant stallion. Indeed, the wayward Sagittarian spirit has much to gain from listening to the counsel of Temperance. His extroverted cheerfulness and attraction to abstract ideas and philosophies are the basis of his strengths *and* his weaknesses. At his highest level, the Sagittarian effortlessly walks and talks his truth - confidently, generously, humanely and philosophically - and this level is experienced when the Angel of Temperance has blended her liquids in the proper combinations. Living enthusiastically and loving life tend to bring the Archer success and the fruition of his dreams and ambitions as a natural by-product of this successful blending. However, the Sagittarius knows too well that that same expansive idealism can lead to an excess of abstraction and carelessness. Wastefulness, extravagance, aimlessness, meaningless chatter, wandering attention, and endlessly doing things without apparent direction or purpose, can all result and render his character lazy and recklessly carefree. Used positively, his agile mind can uplift the entire world - and this is Temperance's highest and noblest aim. The wise Archer takes heed, and consequently lives through his true Spirit - with inspiration, leadership, mentorship, self-respect, integrity and courage. Successful blending, moderation and lack of excess are key.

The Temperance card also resonates with Sagittarius through its religious connotations and symbolism. On the angel's chest, we find the Hebrew letters for Yahweh, the God of Israel, and a triangle, symbolic of the three persons of the Godhead: Father, Son and Spirit. Overall, the angel exudes spiritual strength and perhaps an adherence to a virtuous, religious way of living, and essentially imparts the wisdom to be found in the philosophy of moderation.

★ DIVINE MANIFESTATION USING TEMPERANCE ★

You can Divinely manifest things in your experience through tapping into your inner Scales.
Temperance reveals the ability to maintain equilibrium even in the midst of chaotic change. The freedom to discover new aspects of yourself leads you to explore your inner space once more. You become aware that if you are balanced and centred, life flows more smoothly. Enthralling you with the sense of harmony this creates, you discover qualities that can be explored from the inside and then expressed outwardly. If you're considering making a dramatic life change, approach this change slowly and methodically. As well as undertaking intensive self-work around cultivating balance and moderation, this card is also about working in concert with others, and encourages you to see things from their points of view and to work in unison with them for the best results. Extending this compassion, kindness and tolerance are key

to manifesting your dreams! Forgiveness will also allow for healing, which will help bring about the new beginnings you so desire. This card carries with it an enormous power. If its gifts are managed with clarity, wisdom, and love, you can wield enormous power in the creation of your life experience. Use these powers moderately, harmoniously, and wisely, and you can transcend those more extreme pendulum swings of life.

★ EXERCISE FOR TAPPING INTO YOUR INNER TEMPERANCE ★

★ Are you out of balance with something at the moment? Is there anything that you need to find greater balance around in your life? One clue you might be off-kilter is health problems; for example, if you are experiencing headaches, it could be that something is off-balance in your system. Your job is to find what is causing the disharmony and take one step towards bringing it back into harmony. Moderation is key, but many of us find this difficult, especially around eating, drinking, sleeping, emotions, money, working, time, and numerous other aspects of our life experience. Identify one area in your life where you need to exercise moderation, and try to find some balance or middle way.

★ Are you more masculine or feminine? I am not speaking of gender here, I am referring to the universals principles of yin and yang. Do you find that you express more yin qualities or yang qualities? Identify which of the following checklist you identify most with, and that is likely to be your dominant nature: Yin is female, dark, inner, down, Earth, winter, shadow, cold, night, soft, wet, passive, receptive, stillness, and cyclical. Yang is male, light, outer, up, sky, summer, heat, day, hard, dry, active, positive, creative, movement, and linear. If you feel you are dominant in yin qualities, find some ways to balance it out with some of the more yang qualities, and if you feel you are overly yang, find some ways to balance it out with some of the more yin qualities. This really is a powerful exercise that can help bring about greater harmony, moderation, and balance in your life.

★ THE DEVIL ★

Ruled by Capricorn

Number ★ 15
Astrological Signs ★ Capricorn & Cancer

Keywords ★ Temptation, Excesses, Entrapment, Bondage

Magical Title ★ The Child of the Forces of Time, The Lord of the Gates of Matter
Divinity ★ Hephaestos
Spiritual Value ★ Death and The Devil are the two great controlling forces of the Universe, the destructive and reproductive, the dynamic and the static. You may use this Arcanum to balance your inner being and to release any fears you have around the transmutation process. It will help you to realise that this very fear of change and disintegration is necessary to stabilise your life force and preserve the continuity of your renewal.

★ KEY THEMES ★

"Knocking on Hell's Door"

Temptations ★ Bondage ★ Compulsions ★ False Sense of Entrapment ★ Dependency ★ Bad Influence ★ Overly Focused on Material Things ★ Negative or Fear-Based Thoughts ★ Guilt ★ Refusal to Face the Truth or Take Responsibility For a Situation ★ Addictions ★ Off-Balance ★ Excess ★ Irrepressible Urges ★ Instincts ★ Power Expressed in the Physical and Material World ★ A Passionate, Creative Person, Either Productive or Destructive, Ready to Use Any Possible Means To Reach Desired Ends ★ Firm Willpower ★ Strong Psyche ★ Financial and Material Aims and Achievements ★ Selfish Desire

Meditation ★ "I am confronting my shadow self, and shall not succumb to greed, temptations or obsessions that are ultimately of my own creation. I acknowledge that I crave inner peace through having the courage to meet with my dark side, and that a more spiritually enlightened Path awaits me. I am abandoning my material desires in order to seek the proper Way."

★ *When Working with this Card* ★

MAIN ENERGIES ★ Release, Banishment, Transcendence, Freedom, Empowerment, Self-Mastery
MAIN GOD OR GODDESS TO INVOKE ★ Anubis
CANDLE COLOUR ★ Black
MAGICAL TOOL OR SYMBOL ★ Sword, Black Upright Pentacle
CRYSTALS ★ Jet, Smoky Quartz, Black Tourmaline, Black Obsidian, Apophyllite

ASSOCIATED BEINGS, GODS, GODDESSES & ARCHETYPES ★ The Sorcerer, the Trickster, the Goat of Mendes, Anubis, Min, Seth, Pan, Erebus, Baphomet, Dionysus, Lucifer, Hades, Pluto, Loki, the Shadow Self.

> You are the unconditioned spirit that is trapped in conditions, the boundless spirit that is trapped in boundaries, like the Sun and an eclipse.
>
> **Rumi**

ARCHETYPES ★ The Devil is the dark, shadowy side of our natures and existence. But he is cruel to be kind, and demonstrates how a selfish devotion to and fixation upon material possessions and misguided passions can chain us up, tie us down and keep us from true happiness. He is the Outlaw, the Dictator, the Rebel, the Shadow.

> Expose yourself to your deepest fear; after that, fear has no power. You are free.
>
> **Jim Morrison**

CHAKRAS ★ Use this card to balance and meditate upon the Sacral and Crown chakras.

Sacral ★ Below the Navel ★ Orange ★ Water ★ Physical, Sexual, Creative & Material Desires

Crown ★ Top of Head ★ Purple ★ Thought/Knowing ★ Spiritual Wisdom & Enlightenment

> Monsters are real, and ghosts are real too. They live inside us, and sometimes, they win.
>
> **Stephen King**

TREE OF LIFE ★ In western magic, which combines the Tarot paths of the Major Arcana with the ten sephiroth on the Tree of Life, the path of The Devil connects Hod and Tiphareth.

> Men are not prisoners of fate, but only prisoners of their own minds.
>
> **Franklin D. Roosevelt**

THE FOOL'S JOURNEY ★ Even with all his newfound knowledge, The Fool continues to harbour internal demons, petty things that could undermine his existence, such as obsessions, doubts or uncontrollable impulses. This card serves to remind us once again of our shadow side and the evil we can do to ourselves if we fail to break free from our chains and bondages.

> Ultimately we know deeply that the other side of fear is freedom.
>
> **Marilyn Ferguson**

THE STORY ★ The Devil is the archetypal face of evil. He compels us to look deeper into ourselves to examine our motives and untamed desires. Blinded to his spiritual nature, The Devil looks down on his captors, his slitted eyes suggestive of a complete obsession with and surrender to the material world. The Devil expresses the worst side of human nature: following decadent impulses blindly and judging things only by their surface value or purely by what they can offer him. This is the dark side of the soul, ignorant of what is 'real' and valuable. Though he may be merely mischievous at times, he will try to take advantage of any situation and cannot be trusted. Capricorn, the cardinal Earth sign attributed to The Devil, represents these manifestations in the continual attempt to scale peaks, sometimes at any cost. If Capricorn's competitive and ambitious streak turns to selfish gratification and an unquenchable hunger for power and wealth, it can become destructive.

> The Devil is the playful capacity to be our own Devil's advocate,
> liberating us from rigidity or negativity in our thinking.

Paul Hougham

THE MESSAGE ★ The Devil is a complex card full of paradoxical meanings. In Jungian terms, we could regard The Devil as the collective 'shadow' that our culture has projected onto us, a symbol of societal bondage and power. Traditionally, and particularly to the common medieval psyche, The Devil was a living force of evil and thus greatly feared. However, in modern Tarot decks, the meaning of this card is more in line with Cabbalistic thought, which sees The Devil as the 'tester' or the quality controller - indeed a negative force, but one which provides the challenges and hardships against which you have to strive in your life. For without this active, discordant force, there would be nothing to strive *against*, and therefore little chance to progress. The main idea in this card is that of bondage and this can take many forms, most of which tie you down or give you the feeling of being trapped. It can indicate enslavement to something or someone, and could be an idea, a relationship, a way of life, an unhappy job, a bad habit or a self-destructive pattern. But this card's message is that this perceived entrapment isn't real; it isn't based in reality, but rather it is based in the ego and the shadowy self that lurks deep within. Your trap is of your own making and, even though you may imagine you can't escape its constriction, there is a way out if only you can see it. You will remain enslaved to the challenging situation until you acknowledge that you are in fact your *own* imprisoner and *you* therefore hold the key to unlock your chains.

> If you don't have any shadows you're not in the light.

Lady Gaga

THE AWAKENING ★ The Devil in traditional form, puts fear into our hearts - but for our own good. He shows us the error of our ways and highlights the failings and trappings of ignorance and excess. An encounter with The Devil brings back your deepest primal fears. To overcome these, you need to change your emphasis from physical concerns, to those of the spirit. The first step in breaking out of the chains is to protest, by saying "No!" for example, which requires courage and conviction, a strong belief in self, and an unstoppable impulse toward freeing the wild spirit within. Saying "No!" to private thought forms and thinking habits that cripple us emotionally is empowering. Every person who has given up an addiction or said no to a pressing temptation, understands what effort and victory truly mean. You have within the power to change and use your beliefs, through visualisation, new habits, actions, free will and affirmations that are in harmony with natural and cosmic laws. In essence, The Devil may exist in some form in each one of us, but it can always be exorcised.

> I am only interested in the basement of the human being.
>
> **Sigmund Freud**

THE LESSON ★ The Devil suggests the possibility of great power if energy can be released rather than imprisoned. The image of The Devil as the Greek god Pan, who was worshipped as a fertile, life-giving god of abundance, has attained a bad reputation over the centuries and, as a result, we have learned to feel ashamed of our instinctive urges. The Devil card points out that it is necessary to accept all aspects of our nature - dark, shadowy *and* light - so that our repressed fears can be released to give way to positive, liberated energies. If we don't allow this, inhibitions and phobias can develop in the unconscious, preventing healthy growth and expression. The 'devil' in us must therefore be faced so we can come to terms with him and put his forces to better use. Whether you are the one wielding the power or the one feeling the effects of submission, your soul is in need of liberation. The Devil carries the message and lesson that if such blocks can be overcome, the prospects for growth and progress are much brighter.

> We must be afraid of neither poverty nor exile nor imprisonment;
> of fear itself only should we be afraid.
>
> **Epictetus**

SYMBOLISM ★ The Devil card may evoke an initial response of fear, but its actual message is that you can overcome your inner 'demons'. The Devil symbolises the fearful, shadowy aspects of the psyche, and reflects what can occur when you are governed by the unconscious, ruled by the primeval mind, rather than by logic, intuition and wisdom. He symbolises that you are being controlled by your inner forces and fears, signifying obsessions, sexuality without love, and a sensation of being powerless.

The chains around the 'captives' at his feet are loose enough for them to break free, indicating that they should have the courage to do just that, and that in any case, they have the choice to break loose from the ties that restrict them.

OVERALL ★ CONNECTING IT ALL UP ★

> Our deepest fear is not that we are inadequate. Our deepest fear is that we are powerful beyond measure. It is our light, not our darkness, that most frightens us. We ask ourselves, who am I to be brilliant, gorgeous, talented, fabulous? Actually, who are you *not* to be? Your

playing small does not serve the world. There is nothing enlightened about shrinking so that other people won't feel insecure around you. ... As we let our own Light shine, we unconsciously give others permission to do the same. As we are liberated from our own fear, our presence automatically liberates others.

Marianne Williamson

The image of The Devil is a familiar if sinister one. This is the card of the dangers of materialism. The Devil rules the tyranny of the physical body and the senses and is the bearer of the inevitable, such as disasters and misery.

The Devil is commonly depicted in the Tarot as half-man, half-goat, with bat wings and horns, which connects him with the Greek god Pan, who was the god of untamed nature and sexuality. Lustful and sensual, he was not malicious or evil, however, he represents our natural urges which, if left to their own devices, tend to be more troublesome than if they are managed and owned. This is symbolised by his naked prisoners, whose chains hang loosely and could be broken free from if they chose to do so.

At this stage of the Tarot journey, you are confronted with the fact that the equilibrium you have been experiencing is found to be more fragile than you first realised, and you are forced to face your fears. Temptations appear that are difficult to resist or overcome and your strengthening self-awareness battles to prevent you becoming ensnared by issues of obsession, sexuality, materialism or power.

The two characters chained to each other at The Devil's feet in this card are, it would seem, prisoners of The Devil. But in reality, The Devil is a figment of their imagination, their thoughts, their desires and their wishes, hence lends the sense that their entrapment and imprisonment is merely an illusion. These two figures represent humanity; he has apparent power over them, but in his wisdom, he has made their shackles loose enough for them to escape. It is they who are foolish if they do not take advantage of this, and release themselves from their situation. He makes us aware that only oneself can rid oneself of the psychological bonds inhibiting oneself. Although The Devil is the tempter, who preys on your fears in order to gain power over you and chain you to an illusion, in essence, he really insists that you are not as trapped in your problems or situation as you might think.

This card reveals an excess, an imperious desire, a blind impulse, a pressing or irrepressible need to act, to reach one's aims or to satisfy them. This need is often blocked and if it is released it needs careful guidance to realise the positive aspects of the desire and thus encourage growth.

Its divinatory meanings are subordination, ravage, possessive instinct, bondage, malevolence, downfall, inability to realise one's goals, violence, shock, intense creativity, fatality, self-punishment, temptation to evil, self-destruction, unrealised success, power, weird experiences, bad outside influence or advice, black magic and unexpected failures. It is connected with lust and greed, with a refusal to recognise anything else but pleasure for its own sake. It signifies unyielding power, discontent, depression, overwhelming forces and an immovable object which cannot be overcome yet may be worked around. It is actually a good omen for marriage as it symbolises unbreakable bonds.

The Devil is associated with Pan, the mythical god of music, nature, shepherds and sheep. Pan was a god of physical indulgences, including sex, lust, food, and drink (he was a close associate of Dionysus, the god of wine) and was wild, sometimes giving rise to panic. Because of this connection with Pan, The Devil has come to symbolise erotic pleasures, wild behaviours, unchecked addictions, and unbridled desire.

This is one of the cards that may indicate curses are afoot in your life. Sorcery of the worst kind can be suggested by The Devil card. This is dark magic and one with a mind all its own. Your 'enemy' has unleashed dark forces, over which they have no control themselves. A pact has been made and you are right in the centre of it all. Watch for an unseen presence and supernatural disturbances.

Having said all this, the entrapment that you are feeling tangled up in isn't real. Indeed, a lot of your feelings are stemming from anxieties that aren't based in reality. You may also be focused too much on the material plane and although everyone has needs, your attention to the accumulation of material possessions is out of balance. This card compels you to examine why you wish to acquire these things or experiences. Perhaps you are trying to fill an emotional void, or escape a painful truth, but what you are really craving is inner peace through a spiritually enlightened Path. Before you can do this, your shadow side signified by The Devil must be confronted.

In meeting with your darker self, this will signify the beginning of freedom, release from bondage, the throwing off of shackles, a light at the end of the tunnel, the undertaking of more charitable deeds and thoughts, the recognition of your needs by another person, the overcoming of severe handicaps, the beginning of spiritual understanding, and the overcoming and conquering of bad habits, thoughts or addictions that have kept you limited for so long.

★ HOW THIS CARD RELATES TO CAPRICORN ★

The Devil, the embodiment of physical and material temptation, is assigned to Capricorn, the sign of business, career success, and worldly status. If anyone could beat The Devil at a game of cards, it would be a Capricorn. Both understand all too well the trials and temptations of the material world. He knows that wealth and material success can liberate us - or enslave us ... The mountain-climbing goat associated with the sign bears a striking resemblance to some depictions of the Devil himself.

Corrine Kenner

The Devil archetype can be found in such forms as the horned goat (Capricorn's animal) and in most cards, he shares many features of a goat. The Devil is linked to the sign of Capricorn through his tendency to be seduced by the temptation of materialism and greed. Of all the signs, with the exception of perhaps Scorpio, Capricorn is the most power-hungry and controlling, and these very traits can lead to her downfall - as they can The Devil's. Indeed, this is the very essence of The Devil card's meaning - downfall through an excess, obsession or addiction. Capricorn, as is The Devil, can be ruthless, spiritually oppressive (of the self and of others), cunning and unaffected by others' plight, and will often overlook these in her quest to reach the top or achieve purely self-serving desired ends. The more evolved Capricorn will understand that keeping people as slaves to her needs by symbolically linking them to her by chains to keep them submissive, under her orders and satisfying her needs, however subtle or secretive her tactics, can only be a lose-lose situation. And she holds the key to set her captives - and certainly herself - free if she chooses to do so, by not succumbing to the avarice, selfishness, manipulation, force and compulsions that The Devil card represents.

★ DIVINE MANIFESTATION USING THE DEVIL ★

You can Divinely manifest things in your experience through tapping into your inner Light.

We have to acknowledge that within each of us resides an invisible, wild, gratification-seeking spirit, wanting expression, yearning for freedom. The outcome of the repression of this wildness can lead to robotic, dull, mechanistic, monotonous ways of living, which eventually manifest themselves as violence and aggression, often unpredictable, for when this free spirit breaks free from its reins, we often use expressions such as: "The Devil made me do it." Demanding instant satisfaction, love is lacking in The Devil for he sees it as a sign of weakness and distraction. However, he *will* set free those who choose to see beyond their own damaging material and selfish desires. In doing this, you will see the light of Truth and it will pave the way for your deepest, unselfish desires to manifest, for everyone's highest good, including your own. Your bondage is the result of your limited beliefs about the world and resorting to deceit or avarice to get what you want. The first step to overcoming your addiction to addiction, to use an example taken from the 12-step program that Alcoholics Anonymous advocates, is to acknowledge that you may be powerless over your shadow self's innate and destructive compulsions. Then, hand it over to your higher powers to transmute your dark complexes into their more positive expression, and follow your higher spiritual guideposts, for your Higher Self's instincts will lead you out of the Garden of Temptation and into the light of virtue.

★ EXERCISES TO TAP INTO YOUR INNER DEVIL ★

★ Make an honest assessment of the behaviours, habits and choices you make on a regular basis that diminish your self-image or cause you to feel bad about yourself. Write them down in brief dot point form. You do not need to share these with anyone else, but make sure you do this exercise, as sometimes writing things down can bring to consciousness things we wouldn't otherwise have thought of or been aware of. If you want to, tear the paper up afterwards, knowing that your darker nature has risen to the surface of your consciousness and can now be more effectively dealt with.

★ Buy a key to carry around with you. Every time you entrap yourself with negative feelings about something or someone, remember your key. Symbolically use it to open the lock that is, after all, of your own making, and break the chains. If you have a destructive habit, addiction or unhelpful behaviour or disempowering thought pattern that you regularly engage in, take one step to break free from it, e.g. enrolling in a hypnotism course to give up smoking, making an appointment with a relationship counsellor. In taking these kinds of steps towards freedom from your destructive desires or needs, you have effectively unlocked the padlock that binds you. Now just unravel that chain and throw it as far as you can!

★ Meet your shadow self! Make a date with him or her and keep the date, dressing up for the occasion if you must (but be prepared to strip bare). Your shadow self can be a confronting and scary person that you will probably not even recognise. Be daring, be bold, but above all, be truthful with yourself. No one need know about this very private meeting, so there is no need to lie to yourself or evade the tough questions that will inevitably arise from the depths of your soul. After all, if you deny your shadow self's existence, you are only cheating yourself out of a very powerful experience that carries deep and lasting healing potential, and indeed the potential to change your whole life. Acknowledge honestly if you are really lying to yourself by denying his or her existence. Some deep work around this will inevitably bring about painful truths but ultimately, the capacity for profound healing.

★ THE TOWER ★

Ruled by Mars

Number ★ 16
Astrological Signs ★ Aries & Scorpio

Keywords ★ Collapse, Upheaval, Awakening, Rebuilding

Magical Title ★ The Lord of the Hosts of the Mighty
Divinity ★ Zeus (second aspect)

Spiritual Value ★ The Tower symbolises the beliefs of a lifetime that make up the Ego. These are sometimes blasted by the Lightning Flash of Sudden Illumination, so that you may release any outmoded beliefs and perceived realities. This occurs to make way for new forms to emerge. The Tower's force can be seen as energy attacking inertia; it shakes us up, wakes us up from a long slumber or our blind ignorance. It is the impetuous ejection of those who enclose themselves in the walls of ease, tradition and too much comfort. This Arcanum can be used when you need a sudden boost in strength, inspiration, courage or illumination.

★ KEY THEMES ★

"Rising From My Ashes"

★ Liberation ★ Awakening ★ Unforeseen Calamity ★ Upheaval ★ Destruction ★ Upset ★ Blessing in Disguise ★ Drastic Change ★ Relief ★ Inevitable Collapse ★ A Significant Life Event ★ Time Running Out ★ Confusion ★ Collapse and Ruin ★ A Chance to Rebuild ★ Shattering ★ Total, Inevitable but Salutary Change ★ Evolution ★ Necessary Crisis or Break ★ Catastrophe ★ Sudden Awareness

Meditation ★ "I trust that whatever disaster or unexpected events befall me, they occur for my ultimate higher good. I understand that all adverse happenings, without exception, allow me a chance to rebuild."

★ *When Working with this Card* ★

MAIN ENERGIES ★ Wisdom, Philosophical Outlooks, Optimism, Empowerment
MAIN GOD OR GODDESS TO INVOKE ★ Mars
CANDLE COLOUR ★ Dark Red
MAGICAL TOOL OR SYMBOL ★ Ashes
CRYSTALS ★ Emerald, Moss Agate, Black Tourmaline, Malachite, Moonstone

ASSOCIATED BEINGS, GODS, GODDESSES & ARCHETYPES ★ Fiery or Catabolic Angels, Solar Archangels, Minerva, Apollo, Mars, Belatu-Cadros, the Morrigan, Innerworld Beings associated with Destruction, Purification and Resurrection, the Destroyer, the Martyr.

ARCHETYPES ★ The Tower is a forceful clearing of pent-up energy that strikes heavy, suddenly and hard. It's a bolt from the blue, and it can shake any structure to its foundation if the foundation is no longer serving us. It is the Destroyer, the Miser, the Shadow, the Sorcerer, the Teacher.

CHAKRAS ★ Use this card to balance and meditate upon the Root and Crown chakras.

Root ★ Base of Spine ★ Red ★ Earth ★ Security & Survival

Crown ★ Top of Head ★ Purple ★ Thought/Knowing ★ Spiritual Wisdom & Enlightenment

TREE OF LIFE ★ In western magic, which combines the Tarot paths of the Major Arcana with the ten sephiroth on the Tree of Life, the path of The Tower connects Hod and Netzach.

> (The Tower) depicts the arrogant attempt by people to scale the heights of heaven ... The Tower is also in some degree a phallic symbol and the energy of the thunderbolt is the magical equivalent of the kundalini.
>
> **Nevill Drury**

THE FOOL'S JOURNEY ★ The Fool learns that sometimes lightning can strike without warning, and The Tower serves to remind us that sometimes change can come out of the blue. Sometimes it's change for the good, and sometimes it can be more difficult. Adverse things can and do happen to us all, sometimes suddenly and without apparent cause or warning. But, when surveying the ruins, The Fool experiences the wondrous awakening that out of bad can come good - in this way, he begins to reassess what he once through was stable or sustaining, is in fact not. And from the ashes of his shattered illusions or false loyalties, he can emerge shiny, new, rebuilt and triumphant. A wonderful haiku to put The Tower into perspective is: "My barn having burned down, I can now see the Moon."

> The human spirit is stronger than anything that can happen to it.
>
> **C.C. Scott**

THE STORY ★ A sturdy tower erected on a hill is struck by lightning and explosively blown apart. The castellated top of the tower is lifted by the blast, fire strikes deep within, and flames roar from the narrow windows as two figures fall from their ruined refuge. The security afforded by this strong, old structure, has been reduced to ruin by the forces of natural law. Flames erupt and smoke fills the air, sparks and debris fall on either side; there has been a dramatic reversal of fortune. Future plans have been aborted. The Tower represents the shock that shatters your illusions, removes the rug from beneath your feet, and clears away the refuse. A sudden catastrophe may break down all your previous conceptions about yourself or others. You feel as if there is no firm foundation upon which to rest your life as the veils of illusion are torn away. This forces you to face painful truths, but also liberates you from the past and provides sudden insights. The Tower tears down your world but in doing so provides a new focus. And once the storm settles, you are free! Lightning may have destroyed your world, but enlightenment is sure to rise from the ruins.

> The Tower is the discipline of surrender as we allow the rhythms of our emotions and our fallibility of mind to unleash the splendour and victory of both.
>
> **Paul Hougham**

THE MESSAGE ★ The Tower is representative of destructive and cataclysmic change - an earth-shattering stroke of illumination, a powerful revelation that leads to change, and the end of a structure once thought to be secure or solid. Liberation, upheaval and relief are all connected with this card. The Tower denotes the necessary breaking down of existing forms to make way for new ones; the destruction of the old always precedes the building of the new. This card indicates the needs to find fresh ways to do things, as the old have become rigid and imprisoning. We often live our lives as we have been conditioned to, never examining closely whether our lifestyle really suits us, until this complacency comes crashing down around us and forces us to re-consider and revaluate. The lightning that strikes The Tower on the card represents the new visions and possibilities which await us, and which will soon be brought to our attention through an upheaval or crisis.

> When written in Chinese, the word 'crisis' is composed of two characters – one represents danger and the other represents opportunity.
>
> **John F. Kennedy**

THE AWAKENING ★ Breakdown precedes breakthrough. Mounting pressures must be released or there will be a sudden reversal of all the work carried out so far. There has been a dramatic turn of events and established patterns of thought will be changed. Whether inevitable or not, this explosion of the old monument can be beneficial. It tells you that placing exclusive faith in the security of material objects can lead to disaster and collapse. The Tower foretells an upheaval, the reversal of a situation, and a necessary and inevitable change in your behaviour, your state of affairs or your life. Because it is associated with falling and even death, it tends to have a bad reputation; however, in reality, it reveals that events to come will actually have a clarifying, purifying and ultimately freeing effect. It can be likened to a storm that brews as a result of the building up of excessive atmospheric pressures and volatile conditions. Once the storm has passed, one feels free, relieved, fresh, re-charged. It is true that these events can be destructive and that little can be done to stop them, but they must unfold, or no evolution would be possible. In essence, the sudden, total change and the collapse that this card represents, allows new shoots to sprout.

> Never to suffer would be never to have been blessed.
>
> **Edgar Allan Poe**

THE LESSON ★ The tumbling tower pictured on this card symbolises the excessive pride of people who, in ancient times, would build tall towers, sometimes on the tops of mountains, in an attempt to get closer to the gods and heavens, to grasp and channel their powers towards the Earth. It can be assumed that these people did not reach their god by climbing up high and getting closer to the sky, but by sowing and cultivating the grain of wheat, the wheat germ - whose shape resembles an eye - within themselves, in their own *inner* Earth. Therefore, The Tower teaches us that the higher we try to rise in this physical, material world, the more we fall victim to our pride, and the more we expose ourselves to destruction, ruin and Divine wrath.

You must have chaos in you to give birth to a dancing star.

Friedrich Nietzsche

SYMBOLISM ★ The Tower symbolises the rebuilding of life upon firmer foundations after it has broken down or collapsed in some way. The Tower itself is a symbol of imprisonment and limitation; it is narrow and restrictive which, on an inner level, translates to emotional restraint. Through the effects of The Tower, your illusions are shattered and your 'world' falls apart. Yet this creates space for a new, more solid foundation upon which to rebuild.

The lightning that strikes and destroys the tower symbolises the destruction of the structure and foundation upon which the falling figures have built their lives. One figure lies on the ground, while the other tumbles to join him. The lightning bolt can also signify the power of Divine justice and the impetus for change. The golden 'rain' symbolises the regenerative energy that can follow devastation. The message of this card is that, ultimately, sometimes only a shock or catastrophe can provide the wake-up call that is needed to push you from complacency into full awareness about your situation. It also symbolises a sudden flash of insight or 'lightning bolt' inner revelation that can show you a clearer way forward. The Tower is a symbol of safety; too much trust had been placed in its thick walls. It ultimately reflects the fact that nothing can stand against the will of the inevitable or the Divine.

OVERALL ★ CONNECTING IT ALL UP ★

Only after disaster can we be resurrected. It's only after you've lost everything that you're free to do anything. Nothing is static, everything is evolving, everything is falling apart.

Chuck Palahniuk, *Fight Club*

The Tower depicts a solidly built tower that has been struck by a bolt of lightning, causing shock and disaster to its inhabitants, who are falling to the ground. The destruction of The Tower symbolises the sudden ending of something in your life, and the possibility of new and better opportunities. A crown is often shown falling from the top of The Tower, representing the danger of vanity, conceit and pride. Its small windows suggest a self-protective element is present that can lead to a limited outlook on life.

This is one of the cards that may indicate curses are afoot in your life. The Tower warns you that you are in danger of taking serious risks. It is telling you to be more cautious and careful in all your dealings - financial, emotional and physical. It can indicate you are accident-prone at present, so you must consciously slow down - especially while driving or handling dangerous things. It indicates an important and unexpected change, perhaps even a complete break from what you have built up over a sustained period of time. If you are already cautious in all areas of life, The Tower indicates that you will benefit from any clean sweep you make.

The Tower can also suggest that destructive 'magic' has been worked in the situation in question. The aim is to destroy and undo all the good in your life and to undermine your accomplishments. The curse may come upon you suddenly and something may fall apart or destruct. This is cruel and swift magic, but allows for a chance to rebuild once the dust has settled.

Its divinatory meanings are complete and sudden change, breaking down of old beliefs, abandonment of past relationships, severing of a friendship, changing one's opinion, unexpected events, loss of stability, bankruptcy, downfall and loss of security.

If its message is not heeded and acted upon and/or learned from, The Tower will ensure continued oppression, the following of old ways, living in a rut, entrapment in an unhappy situation, and the sustained inability to effect any worthwhile change.

This card is giving you the message that a recent event has been a wake-up call for you to make some life changes. This may be a new revelation or something you've known for a time but have been procrastinating about. Now you've realised that this situation cannot be ignored any longer and action is necessary.

This is a moment of both freedom and awakening. It signifies liberation, a sudden flash of the 'truth', and rapid, inevitable change is upon you. Time is running out. The way you see yourself and the world has forever changed, bringing you growth and encouraging you to spread your wings. Allow these new insights to motivate you to embrace the Path of your intuition and your heart's true desires.

★ HOW THIS CARD RELATES TO MARS ★

The Tower, perpetually guarded and under attack, is assigned to Mars, the planet of energy, war, aggression and assertiveness. The astrological glyph associated with Mars is a shield and a spear.

Corrine Kenner

Mars represents everything that has the potential to be volatile, explosive, aggressive and spontaneous. The Tower is a prime example of this masculine force, which can sweep through and clear everything up without warning, even without provocation, with no subtlety whatsoever, and with little regard for the effect of its actions on those whose personal experience it touches. Mars doesn't reflect, Mars acts - and oftentimes, he acts on impulse. The Tower serves to remind us that some things that exist in our lives are not always as solid or secure as we thought they were, and Mars reinforces this idea. Mars does not dabble in that which is consistent or sturdy; he can blow his top at any time if he feels it is fit for the situation. In the case of The

Tower, the warrior planet is in full attack mode, and the fort is under assault from the four elements of nature. Both this card and the planet symbolise quick, sudden bursts of energy and power, mostly unpleasant and shocking in their intensity and potency. But they are also bringers of inspiration and provide the impetus for change, for they represent the ensuing enlightenment, revelation, purification, release, liberation and renovation that such change can bring about after a time. Mars, like The Tower, confronts us with the truth, even if it is painful. But we must know that Mars, like The Tower, may destruct things in a blaze of enraged fury, but is quick to pick himself up and move swiftly on afterwards. For his blessings are as mighty as his curses, and he instinctively knows that every negative also has a positive; he balances the bad out with his indiscriminate passion, bravery, courage, immense power and above all, the resilience to overcome and rise victorious once the storm has settled.

✶ DIVINE MANIFESTATION USING THE TOWER ✶

You can Divinely manifest things in your experience through tapping into your inner Rebuilder.

If you have recently experienced an upheaval, a sudden catastrophe, an accident, a hurt, a disappointment or a setback, this may be serving to break down all your previous conceptions about yourself or others. The change may be something that happens to you, an event or situation that transforms you. You may suddenly just know your marriage is over, your job is ending, or the time has come for a move. You may have a sudden lucid understanding of your own destructive behaviours or addictions and the need for an immediate and radical overhaul. These insights may be momentary, like a lightning bolt, but the effects are far-reaching and enduring. If possible, open yourself right up to the power inherent in The Tower card. You may feel as if there is no firm foundation upon which to rest your life as the veils of illusion are torn away, but must understand that this is ultimately paving the way for a new path that will lead to a better life for you. The Universe is always working for your higher good, even if it does not seem so after this shake-up. Events of your past that have appeared to crumble you, may have actually instead been the catalyst for profound healing and change: in forcing you to face painful truths, they have also likely liberated you from the bondages of your past, and provided sudden insights that point the way to the achievement of your desires. The Tower tears down your world but in doing so clears the path, cleans the slate, and provides a new focus and direction. And once the storm settles, you are free! Lightning has struck, but enlightenment is sure to follow. This will clear your path for dreams to be grown out of the new fertile soil and ultimately realised. The time has come and the way is shown for you to rebuild a better building than the one that was shattered before your eyes.

✶ EXERCISE TO TAP INTO YOUR INNER TOWER ✶

✶ Can you recall an event in the past when something unfortunate, shocking or unexpected happened to you? Reflect on this misfortune, from how you felt when it first occurred, to a few weeks, months or even years later when things had settled down again and you looked back on it. How did it serve as a powerful lesson for your growth (if at all)? Could you rebuild again and find some positives or at least some lessons from the experience? In retrospect, how do you feel about that event or feeling it evoked in you right now as you think about it? Would you change anything about the whole experience? Why or why not?

★ THE STAR ★

Ruled by Aquarius

Number ★ 17
Astrological Sign ★ Aquarius

Keywords ★ Renewed Hope, Inspiration, Dreams, Optimism

Magical Title ★ The Dweller between the Waters, The Daughter of the Firmament
Divinity ★ Aphrodite
Spiritual Value ★ The path of the Star is the path of meditation combining focused effort and will, knowledge, and imagination in search of the Divine Light. This Arcanum can help you to plan and develop projects. It enables you to manifest and nurture your authentic inner personal treasures, which you may have troubles accessing. She allows you to reveal the best and truest part of yourself, and to understand the meaning and purpose of your incarnation.

The Star guides the glistening ecstasy within our shadow into the stardust of our potential.

Paul Hougham

★ KEY THEMES ★

"A Bright New Dawn"

★ Hope ★ Inspiration ★ Creativity ★ Happiness ★ Good Luck ★ Rebirth ★ Renewal ★ Light After Darkness ★ The Calm After the Storm ★ Restored Hope, Faith, Inspiration and Promise ★ A Bright Future ★ Imagination ★ Creation ★ Idealism ★ Good Prospects

Meditation ★ "The energy, hope, faith and love I intend to summon and pour forth today will light up my whole future."

★ *When Working with this Card* ★

MAIN ENERGIES ★ Hope, Optimism, Rewewal, Healing, Restoration, Faith
MAIN GOD OR GODDESS TO INVOKE ★ Nut
CANDLE COLOUR ★ Yellow
MAGICAL TOOL OR SYMBOL ★ Eight-pointed Star
CRYSTALS ★ Citrine, Aquamarine, Emerald, Yellow Topaz

Hear the words of the Star Goddess, the dust of whose feet are the hosts of heaven, whose body encircles the Universe: 'All acts of love and pleasure are My rituals. Let there be beauty and strength, power and compassion, honour and humility, mirth and reverence within you … I have been with you from the beginning, and I am that which is attained at the end of desire'.

Starhawk

ASSOCIATED BEINGS, GODS, GODDESSES & ARCHETYPES ★ Archangels, the Enchantress, the Magical Helper, Nut, Isis, Hathor, the Holy Spirit, Phosperos, Aphrodite, Hesperos, Astraea, Bast/Bastet, Apollo, Lugh, Belenos, Eve in Paradise, and Stellar Entities Sirius *, the Star of Bethlehem, the North Star, the Visionary, the Mystic, the Poet, the Star of the Magi.

* The star Sirius has held considerable significance for humankind since the earliest recorded times. The Dog Star, as it is colloquially known, has enjoyed many names and titles throughout the magical and religious history of our world. This luminary is a white star in the constellation of Canis Major, some eight and a half light years away from Earth. It has the lovely reputation of being the brightest star in our night sky (unless we consider a more recent discovery in the Tarantula Nebula). According to old traditions and teachings our Solar system was seeded from Sirius, which means that cosmic impulses must have gone out from that direction in the infancy of our Sun.

ARCHETYPES ★ The Star is a shining light at the end of a dark tunnel. Like the Goddess of the night, she's the winsome spirit who offers hope, inspiration, illumination and guidance. She is the Enchantress, the Mystic, the Scribe, the Goddess, the Innocent Child, the Maiden, the Priestess.

CHAKRAS ★ Use this card to balance and meditate upon the Solar Plexus, Heart, Third Eye and Crown chakras.

Solar Plexus ★ Behind the Navel ★ Yellow ★ Fire ★ Personal Power, Confidence & Control

Heart ★ Heart Region ★ Green ★ Air ★ Love & Compassion

Third Eye ★ Between the Eyes ★ Dark Blue ★ Light ★ Clairvoyance, Wisdom, Intuition & Vision

Crown ★ Top of Head ★ Purple ★ Thought/Knowing ★ Spiritual Wisdom & Enlightenment

TREE OF LIFE ★ In western magic, which combines the Tarot paths of the Major Arcana with the ten sephiroth on the Tree of Life, the path of The Star connects Yesod and Netzach.

> Seventeen is the number of the Star; it is that of intelligence and love … I believe because I know why and how one must believe, (and) I believe because I love.
>
> *The Key of the Mysteries,* **Eliphas Levi**

THE FOOL'S JOURNEY ★ After The Tower crashed down around The Fool in the previous card, he finds a glimmer of hope and renewal amid the destruction. The Star of the Sun will still rise, and life will go on - but this time The Fool will walk the Path before him with a fresh sense of healing, purpose, faith, freedom, flow, optimism and inspiration.

> Dreams are illustrations ... from the book your soul is writing about you.
>
> **Marsha Norman**

THE STORY ★ The last five Major Arcana cards can be found in the heavens and, as the haiku of The Tower card reminds us, there's always hope no matter how dark the road might seem. The Star represents the idea that hope, courage and inspiration will bring the promise of better times to come, and that there will be peace after a storm. A star of hope and wonder shines in the heavens, promising spiritual illumination and inspiration. Below, with one foot on the land and the other poised magically on the surface of the stream of the unconscious, a near-naked maiden stands entranced, joyously receiving the waters of the pool, which rise up to her as she pours an endless shower of liquid from her two containers. She demonstrates that as heaven nourishes the earthly planes, the wonders of the physical world nourish the heavens. The star in her is a star upon which to wish for pure miracles, with the guilelessness of a child. In the realm of The Star all is fresh and new, and all is innocence and purity and hope. The maiden's language is poetry and art and she is in perfect accord with her spiritual gifts. The Star is a symbol of the cleansing and purification that occurs when we allow the upheavals of life to wash over us and dissolve. It ultimately stands for the sense of wonder that heralds the restored belief that dreams can - and do - come true.

> Happiness is as a butterfly, which when pursued, is always beyond our grasp, but which if you will sit down quietly, may alight upon you.
>
> **Nathaniel Hawthorne**

THE MESSAGE ★ The Star gives us a vision beyond the roles we play in life to who we really are. She is the bright and luminous muse, who restores hope and inspiration after the storm. You rest, gather your strength and tap into a newfound sense of inner peace and tranquillity. A healing process takes place, which is experienced within all levels of yourself. The future brightens as you feel refreshed, renewed and revitalised. You are full of hope, and have every reason to be - or soon will.

> The countenance of the Star Goddess is one of unearthly beauty as she looks down, a faint smile curling her lips. And as the sea of upturned faces observe the vision, a mystical union occurs between the Star Goddess and every soul on the plateau – a unique and personal communion to be treasured for all time.
>
> **Patricia Crowther**

THE AWAKENING ★ Take time to recharge yourself with a period of relaxation. Enjoy being 'the star' of your own life journey. This is the time for the allowing, acceptance and enjoyment of spiritual ideas and concepts. Let your ideas pour out to nourish those around you. Allow your mind to dwell on what is pleasant in your life and avoid negativity for a time. It is important for you to express your deep creative urges by either creating or enjoying art.

> You are never too old to set another goal or to dream a new dream.
>
> **C.S. Lewis**

THE LESSON ★ Wish upon a Star. It suggests that you should be more positive in outlook, and that while you may look to the stars for guidance, you should also make a practical effort to achieve your heart's desire. Avoid daydreaming and nurturing unattainable fantasies. The Star is a brilliant and positive influence, so take her advice and you will gain in self-confidence and travel far along life's wondrous, awe-filled Path.

> When I look into the future, it's so bright it burns my eyes.
>
> **Oprah Winfrey**

SYMBOLISM ★ The Star symbolises your ability you connect or reconnect with the source of life, optimism, renewal, hope and inspiration, which will propel you forward. This card follows The Tower card, and embodies the calm that comes after a hurricane, the inner peace that arises after a difficult time. It represents your ability to recapture and rediscover your dreams and to focus on bringing these dreams to fruition.

In the lady's left hand, she holds an empty jug that she is about to fill, which symbolises an awareness that energy needs to flow in both ways, and should be used to replenish the spirit as well as the material aspects. The water in the pool is the source of life. Pouring water into the pool replenishes the energy source from which the lady has drawn.

Above her, eight stars (all eight-pointed ^), symbolising the heavenly or higher realms, shine brightly against the backdrop of a milky night sky on the cusp of daybreak, while a bird perches on a tree in the background and a butterfly flutters overhead. The large star is the one seen by the Magi, while the smaller stars represent hope. The feature star emits rays of light towards the Moon and rising Sun, emphasising the subtle interconnectedness between all life and the Universe. As the maiden reaches out to touch the oneness of all life and all the Universe, the same light that radiates from the stars overhead, glows from her.

The bird sitting in the Tree of Life is the ibis of immortality, a sacred bird, a symbol of the soul's ability to rise to higher levels of emotional and spiritual consciousness. It also represents a symbol of our spiritual self, waiting to drink from the wisdom-bestowing waters of the lake. The butterfly stands for transformation and resurrection. Like its animal symbols, this card comes after a crisis or 'storm', standing for light coming out of darkness, and offers peace, flow and freedom.

^ The eight-pointed star is an attribute of Mars and is mostly used in talismanic magic to invoke the powers of that planet and to subjugate the person to will of the magician. It has also been identified with the Star of the Magi, a symbol of hope, and with the *etiole flamboyante* or flaming star of Masonic symbolism. Other schools of thought regard the eight-rayed star as a symbol of the law of equilibrium; the balance between spirit and matter, yin and yang, and the inner and outer bodies. Its associations with The Star Tarot card and its principle meaning being hope, many occultists use the eight-pointed star symbol for spiritual enlightenment and general protection. This great yellow star can also be interpreted as a symbol of the Quintessence, or Fifth Essence, of the alchemists. The seven lesser stars are also eight-pointed, to show that they are manifestations of this same Quintessence. They may represent the seven alchemical metals: Lead, Iron, Tin, Gold, Silver, Copper and Mercury, or the seven astrological planets: Saturn, Mars, Jupiter, Sun, Moon, Mercury and Venus. Therefore, they are symbols of the seven interior 'stars', or chakras, which are centres through which the One Force manifests itself in the human body.

OVERALL ★ CONNECTING IT ALL UP ★

Without leaps of imagination, or dreaming, we lose the excitement of possibilities. Dreaming, after all, is a form of planning.

Gloria Steinem

The Star is a good omen. A fortunate card, it indicates the hope and renewal that occurs after calamity, promising new and rich horizons, perhaps in previously unforeseen directions, but only after you have been tempered and expanded by having come through the storm. It expresses hope, a sense of healing and a return to wholeness, especially after emotional storms, for after the storm, there is peace. This card is the perfect symbol of wholeness, calm, oneness and healing. It depicts a beautiful naked maiden, sometimes depicted as Persephone of Greek legend, who spent one-third of every year with Hades, god of the Underworld, and two-thirds with her mother, the Earth goddess Demeter. She pours water from two pitchers; one flows into a pool, representing the depths of the unconscious, and the other onto dry land, representing the conscious mind. She revives the land with the water from the pool, while the morning star heralds the beginning of a new dawn, new life and new hope. In The Star, we see the inner self joyfully experiencing itself. The Star is *free*.

Aquarius, the sign attributed to The Star, is the fixed air sign of the Water Bearer and represents the healing force in the universe, as well as group understanding, collective sympathies, psychic sensitivities, and universal friendship. Aquarians tend to be visionary in their outlook, and The Star prepares one for initiation, making it an effective symbolic tool for initiating oneself towards a brighter future - one that the Aquarian often envisions in his or her mind and spirit long before anyone else.

A card of enlightenment and enhanced awareness, The Star is symbolic of our faith, our belief in our hopes, and our desire that our wishes will come true, providing a sense of purpose and meaning, without which our lives become dull and lacklustre. It signifies that redemption is possible, that transformative powers are within our reach. It cleanses and releases all pain, restoring happiness and belief. The Star provides that bit of magic that spurs us on, keeping us going during times of stress or doubt. Indeed, the image of The Star reflects the inner light that can guide us through the darkness. The Star is not a card of action, but of inner calm. For the moment, the journey can wait. Destiny will unfold as it will before you. This card urges you to stay positive, for a goal is at last within your reach.

The idea of wishing upon a star is at the centre of the card's meaning, and it signifies that a wish will come true, something you have hoped for since you were a child. The wish-granting quality of The Star also shows us that the Universe is not the senseless and unjust place it often appears to be. The Star card suggests that there is always something else, even when the going is really tough. It indicates a gesture of affection, perhaps a gift, but the gifts of The Star are not always material. It symbolises insight, understanding and hope for the future, and asks that the spiritual dimension of life should not be ignored.

This card is a good indication that wishes will be fulfilled, not always in the form that one expects, but even so, the unexpected will have a good result. The Star shows good health and that gifts will be given. Some gifts may be in the form of the idea of cosmic power reaching down, blessing our earthly life, bestowing our spirit with joy, and transmitting its healing energy.

Its main divinatory meanings are hope, faith, inspiration, bright prospects, optimism, insight, a mixing of the past and present, spiritual love, astrological influence, fulfilment and pleasure. It signifies the divine balancing of desire and work, love and expression, and hope and effort. It delivers a message of promise, good fortune and joy. It suggests inspiration, a deep sense of purpose, an inner knowing that things will turn out for the best, an intuitive belief in magic, and the renewal of life's force and energy. It promises and encourages imagination and a positive attitude, even when times are difficult or trying.

When you get The Star card in a reading, you know you have passed to a new level and something in you has opened to a higher plane. You are ready to ask for help, and you will receive it. A certain grace comes over you which allows you to see the future with renewed faith, and you trust in the ability of the universe to heal you. You are ready to begin the process of transformation.

This may indicate a time when you have become aware of a divine or higher spirit 'touching' you or drawing you in, and perhaps it is fitting that you choose or are chosen for, a new name for yourself, to signify the newness of your-self. Those who have been transformed through the powers of The Star symbolism, have often thereafter adopted a spiritual, ritual or otherwise special name. Listen for yours. It will be unique and have deep symbolic significance for you. Above all, it will represent your reborn, renewed and refreshed self.

The Star is an image of hope and promise. It indicates a sense of purpose, a goal to reach for and an ambition to aim towards. The sight of the stars at night have long been associated with awe and magic, and The Star appearing in your reading brings with it the hope and belief that things will come right, even when they have been very difficult. The Star can provide you with a positive outlook and a welcome source of optimism and expectation that will carry you through stormy times.

When working with this card, ask yourself what insights flow from the waters of your unconscious? Now that The Star has lit up your spiritual darkness, it is only a matter of time before you reach the ultimate heights of your journey. The world needs your light and your happiness. Make it a point to shine brightly like the stars this card depicts, and you will reap the benefits from sharing your joy, wisdom and higher self. Ultimately, this card conveys the hopeful message that when we wish upon a star, our dreams come true.

★ HOW THIS CARD RELATES TO AQUARIUS ★

Aquarius is jointly ruled by Uranus and Saturn. These two planets are represented by the first and last Keys of Tarot. Uranus is The Fool, and Saturn is The World. Here is a hint that the practice of meditation will eventually bring about answers to every question, from the most abstract to the most concrete. The title The Star refers directly to the Universal Light-energy which condenses itself into stars as the Reality behind their physical forms.

Paul Foster Case

The Star, a glimmering light of hope and inspiration, is assigned to Aquarius, the airy sign of social groups and futuristic thinking.

Corrine Kenner

The Water Bearer pours the *aqua nostra* or Waters of Life and Renewal, down upon the Earth at the beginning of the new year. In occultism, the twin streams are seen as blood and water and represent the magico-mystical energies - the magnetic fluids of new life. They are intimately connected with the mysteries of Maat - the Star Goddess - the star in question being Sirius, and having thirteen points.

Patricia Crowther

"We are all in the gutter, but some of us are looking at the stars," quipped fellow Air sign Libran Oscar Wilde. The eternal idealistic optimist, the Aquarian soul is the most likely to be the one looking up at those stars. For Aquarius doesn't just believe like Pisces does, he *knows*. He knows that things will always get better, that there are no rainbows without the rain, and that when nothing else is available, there is always hope. The Star's concepts share many characteristics with the socially conscious, future-oriented Water Bearer. Aquarians are naturally altruistic visionaries, revolutionaries and idealists who dream of a brighter tomorrow.

The lady depicted in The Star card could very well be Nut, the Egyptian goddess of the night sky, her name meaning 'night'. Arching protectively over the Earth, covered in stars, she served as a barrier between chaos and the orderly workings of the cosmos. Each evening she would swallow the Sun so she could give birth to the morning, a myth which has lovely links with the meaning of The Star card, and the hopeful outlook of its ruler Aquarius.

Aquarians are dedicated and humane champions of their many causes, with strong ideals and convictions, and above all, forever chasing rainbows, hopes and dreams - which always resides in the future - where The Star firmly dwells and shines at her very brightest. After all, Aquarius *knows* that The Star is the main source of light for his magical Path, leading all the way into his bright future.

★ DIVINE MANIFESTATION USING THE STAR ★

You can Divinely manifest things in your experience through tapping into your inner Dreamer.

What better card is there in the Tarot, than The Star for Divine Manifestation? The Star is a symbol of the cleansing and purification that occurs after the storm of life's upheavals calm down; it ultimately stands for the sense of wonder that heralds the restored belief that dreams can - and do - come true. Take time to recharge yourself with a period of relaxation, to allow your dreams to germinate. Enjoy being 'the star' of your own life journey. This is the time for the allowing, acceptance and enjoyment of spiritual ideas and concepts. Let your ideas pour out to nourish those around you. Allow your mind to dwell on what is pleasant in your life and avoid negativity for a time. It is important for you to express your deep creative urges by either creating or enjoying art. The Star's character is someone who hopes to achieve or tries to make their thoughts, ideas, plans or beliefs a reality. This character adopts the virtues of faith, trust, magic and a deep sense of personal Truth to allow their dreams to manifest on the material plane. A combination of circumstances favouring your hopes and aims ensures that your prospects are bright. Possessing a profound and unwavering belief in the unseen, you elevate yourself to ever greater heights. So, under the star-spangled sky above you, make that wish, and always remember and keep the faith that dreams *do* come true.

★ EXERCISES TO TAP INTO YOUR INNER STAR ★

★ Wish upon a Star! Do a bit of research on your zodiac sign's constellation and if it is visible in the night sky (and indeed in your Hemisphere), try and find it! Then, make a wish and keep the faith that it will come true for you if it is for your highest good. Trust.

★ Light a candle of hope for someone who needs healing and a replenishment of the spirits. Visualise this person as you wish them to be - happy, healthy, fulfilled, and full of hope and promise for a bright future. It doesn't even have to be someone you know personally, just that anyone you wish new hope, fresh starts, renewal, and healing for. Telepathically, though not always consciously, they will receive your message and your thoughts will heal not only the other person, but yourself, too.

★ THE MOON ★

Ruled by Pisces

Number ★ 18
Astrological Signs ★ Cancer & Pisces

The dark realm of Hecate is illustrated here. At the foot of the card is a crayfish, symbol of the primitive devouring forces of the unconscious which have to be overcome. In the middle distance are the wolf and dog, guides to the land of the dead, who are also unstable and not to be trusted. Behind them are the pylons of the gateway to Hades, the portal of the dark womb, whilst above all hangs the Moon itself, drawing souls to it with its irresistible magic power.

Alfred Douglas

Keywords ★ Hidden Depths, Betrayals, Illusions, the Subconscious

Magical Title ★ The Ruler of Flux and reflux, the Child of the Sons of the Mighty
Divinity ★ Selene
Spiritual Value ★ The Moon card contains the troubled waters of Night, wherein the crayfish, counterpart of the Scarab, lurks. The barren hills in the distance of this image, are surmounted by the gloomy fortresses that appear to guard the way to attainment. This Arcanum, representing the unconscious part of your psyche, can help you change the conditions that hold you back from realising your dreams. She opens up the Divine pathway for your goals to manifest, as she is the original power present in your subconscious which creates all mental forms and brings the manifest world into existence. Her character bypasses the use of logical analysis; she represents that knowledge that will remain hidden to you if your heart is not pure or well-intentioned.

★ KEY THEMES ★

"Daring to Plunge into the Depths"

★ Dreams ★ Illusions and Disillusions ★ Subconscious Mind ★ Betrayal ★ Bad Influence of Friends or Family Circle ★ Private Life and Thoughts ★ Self-deception ★ Time of Uncertainty and Confusion ★ Unforeseen perils ★ Intuition ★ Lack of Clarity ★ Psychic Awakenings ★ The Primitive Subconscious ★ Premonitions

Meditation ★ "I trust my intuition; it always knows what to do. I dare to be vulnerable and to bare my soul, even if this is frightening, as doing this will enrich me beyond measure."

★ *When Working with this Card* ★

MAIN ENERGIES ★ Inner Searching, Introspection, Discernment, Wisdom

MAIN GOD OR GODDESS TO INVOKE ★ Hecate
CANDLE COLOUR ★ Silver
MAGICAL TOOL OR SYMBOL ★ The Triple Goddess, Silver
CRYSTALS ★ Amethyst, Moonstone, Selenite, Opal, Aquamarine, Pearl, White Howlite

ASSOCIATED BEINGS, GODS, GODDESSES & ARCHETYPES ★ The Guide, the Guardian, the Shaman, the Mother, the Priestess, Nature Spirits and Elementals, Fairies, Ancestral Beings, Beings from Other Worlds, Diana, Selene, Arianrhod, Danu, Sophia, Cybele, Artemis, Ceridwen, Hecate *, Sin, Khonsu, Isis, Luna, the Earth Mother, and all Goddesses of Nature, Birth, Life, Death, Prophecy & Fertility, Prevision & Magical or Supernatural Practices.

* Hecate has an obscure nature as far as mythology goes. She is mostly mentioned in writings on witches and witchcraft (even Shakespeare's witches of *Macbeth* petitioned this triple goddess), and is viewed as having three faces, one looking to the Underworld (land of the dead), one looking to the Middle World (Earth), and one looking to the Upper World (spiritual plane). It is because of this triple vision that Hecate is often called 'the far-seeing one'. Although considered a minor deity in comparison to the other Olympian gods and goddesses, she is the most powerful of all deities in the realm of magic and mystery, her power being second only to Zeus, the 'god of all men'. Hecate is a mysterious goddess around whom secret orders and ideas of magic can easily develop, but a relationship with her is a two-way street: she provides for you, but when she is in need of a favour she expects to be treated in kind. Although a wondrous goddess, she is a harsh teacher and very demanding.

ARCHETYPES ★ The Moon is the ever-shifting shimmery mirror of the Sun, and a symbol of the otherworldly mind. From its vantage point in the night sky, The Moon represents secrets and mysteries that may not be clearly understood – or even recognised. It is the Goddess, the Mystic, the Shaman, the Guide, the Psychic, the Shadow, the Wanderer.

> The patron goddess of art is Diana, the Moon goddess, whose knowledge is knowledge of the Night, whose *light* is the light of the Night. To walk this path, we must not fear the Dark, must not draw back from wrestling with the Shadow, must not be shy of the deep pain and the often-life-threatening danger that entails. The artist often thrives because he or she is willing to look at aspects of the psyche or the culture or the species that others would reject.
>
> **Danah Zorah and Ian Marshall**

CHAKRAS ★ Use this card to balance and meditate upon the Root and Third Eye chakras.

Root ★ Base of Spine ★ Red ★ Earth ★ Security & Survival
Third Eye ★ Between the Eyes ★ Dark Blue ★ Light ★ Clairvoyance, Wisdom, Intuition & Vision

TREE OF LIFE ★ In western magic, which combines the Tarot paths of the Major Arcana with the ten sephiroth on the Tree of Life, the path of The Moon represents Malkuth to Yesod and is associated with sexuality and the cycles of fertility.

THE FOOL'S JOURNEY ★ By the light of the Moon, The Fool gets the ominous sense that things aren't always what they seem. The Moon reminds us that illusions and hidden forces can obscure what's really happening. But this card also represents our psychic, imaginative, or emotional sides, and if we use these oft neglected parts of ourselves to know ourselves better, we can then ascend with the next Rising Sun. In doing this, The Fool also realises that darkness never lasts forever.

> There are nights when even the wolves are silent and only the Moon howls.
>
> **George Carlin**

THE STORY ★ The Moon is the card of hidden emotions. The Moon tells us that there is illusion all around us; the waters can mislead and confuse. The waters around you might look calm on the surface but a powerful current might be brewing just beneath. The water can tell us about looking past illusion, into the vision of what is really there. Its reflective surface challenges us to look at ourselves and the image we present to the world. It also tells us that only a person of truth will have the truth shone back at them. This card signifies that the landscape beneath the Moon is full of threats. It is the card of hidden meanings, and represents frustrated and seemingly impossible desire. But the Moon's light can also reveal a great deal. Its link also with the star sign Cancer shows that a tough shell cannot conceal or stifle tender love, and that illusions can blind us to what lurks beneath.

THE MESSAGE ★ The Moon is the intuitive clairvoyant, who opens you up to your deeper self and uncovers your hidden depths. The kingdom of darkness represents all that is concealed, buried and deep inside each one of us. The darkness contained within the night symbolises the hidden side of our personality, the Divine part of ourself. When the symbolic dark intervenes in our lives through hardships, setbacks, trials and obstacles, it tests our strength and self-knowledge. Trials lead us to question ourselves but also to search for the light - which we would not do if life was smooth, serene and going well. Everyone experiences times in their lives when they are fearful or insecure. Sometimes these fears are based on the 'seen' and that which we can recognise, while other times they stem from the unknown, irrational, hidden or illusory forces. In both cases, it is important to go within and be guided by your intuition. Ask your inner self about the true source of your fears, and trust its answer.

> Follow your inner moonlight; don't hide the madness.
>
> **Allen Ginsberg**

THE AWAKENING ★ This is the darkness before the dawn. You must separate illusion from reality. Even though the Path may seem daunting and treacherous, you need not fear the mysterious unknown. Your natural intuition can guide you to hidden opportunities. Remember to save your energies for the challenges and obstacles ahead, and not squander them with needless worrying. The freedom allowed by the previous card The Star takes you deeper within yourself. You become more reflective, aware of the messages of your subconscious mind, intuition and dreams. This leads you to explore a profound sense of connection within yourself and to see the threads of your life woven as a rich tapestry - you need only to join them all up through the use of your imagination.

Everyone is a moon, and has a dark side which he never shows to anybody.

Mark Twain

THE LESSON ★ The Moon's face on this card is beautiful but the light she sheds on the world is deceptive; under it we tend not to see things as they really are. The wolf-dogs baying at her do not trust her influence. But she is teaching us that we should allow ourselves greater freedom and avoid holding back or suppressing feelings, as the crayfish emerging from the water in the picture is prone to doing. You may also be living under some sort of delusion or denial by refusing to see things as they really are. In the long-term, this self-deception will harm you. The Moon also warns you to be wary of outer-deceptions as well - your friends or family could be much less trustworthy than you imagine. This card will show up when you are encountering difficulties, conflicts, disappointments or disillusionment in your life, which have originated from your errors and shortcomings. They manifest themselves in your life as a test, so that you may become aware of them. Outside, under a waning Moon, visualise a circle of protective white light around yourself as you stand by a body of water. Concentrate and project a specific and deep-rooted personal fear into a special stone, then strongly hurl it out of your circle of light into the body of water as you chant: "With this stone, fear is banished, into the water it has vanished."

SYMBOLISM ★ The Moon reflects the realm where the unconscious meets the conscious. In astronomy, the Moon reflects the light of the Sun. Its mysterious, veiled qualities reveal only portions of itself and this symbolises the need to use the power of our imagination to move into that mystery and attempt to decode it.

The Moon card seethes with desolation. In the foreground is a stagnant, eerily still pool, from which the crayfish emerges, and from this pool is a winding Path that leads to the desolate mountains in the background. In the middle a dog and wolf are baying at the Lunar sphere above, and behind them are two pillars or gates which open onto the stark, bereft wilderness, which possesses an air of loneliness, emptiness and bareness.

The crayfish or crab emerging from the water is a symbol of the deepest fears that haunt us yet never fully materialise. It represents the surfacing of our inner nature, which we often push back down into the depths again. Therefore, the Moon highlights the need to face our fears by bringing them to the surface rather than keeping them hidden and submerged.

OVERALL ★ CONNECTING IT ALL UP ★

One does not become enlightened by imagining figures of light,
but by making the darkness conscious.

Carl G. Jung

This card's symbolism can suggest unforeseen perils and deception, but is also shows great possibilities can be accessed through intuition, latent psychic powers, and astral travel. Its other divinatory meanings are twilight, disillusionment, danger, obscurity, bad influence, ulterior motives, frustrations, false friends, selfishness, insight/intuition, craftiness, deceit, slander, disgrace, unknown enemies, libel and superficiality.

The Moon card depicts two animals, a dog and a wolf, baying at the Moon, and in the foreground a crab or crayfish crawling out of a pool disturbs its waters, symbolising that the innermost fears are forcing their way to the surface of consciousness. The idea of dogs and wolves baying at the Full Moon is a powerful image suggesting madness or lunacy, and the two animals represent our 'animal self' roused by the Moon. A werewolf howling under a Full Moon is a vivid metaphor of the power of the unconscious to bring out the primitive, 'unknown' side of ourselves. The Moon rules the waxing and waning rhythms of life, of tides, and all natural cycles, particularly the feminine ones. It also symbolises feelings and emotions that are by their nature often volatile, nebulous and uncertain. But it also represents the power and mystery of women's fertility, and power does not have to be destructive, threatening or frightening.

Indeed, if respected, this lunar psychic awakening enriches life. Ruling the realm of subconscious thoughts, fantasies and dreams, these aspects, when made conscious, can become wisdom. This card indicates that both our primitive animal instincts and our tamed mundane domesticity are a trap, in that the truth lies between them on the rocky narrow road that leads over the horizon under the watchful gaze of the silent and mysterious Moon. The idea of the crayfish in the foreground forcing its way onto the land from out of the depths of the water, is symbolic of our innermost fears emerging from the depths of our souls and rising to the surface. This crayfish might represent childhood fears reappearing in adult life, still managing to cause fear and anxiety even when these fears have lost their rationality or logic. As the crayfish crawls up into our consciousness, we often try to push it back down into the subconscious. However, when we do this, it continues to exist and persist there, still giving rise to vague fears and unacknowledged stress until such a time arrives during which we allow it to fully emerge and in turn, confront it.

The meaning of The Moon card is telling us to take care, as all is not as it seems, and you need to use your intuition to deal with a deceptive situation. It indicates that you may be being lied to, so it is important to examine the situation and ask more questions. It also suggests that you should allow yourself a greater freedom of expression and avoid holding back or suppressing your feelings, as you may be unwittingly inviting trouble by keeping emotions hidden under the illusory veil of the shimmery water's surface. This card hints that you may be allowing your emotions to affect your judgement, or that you may be failing to see things as they really are. It also warns you not to readily consult your friends, as their counsel may be untrustworthy at this time. Other questions to ask yourself include: Am I being illogical at present? Have I looked at my problems from a purely practical point of view? Has someone had too much influence over my judgement? Is my imagination running away with me? Am I overreacting to a situation? And the ultimate question involving deeper self-examination: Am I holding back when I should let my feelings be known? You may be unknowingly deceiving others if you are withholding your truthful and open expression.

As its imagery suggests, The Moon symbolises our insecurities and fears, often borne out of that which is hidden or lurking in the shadows or unseen depths. Representing the metaphor of the rocky landscape of memory of feeling - brilliantly illuminating when she is Full, but dark and shadowy when her face is concealed from view - The Moon describes our sensitivities, our instinctive responses to threats and triggers, and our embedded early childhood memories. The Moon card usually points to a period of fluctuation, change, uncertainty and illusions. It can also suggest that solutions to problems can be found through dreams and intuition rather than logic and reason. The Path you are on is difficult and may cause fear, but continue along it even if you are doubtful, because all will eventually turn out well. If you are involved in a secretive love affair or harbour secret feelings for someone, this card is favourable.

Concerning love, The Moon card can suggest that a relationship is not yet reaching its potential because your real self is very different from what you, and others, currently believe yourself to be. You are keeping a safety blanket of ice over your emotions, and although this may protect you from disappointment, it can hinder the deeper pleasures of love. You have creative love skills, and a rich and sensual imagination, and The Moon card tells you these should be used to melt the ice and open your heart to real feelings. If you are in a relationship, it is time to talk about what you want and let your heart reveal the real you and your real desires. When this card appears in your life, it can mean that both you and your partner may be hiding what you truly feel and that you need to strengthen your bond by communicating. It is also important not to dwell on old hurts.

It can take on the Piscean quality of sacrifice, by urging you to be more introspective, to turn away from outer concerns, to give up some specific activity or simply allow a period of withdrawal. The Moon reminds us that The Star and the Sun give off their own light, whereas the Moon herself reflects the hidden light from the Sun. In fact, the Tarot Sun comes after The Moon, suggesting that simplicity can only be appreciated after a journey through dark, strange Lunar landscapes. Ultimately however, The Moon can be our guide if we let it, and the road leading towards the horizon between the two mountains, need not always be perilous if we can join the unconscious and conscious forces of the mind together harmoniously to create a well-integrated personality.

All the irrational, supernatural associations of the Moon can make this seem an unfortunate card for the rational person, because it indicates a time when only intuition, the non-rational side, can overcome obstacles. Yet the non-rational must be used with care, for it can lead towards a dangerous fantasy world. On the other hand, it warns against fearing this non-rational side of ourselves, in case we settle for a life of sterility and stagnation.

It is time to ask yourself: What about me seems murky or polluted? What can be done to clear up the waters of my inner channels? Now is the time to take stock of the current you are standing in. Where does it pull you? How strong or gentle is its force? Sometimes it feels as if we are swimming with the current and towards our authentic self, but others it feels as though the waters around us will never be clear enough to peer into. In other words, it can seem like nothing is true and all around us is merely an illusion. Communion with water and The Moon can empower us to see past the façade and down into the bedrock of the ocean floor. What sits there, in its truest, clearest form? Trust your gut - for water always knows where it's supposed to go.

★ HOW THIS CARD RELATES TO PISCES ★

The Moon, which rules the night, is assigned to Pisces, the sign of the mystical and the subconscious. The Pisces fish swim in the reflecting pond that's pictured in most versions of the card.

Corrine Kenner

The positive aspect of The Moon card is that we are reminded of the aspect of our deep inner selves that Jung labelled the 'shadow'. To be genuinely integrated and in touch with our pure life force, we must acknowledge and confront this shadow self. Pisces possesses the most self-deluding and arguably 'hidden' characters of all the zodiac. Her urges to escape, especially when faced with her own dark emotions, as portrayed by the crayfish emerging from the water in The Moon card, is well-known. If Pisceans are able to summon the courage to face the deep feelings and rampant demons that this card represents, they can live a life of greater integrity, truth and strength. But all too often, Pisces plays the victim, buries her feelings in favour of escapist behaviours such as self-delusion, denial and addictions, and consequently becomes engulfed by 'woe is me' thought patterns, which only further reinforce the negative and vicious cycles inherent in her oft unexamined experience. The Moon relates to and speaks to Pisces in a strong voice, and people of her personality type need to be cautious, for the ultimate negative feature of The Moon card is for Pisces to deny the message this card is trying to teach her.

★ DIVINE MANIFESTATION USING THE MOON ★

You can Divinely manifest things in your experience through tapping into your Instincts.

The Moon is the intuitive clairvoyant, who opens you up to your deeper self and uncovers your hidden depths and Truths. This is that darkness just before the dawn. Ask your inner self about the true source of your fears, and trust its answer. The Moon card appears when we are experiencing times that open us up to our intuition and psychic abilities through increased self-awareness and the acknowledgement of past blocks that have held us back - or things which have been suppressed and need to rise to the surface to be transmuted. It is from our shadow selves that we must endeavour to draw regenerating energies so as not to become overcome by our emotions or ravaged by insurmountable circumstances. The Moon's main message is to encourage us to face the unknown without being afraid, to acknowledge our anxieties, weaknesses and mistakes, and to conquer the inner darkness that lurks within. You need to awaken to the truths about yourself that you have so far kept hidden, and ultimately, to reawaken to your brilliant light and power.

★ EXERCISE TO TAP INTO YOUR INNER MOON ★

★ Explore one aspect of your shadow self (a part of your character or personality that you hide because it is loathsome, or you fear loss if you express it to others). Bring it to the surface through gentle meditation, face it, and then seek to gently and lovingly release it. No one need know about this exercise; you do not need to share it with others. Allow the revelations and insights you gain pave the way for deep healing on a soul level.

★ THE SUN ★

Ruled by the Sun

Number ★ 19
Astrological Sign ★ Leo

It (19) is the number of light.

The Key of the Mysteries, Eliphas Levi

Keywords ★ Success, Joy, Vitality, Radiance

Magical Title ★ The Lord of the Fire of the World
Divinity ★ Helios

Spiritual Value ★ The Sun's function is to tap into the intelligent part of your personality which seeks to become more than you are. If you fly too close to the fiery rays of the Sun, you will be burnt. But approached with humility and reverence, the Sun becomes the beneficent source of life. This Arcanum can be used when you are emotionally, spiritually or physically depleted and need to increase your ability to manifest the hidden powers of your character.

★ KEY THEMES ★

"Pure Radiance"

★ Optimism ★ Joy ★ Positive Energy ★ Merriment ★ Exuberance ★ Clarity ★ Positive Outlook ★ Freedom ★ Blossoming ★ Public Recognition ★ Great Personal Insights ★ Vibrant Health ★ Fulfilment ★ Play ★ Success ★ Abundance ★ Enlightenment ★ Pure Feelings ★ Perfect Happiness ★ Radiance ★ Rejoicing ★ Satisfaction ★ Delight ★ Charisma ★ Magnetism ★ Affinities ★ Union ★ Profound and Complete Joy

Meditation ★ "I express immense gratitude for the sheer joy of being alive. My heart is open and my soul streams out in an uninhibited flow of endless luminosity, love, generosity, radiance and spirit. I am pure happiness."

★ *When Working with this Card* ★

MAIN ENERGIES ★ Faith, Trust, Purity, Flow, Joy, Love
MAIN GOD OR GODDESS TO INVOKE ★ Apollo, Ra, Sol, Helios
CANDLE COLOUR ★ Gold
MAGICAL TOOLS OR SYMBOLS ★ The Sun, Fire, Gold
CRYSTALS ★ Yellow Topaz, Citrine, Ruby, Sunstone, Clear Quartz, Yellow Sapphire, Diamond

ASSOCIATED BEINGS, GODS, GODDESSES & ARCHETYPES ★ The Creator, the Divine Child, the Visionary, Masters and Saints, Archangels Michael and

Uriel, Illuminated Ones, Apollo, Ra, Sol, Sunna, Amaterasu, Mithra, Dazhbog, Sekhmet, Belenos, Arinna, Belisama, Saule, Helios, Bel, Lugh, the Dagda, Nuada, Shamash, Atum, Oak King, Osiris, Hyperion, Castor and Pollux, Khephra, Hathor, Bast/Bastet, Bran the Blessed, Horus, Sol Invictus, All other Solar Deities, Transpersonal Teachers and Guides, Redeemers and Saviours.

> Were I to choose a religion, I would probably become a worshipper of the Sun. It gives life and fertility to all things. It is the true God of the earth.
>
> **Napoleon Bonaparte**

ARCHETYPES ★ The Sun is a symbol of joy, light, consciousness and action. As the heart of our Universe, it is the source of warmth, illumination, enlightenment and all life on Earth. It is the Animus, the Father, the God, the Ruler, the Pure Self.

> Keep your face always to the sunshine, and the shadows will fall behind you.
>
> **Walt Whitman**

CHAKRAS ★ Use this card to balance and meditate upon the Solar Plexus and Heart chakras.

Solar Plexus ★ Behind the Navel ★ Yellow ★ Fire ★ Personal Power, Confidence & Control

Heart ★ Heart Region ★ Green ★ Air ★ Love & Compassion

TREE OF LIFE ★ In western magic, which combines the Tarot paths of the Major Arcana with the ten sephiroth on the Tree of Life, the path of The Sun connects Yesod and Hod.

THE FOOL'S JOURNEY ★ The Fool instinctively and wisely knows at this stage of his journey, that the darkest hour is just before the dawn, and in the light of the Sun, The Fool has come out of that darkness into a new awareness and strength. Revitalised by the power of life's journey, he is at his strongest, ready to shine.

> I am not young but I feel young ... J'aime la vie! I feel that to live is a wonderful thing.
>
> **Coco Chanel**

THE STORY ★ Two almost naked children, perhaps the celestial Castor and Pollux, the Gemini of the zodiac, are standing in front of a wall with the Sun above casting down radiant rays, falling like drops of gold around them. Some decks show a beaming Sun gazing down on a single naked child riding a white horse. The child holds up a banner, and behind him is a wall, over which sunflowers, the ultimate symbol of the Sun, can be seen. Whatever its imagery, The Sun symbolises the Divine, wise child, who reminds you how to frolic. This motif is an appeal to us to re-realise the passionate simplicity of the unfettered child, serving as a potent reminder to laugh, play and *love* more. The Sun card reminds us of times when we were or are at our happiest, and brings us back to basics. In idyllic scenes from childhood, everything is open and always flooded with the Sun's rays. This card allows you to freely open your heart to the world and simply to feel good. There are no boundaries and no secrets. The Sun in the card casts strong rays of light on a loving couple, child or children, who represent love, friendship and rapport. They are protected from outside evil influences by a sturdy, well-built but quite low wall. However, we may get the impression that the characters are becoming overheated by the Sun's powerful energy, serving as a reminder that although the Sun is a cheering presence, it can also burn you; you must beware of over-exertion as it can lead to burn-out. The other potential negative of The Sun, is that when we are the laughing child we may fail to see, or we may forget, the adversities around us and the suffering of others.

> Perfect is what I have said of the work of the Sun.
>
> **Hermes Trismegistus, *The Emerald Tablet***

THE MESSAGE ★ The Sun represents rebirth - the emergence of the butterfly out of the cocoon, the soul's appearance in all its radiance. The Sun card indicates that now is a marvellous time for all who bask under its rays. Any endeavours undertaken or beginning at this time will be blessed with abundance and success. This is a time for shining in every sense of the word; keep your thoughts positive and turned to the Sun, and your brilliant ideas will turn out magnificently. The spiritual and personal work you've been doing is yielding results and is bringing astounding changes to your life. Indeed, you are well on your way to spiritual enlightenment, as well as the perfect gifts of powerful physical and emotional health.

THE AWAKENING ★ Everything will be sunny and bright. Love, relationships and friendships of all kinds will be highlighted. This is a time to emulate the Sun's active, creative ability to realise new works of art or love, and to be a dynamic, inspiring and influential leader whose lights shines for all to see and be warmed by.

> There is no duty we so much underrate as the duty of being happy.
> By being happy we sow anonymous benefits upon the world.
>
> **Robert Louis Stevenson**

THE LESSON ★ Quite simply, The Sun urges you to give in to satisfaction, contentment, spontaneous and pure feelings, and to be yourself. The presence of The Sun is a good omen, and a sign of relief, clarity, success and abundance. It suggests that you should also encourage others to enjoy life. If you are thinking of starting or increasing your family, The Sun gives you this blessing. It also tells you that all that is true, good, just and beautiful will triumph.

> Do anything, but let it produce joy.
>
> **Henry Miller**

SYMBOLISM ★ Just as the Moon is the deeper female aspect, the Sun is the overt masculine principle, the creative element that impregnates the female to bring forth life. Without the union of male and female there is only sterility and stagnation. Having received a glimpse of the female archetype in The Moon, the Tarot traveller is now shown the male archetype of the Sun.

The Sun card symbolises happiness, growth, the light of knowledge, freedom, wonder, blossoming, life-affirming energy, joy, playfulness, creativity and pure love.

The Sun in the card shines upon the young couple and landscape below, yet its brightness is directed indiscriminately, which shows that its light is available for the use of everyone. It represents the knowledge that we are all connected by the eternal rays of the life force, that life is a joyous circus and everyone is in the ring together. The Sun card employs generous imagery - the sunshine illuminates all that it falls upon, and spreads it far and wide.

Some cards may include a butterfly, which is the archetypal symbol of rebirth and metamorphosis. Through learning of its process of moving out of a chrysalis state and into the light, transformed, we can experience the miracle of the butterfly - emerging from our cocoons, we unfurl our wings, and soar into the Sun-soaked heavens, utterly changed.

OVERALL ★ CONNECTING IT ALL UP ★

I will follow the Sun through the zodiac, and as each sign is illuminated, I will seek to discover its inner meanings and its message. At each new station, a new adventure and a cosmic truth, revealed.

Patricia Crowther

The Sun is the nineteenth card of the Major Arcana, and heralds a time of joy and progress. While The Moon signifies uncertainty and doubt, The Sun symbolises clear vision, a positive attitude and confidence. The Sun is a symbol of masculine energy, and its divinatory meanings are success, satisfaction, accomplishment, contentment, love, joy, favourable relationships, devotion, selfless sentiment, engagement, a happy marriage, pleasure in daily existence, warmth, high spirits, a good friend, sincerity, simple pleasures, creative achievement and liberation. Enthusiasm and joy are positive aspects connected with The Sun, but if they are not kept in check, they risk turning into negatives, in the form of insensitivity, over-confidence, extravagance, and a lack of awareness of one's limits. And although the Sun ripens the fruit, if its rays are too strong for too long, moisture can evaporate quickly and it can burn the fruit. Overall though, this is the card of success, clear skies ahead, and the promise of a sun-kissed future. Double warmth comes from its astrological link with the Sun itself, focusing on personal potential, and the dazzling light of complete self-knowledge - *magic luck*.

In some cards a huge, brilliant Sun hangs over the Earth, dropping beads of sparkling dew, brightening and ripening everything - and everyone - beneath it. In other decks, The Sun frequently shows a naked child riding a white horse. The child is a sign of new life and hope. Behind him is a wall, over which sunflowers are seen, or the sunflowers may be shown on open ground. In some decks, the child actually holds the Sun, while in others a massive Sun dominates the sky. Oranges and sunflowers, both Solar images, often adorn the scene. Sunflowers can be said to symbolise the four elements of Earth, Air, Fire and Water.

The Solar journey takes a year, unlike the Moon's monthly cycle, and involves a recurring theme of death and rebirth. The Sun's rays are at their weakest at the winter solstice, which represents the dying god. After this point, the days gradually get longer, marking the birth of a new god. At the summer solstice, the Sun is at its strongest and is seen as the celestial ruler in his prime. The Sun's passage through the seasons of spring, summer, autumn and winter reflects life's journey through birth, youth, maturity and old age.

The Sun is obviously a daytime card and, as such, is connected with brightness, energy and clarity, unlike the dark, mysterious, shadowy night-themed card The Moon. The Sun and Moon who, in mythology, were twins, make up two halves of the whole; either one on its own would be unstable and upset the balance.

The mood of this card is buoyant and happy. The glorious Sun bestows the gift of life to all the Universe. The child, without saddle or bridle, represents the perfect control between the conscious and unconscious mind. The child's nakedness shows that he has nothing to hide. Success, glory, achievement, happy reunions, joyful love affairs, pleasure, vitality, good health and children are all shown by this card; perhaps good news concerning offspring will come about, or a longed-for baby will be conceived or born.

The Sun can represent birth - the emergence of the butterfly out of the cocoon. It symbolises consciousness and the active, awakened understanding of, and appreciation for, life. Out of the dark womb of night, The Sun symbolises the soul's appearance in all its radiance. In rebirth, one feels a great happiness, a joy of being alive, a renewed and expanded sense of play. Less attached to desires and expectations, one enjoys a growing feeling of acceptance. The achievement of nonattachment does not imply lack of feeling or disconnection; on the contrary, it signifies stronger links with the oneness that is at the centre of life, and a less personal sense of attachment to all the hurts, pains, irritations and grievances of the daily reality. Indeed, our inner Sun radiates to the outer sphere and heals the fractured parts of the being, bringing together, integrating and harmonising under the guidance of the soul.

Here, the ego is not obliterated or surrendered fully; rather, it is lifted up. What this means for the ego is transmutation. From the Solar Plexus, consciousness is raised up into the heart from which it radiates in a more powerful and balanced flow of vital life force energy. This raised consciousness is the higher octave of the zodiacal sign Leo. When conscious awareness is centered in the heart, personal concerns and petty desires no longer control or dominate the human being but are seen for what they really are - a display of personal ego consciousness and theatrics.

Overall, The Sun is a positive force of illumination, presaging good fortune, health, cheer and worldly success. It promotes growth and inspires vitality, energy and confidence. However, if it is too bright, it can also dazzle and blind you to the truth of a situation. It is a card indicating growth and increased potential, such as progression of relationships, financial expansion, and physical growth (as in pregnancy). The idea and understanding that Divinity is right here, in us, now - in everything and everyone - is extremely liberating.

When this card appears in a reading, it can point you towards fortune, and even fame, in all areas of your life. But you have your part to play - by seizing the opportunities as they arise. You can relax and enjoy yourself, for it's going to be a good day, week or year. You are probably experiencing a great deal of expansion, awakening and pleasure - your Sun is shining. Celebrate! In some way, you have come out of a dark, lonely, confused or sad space, and are now feeling the renewal of energy and friendship. Life seems to open up and offer you new directions. You feel yourself to be part of something bigger than your own individual life, and yet your individuality is emancipated and travelling lighter as well. If you draw this card, you may need to ask yourself: How can I reconcile these two apparently opposite parts of my psyche (the male and the female)? Before you can reach the end of your journey, you must unify these two aspects of yourself, so you can move beyond their duality.

The Sun offers you the confidence and ability to put yourself forward in the world, and allows you to radiate your personal power because you now understand your place in the Universal scheme of things, or are at least on the cusp of embracing this. This should be a creative period for you; allow your ideas to grow, flow and change, and let your true colours show.

★ HOW THIS CARD RELATES TO THE SUN ★

The Sun, the sustainer of life, naturally corresponds with the Sun, the source of energy and enlightenment.

Corrine Kenner

This is perhaps the most transparent card of all, and as such requires the least explanation for how and why it relates to its ruler, the Sun. The Sun is pure radiance, light and energy, and the only negative meaning to this card - if indeed it can be perceived as negative - is that if one gets too close to the Sun, one may get burnt; too much of a good thing is not always good. The Sun Tarot card relates to the luminary Sun in our sky in the simplest of ways: quite simply, it radiates beams of warmth, happiness and indiscriminate love. The bright yellow light emanating from the Sun card *and* the Sun in the sky, blesses the Tarot traveller with an enlivening sense of possibility and positivity. It touches and bestows life upon everyone and everything who dwell upon planet Earth. So above all, ask not for whom the Sun shines: because it shines for us *all*.

★ DIVINE MANIFESTATION USING THE SUN ★

You can Divinely manifest things in your experience through tapping into your Inner Child.

This card allows you to freely open your heart to the world and simply to feel good. With this most luminous of stars, there are no boundaries, no impurities, and no secrets; everything is bathed in the light. Experience your soul as its pure, child-like, innocent self. Emulate the Sun's active, creative ability to realise new works of art or love, and to be a dynamic, inspiring and influential leader whose lights shines for all to see and be warmed by. The Sun is a very lucky omen, and perhaps the happiest, most positive card in the Tarot. Its powers can most easily be evoked through tapping into your Inner Child, that magical Divine being that you so often neglect and unwittingly cast aside. The introspection you experienced in the previous card The Moon, enables you to better understand yourself and serves to open you up to a well of pure joy that bubbles up and overflows throughout all areas of your life. You are brimming with reverence for the world, your energy is increased, and you can now focus on realising your dreams. The Sun gives you the gift of abounding success. Unwrap it and feel the joy.

★ EXERCISES TO TAP INTO YOUR INNER SUN ★

★ Bring your Inner Child out to play! Visit a happy place from your childhood, dance, sing, be silly, play with children, frolic with a bounding dog, eat fairy-bread, and make daisy chains! Whatever makes you feel unhindered, unfettered and free, do it. Be conscious of and present in the experience, reach in and embrace your Inner Child, who still has so much love for you. He/she is still in there, and is waiting for you to re-discover him or her. Restore yourself to that sense of wellbeing and ease, even if it is only fleeting, for every second spent with your precious Inner Child is well worth it.

★ What is one of your happiest childhood memories? For ten or so minutes, close your eyes and bring it to the forefront of your mind in vivid detail. Relive it in your mind and consciously feel the elation, love, innocence, happiness, or excitement of the scenario of that experience. Bring this treasured memory to mind whenever you are needing to restore, replenish or refresh your spirits.

★ JUDGEMENT ★

Ruled by Pluto & the Element of Fire

Baptism by Fire is a classically Plutonic initiatory rite of purification, whereby all that is temporal and conditioned is burnt away.

Caroline W. Casey

Number ★ 20
Astrological Signs ★ Scorpio, Aries, Leo & Sagittarius

The Judgement card has positive and negative aspects. In the positive sense, we are being awakened from a long sleep, a period during which we lacked clarity, and now insight is dawning upon us in a psychic rebirth and resurrection. In the negative sense, we are being called to account for past actions, and to justify in the light of truth what we have done in the past. Judgement speaks of a time of reckoning, a time of bringing to light those things which were hidden.

Edward Aviza

Keywords ★ Evaluation, Self-assessment, Opportunities, New Directions

Magical Title ★ The Spirit of Primal Fire
Divinity ★ Aphrodite
Spiritual Value ★ The impulse to ascend must come from above, but by its power you may transcend your environment and cast aside the burdens of desire. This Arcanum allows you to connect with an upper reality located above the limitations of your rational mind. It enables you to develop your willpower, decisiveness, and conscious powers of demand.

★ KEY THEMES ★

"Confessional Box"

★ Discernment ★ Karma ★ Reaping What Has Been Sown ★ Evaluation ★ Evolution ★ Review ★ Improvement ★ Revelation ★ Renewal ★ Favourable Assessment of the Facts ★ Objectivity ★ New Directions ★ Transformation ★ Legal Situations Resolved Favourably ★ Academic and Examination Success ★ Bonus ★ A Career or Life Change ★ Moving in a Different Direction ★ Sound Decisions Based on Good Preparation and Evaluations ★ Rehabilitation ★ Recovery ★ Promotion ★ Admission of Guilt ★ Good News

Meditation ★ "I stand at the Oracle of Judgement. In its innate wisdom and pure truths, I trust that it will light the way ahead by allowing for my redemption, renewal and rebirth."

★ *When Working with this Card* ★

MAIN ENERGIES ★ Redemption, Resurrection, Wisdom, Enlightenment

MAIN ENTITY TO INVOKE ★ Akashic Records
CANDLE COLOUR ★ Royal Blue
MAGICAL TOOL OR SYMBOL ★ Judge's Gavel
CRYSTALS ★ Amethyst, Clear Quartz, Black Obsidian, Malachite, Peridot, Sapphire, Turquoise, Apophyllite

ASSOCIATED BEINGS, GODS, GODDESSES & ARCHETYPES ★ Supernal Entities, Archangels, Raguel ^, the Great Mother, the Star Father, Osiris, Amit, Saturn, Neptune, Anubis, Sekhmet, Ra, Kephra, Holla, Brigid, Ma'at, Thoth *, Apollo, Lugh, Nemesis, Matrona, the Zodiac, the Guardian Angel, the King, the Magical Helper, the Medium, the Messiah, the Messenger, the Saviour, the Psychopomp.

^ Raguel is one of the seven archangels and is known as the Angel of Ice and Snow. It is said that he will call forth the other angels on the Day of Judgement.

* In ancient Egyptian mythology, when the deceased reached the Judgement Hall, he or she had to swear before Osiris, Ma'at, Thoth and 42 Divine judges that they were free of a long list of sins. The deceased's heart was then weighed against the feather of Truth. If the feather and the heart balanced perfectly, the soul was judged sinless and 'true of voice', and was accordingly admitted to paradise; but if the heart was heavy with sin, the deceased was condemned to oblivion. As Divine judge, his voice was said to possess magical properties. Thoth recorded the verdict. In the *Book of the Pyramids*, one of the oldest on record, Thoth is spoken of as being the eldest son of Ra; in other texts, he is the brother of Isis and Osiris. Thoth is the patron of history, keeper of the Divine archives, lord of karma, herald of the gods. His female aspect is Ma'at, goddess of law, truth and justice. Sometimes he is said to have been married to Ma'at, but according to other legends, his wife was Seshat, a star goddess who was patroness of architects and taught men to build the stars.

ARCHETYPES ★ Judgement reveals all, heralds the dawn of a new world, and stands as a reminder of the power of forgiveness and its role in redemption and renewal. It is the Herald, the Gatekeeper, the Judge, the Rescuer.

CHAKRAS ★ Use this card to balance and meditate upon the Solar Plexus and Crown chakras.

Solar Plexus ★ Behind the Navel ★ Yellow ★ Fire ★ Personal Power, Confidence & Control

Crown ★ Top of Head ★ Purple ★ Thought/Knowing ★ Spiritual Wisdom & Enlightenment

TREE OF LIFE ★ In western magic, which combines the Tarot paths of the Major Arcana with the ten sephiroth on the Tree of Life, the path of Judgement links Hod and Malkuth at the base.

THE FOOL'S JOURNEY ★ Archetypically, Judgement means resurrection, the rebirth that comes with self-examination, assessment of our journey so far, spiritual awareness, and the need for personal change. Arriving at this step on his travels, The Fool understands the possibilities of transformation that may accompany this awakening. The Fool reaches for redemption and enlightenment.

> You have brains in your head. You have feet in your shoes. You can steer yourself in any direction you choose. You're on your own and you know. And you're the one who'll decide where to go.
>
> **Dr Seuss**

THE STORY ★ The Judgement card is the respected mentor, who leads the way to a fresh perspective on life and leaves you feeling elated. Its main divinatory meanings are atonement, judgement, improvement, evaluation and finally, rebirth. In the symbolism of the Tarot, Judgement is not concerned with eternal damnation or heavenly bliss based upon this 'judgement' of your life experience so far, but instead with identifying ourselves the lessons we have learned not only from our archetypal Tarot journey so far, but through our whole life from birth onward. It is not a time for punishment and retribution, but a time of being called to account for past actions and experiences. After facing one's 'moment of truth', one can see oneself with more clarity and acceptance, and is then able to see others in the same way. This acceptance is an understanding of the human condition, human beauty, and embraces imperfections and Divine wisdom alongside each other. Our past, having been reflected upon, ensures that a positive resolution will be reinforced. With atonement and repentance, real advancement can occur. Therefore, Judgement is less about guilt and more about self-knowledge.

> To err is human, to forgive Divine … Haven't you read how in some of the near-death experiences a great golden presence of light arrives that is all-forgiving? And it is very often said that it is finally *we* who judge ourselves.
>
> **Sogyal Rinpoche**

THE MESSAGE ★ Judgement symbolises a time of judgement, when souls rise from the dead to be judged. This card depicts an angel blowing a trumpet to awaken the dead from their graves, and announcing it is Judgement Day. Bodies emerge from their coffins with arms outstretched, often casting off funeral shrouds as they make ready to embrace the new life that is offered to them by the Angel of Judgement. There are usually three figures rising from the dead, perhaps representative of the Mind, Body and Spirit trinity, all of which must be brought forth to be judged. The dead are praying for mercy in the hope that the sins of their lifetimes will be forgiven. They now know that their misdemeanours are being exposed, and they are hoping to be allowed to move onto a higher plane of existence. You're either near the end of a project or at a crossroads, but either way, you are on the threshold of making an important change in your life, and ready to move up to that elevated plane.

THE AWAKENING ★ From deep within the core of your being comes a call announcing that it is time to make an important change. You must concern yourself with finding meaning and purpose, evaluating past deeds and becoming more aware of who you are and who you wish to become. Past events are viewed with the clarity of perspective and you are able to make better sense of them. Your view on life shifts to allow a broader outlook, which prompts you to make sweeping changes and open up your self-expression. In essence, it allows you to more fully express who you are. When this card appears in a reading, it speeds up the pace of the surrounding cards and shows that the outcome will be quicker than you expect. This card may even be your stepping stone to even advance straight to The World!

> The only way to find true happiness it to risk being completely cut open.
>
> **Chuck Palahniuk**

THE LESSON ★ The word 'judgement', derived from the Latin *judicem*, means 'to show or to speak what is right'. But in the context of this card, is has another meaning: discernment. As far as Judgement is concerned, discernment takes the form of distinction, recognition and separation, and all that can be accomplished. The people in the card standing beneath the figure, wearing only their nakedness, show themselves as they are, stripped of any artifice. The light within may therefore now shine forth and they no longer have any need to feel ashamed of their nudity, or to be themselves. They can discriminate between what is true or false, just or unjust. The information that has shaped their existence and made them live in hope or in fear no longer comes from external sources, but from an internal wellspring - from *themselves*. This is a revelation. For we are all assailed by outside forces which are often unconnected with our lives, that leave us feeling powerless and depressed. With such hubbub and chaos surrounding us, it is hard to hear our inner voice (depicted as the angel on this card) and see and feel the light of our own wisdom (represented by the rays of the Sun around the angel). If we cannot hear these things, how can we detect, dissect and discern? Indeed, Judgement foretells a revelation, a renewal, an inner vision that is more accurate, more profound, more objective and more real than ever before. Its presence suggests that we can no longer lie to ourselves or hide the truth from others, bringing a relief, a cure, a reconciliation, a state of trust, a relaxing of tenseness, and total receptivity. It can also reveal a vocation, a promotion, a recognition or a reward that comes about as a result of our newfound inner consultations.

In order to clear your guilt, ask for purification from the depths of your heart. If you really ask for purification, and go through it, forgiveness will be there. To help yourself to forgive yourself, remember the good things you have done, forgive everyone else in your life, and ask for forgiveness from anyone you may have harmed.

Sogyal Rinpoche

SYMBOLISM ★ Judgement brings you a new sense of Self. It renews and restores, and signifies that a rebirth process is taking place within the Self. A wider perspective has become available.

The angel in the card uses a trumpet, as if to call the figures from their sleepy sense of unawareness into full awakening. Attached to the trumpet is a flying pennant. On the pennant is a red cross, which is a Universal symbol of healing. To personally evaluate one's life is a healing process, and Waite said that it has truly been called a card of eternal life - and indeed, any healing we undertake is bound to be ongoing and ever-unfolding. This cross, as well as the cloud, symbolises that this is spiritual in nature. The figures gradually rise - they are becoming released from the bonds of the past, and begin to look upwards towards an all-encompassing, broader and joyous perspective.

In some decks, the tombs are floating in a sea or river, which associates it with the notion that a river must be crossed before reaching the Promised Land. At the point of resurrection, evaluations must be made on each soul's life; therefore, this card portrays the need to reflect on life as it has been lived so far, to decide how one should proceed in the future.

OVERALL ★ CONNECTING IT ALL UP ★

The biggest adventure you can take is to live the life of your dreams.

Oprah Winfrey

This card's divinatory meanings are atonement, the need to repent or forgive, judgement, improvement, rebirth, rejuvenation, promotion, development, the desire for immortality, and the moment to account for the manner in which we have used our opportunities on our life's journey thus far.

Judgement implies the need for evaluation and self-assessment. This is a time for summing up and balancing emotional accounts by looking back over the recent past, in order to bring things into rightful perspective and prepare for the future.

The Judgement card signifies the final settlement of a matter, and a time to pay off old debts in preparation for a fresh beginning. It suggests that that which has been lying dormant will spring to life, as symbolised by the dead rising from their coffins. Judgement also indicates that the rewards for past efforts will soon finally be forthcoming.

The Judgement card indicates that the time is ripe for a period of self-appraisal, which involves taking an honest look at yourself, your motivations and your actions. This means reviewing your accomplishments so far, neither under- or over-valuing them. It also advises that one should carefully consider how present actions affect others around them.

Ultimately, Judgement suggests that it is time to review, evaluate and make some considered and thoughtful judgements regarding your life, and then make empowered decisions. To put it another way, in the words of Henry David Thoreau: "Go confidently in the direction of your dreams. Live the life you have imagined." It is time to practice discernment and then move in a new direction, from that newfound, redeemed, freed spirit.

★ HOW THIS CARD RELATES TO PLUTO & THE ELEMENT OF FIRE ★

Judgement, a last call for awareness, understanding, and acceptance, is assigned to Pluto, the planet of death, resurrection, and unavoidable change.

Corrine Kenner

All of Pluto's key themes relate to those represented by the Judgement card: regeneration, evolution, awakening, transformation, power, renewal, yearning, elimination, metamorphism, eruption, stirred passions, change, penetration, insight, self-mastery, transmutation, subversion, depth, darkness, and psychoanalysis. Pluto and the Judgement card both teach that endings are merely part of the cycle of life, resurrection and rebirth, and that forgiveness and release play a big part in this cycle. The depths to which Pluto will plunge to find its truth and redeem itself, are darker than those qualities of the Fire element, but Fire's characteristics nonetheless form a potent link with the Judgement card also. Fire is regenerative, transformational, destructive, constructive, and has the potential to be life-changing, concepts it shares with Judgement. If we use the powerful energies of all three - Judgement, Fire and Pluto - we can rise anew from our own ashes, more empowered, enlightened and brilliant than ever before. But all three are frighteningly confronting forces, and if we are ready to stand before the Judgement, Fire and Pluto trinity, then we need to be sure we are truly ready to hear their oft unsettling - but ultimately transformative - insights and truths.

★ DIVINE MANIFESTATION USING JUDGEMENT ★

You can Divinely manifest things in your experience through tapping into your inner Redeemer.

Sometimes called the Angel, this card has a very simple but profound meaning - a second chance. The wake-up call of this card, is that we all have to eventually face up to who we are, as an aspect of our maturity. At the heart of this message is the growth that ensues after personal confrontation. Judgement usually portrays an end to suffering and the beginnings of a spiritual resurrection. Through Judgement, you are being offered a dissolution of negative past patterns and a resulting spiritual rebirth, the opportunity to review past events, and to offer forgiveness or make amends. On a spiritual wavelength, this card implies that one particular phase of your soul's journey is ending, and you will shortly assess what you learned and how you dealt with the passing situation, summing up your performance and its value to you. Judgement is telling you that at this point in your life it is time to assess and evaluate yourself, and perhaps address any underlying issues which up until now may have been ignored. To do this, you need simply to become more self-aware. Judgement emphasises that in undertaking this self-examination, you should be fair on yourself and focus on your positive character traits. It is telling you that once you have done this, like the symbolic people on the card, you will be ripe and ready to move in a new direction and onto a higher, more worthwhile plane of existence! You're either near the end of a project or at a crossroads, but either way, you are on the threshold of making an important change in your life.

★ EXERCISES TO TAP INTO YOUR INNER JUDGEMENT ★

★ From deep within the core of your being comes a call announcing that it is time to make an important change. What needs to happen first? What do you need to patch up, make up for, redeem in yourself or your surroundings before you can move forward into that new space?

★ Practice at least one act of self-forgiveness for something you have done in the recent or distant past that you wish you could take back. Visualise the Angel of Judgement gently blowing her trumpet to acknowledge your repentance and atonement over this deed or occurrence and allow it to dissolve in your mind. Realise that you have the key to unlock your own prison and that everything that has happened thus far in your life has happened because it was part of the Divine order of things and that it was meant to serve as a lesson to lead you to your greater purpose. So in essence, your exercise is to reach some level of resolution and acceptance about something that has happened in your life, trusting that everything occurred as it was meant to given your level of knowledge at that time. Better still, forgive someone else for something they have done wrong to you. Forgiveness (of yourself or others) is the ultimate peace of mind, the highest freedom. Set yourself free.

★ THE WORLD/UNIVERSE ★

Ruled by Saturn & the Element of Earth

Number ★ 21
Astrological Signs ★ Capricorn, Taurus, Virgo & Aquarius

Keywords ★ Completion, Attainment, Fulfilment, Success

Magical Title ★ The Universe, the Great One of the Night of Time
Divinity ★ Hera
Spiritual Value ★ Here, we have the keys to the Universe and must use them wisely. Some Tarot scholars make the distinction between The Universe and The World as titles for this Arcanum, as proponents of the former assert that to the ancients, Saturn represented the outer limit of the Solar system. To them, Saturn passing through the spiral path of the zodiac, marked at its cardinal points to form a cross, was a comprehensive glyph of the whole. Therefore, in this card, we find a synthesis of the whole Taro or *Rota*. The World or The Universe, whichever you would prefer, stands for the Kingdom of All. It guides you towards truth, and may help you in finding your initiatory path.

★ KEY THEMES ★

"The Grand Arrival"

★ Arrival! ★ Completion ★ Fulfilment of Hopes and Dreams ★ Crowning Achievement ★ Total Success ★ Dreams Come True ★ Expansion ★ Aspirations ★ Idealism ★ A Prize or Goal Reached ★ Acclaim ★ Graduation ★ Accomplishment ★ Attainment ★ Contentment ★ Gratitude ★ The Path Toward Enlightenment ★ Perfection ★ Freedom ★ A Move to the Next Level ★ Cosmic Awareness ★ Expanded Consciousness ★ Joy ★ Great Outlook

Meditation ★ "I have completed one journey and will now rebirth myself to begin a brand new one. I welcome every chance to grow and learn, and I truly never stop evolving."

★ When Working with this Card ★

MAIN ENERGIES ★ Enlightenment, Wisdom, Knowing, Love, Freedom
MAIN ENTITY TO INVOKE ★ The Universe
CANDLE COLOUR ★ Gold
MAGICAL TOOL OR SYMBOL ★ Circle, Ourobous
CRYSTALS ★ Clear Quartz, Azurite, Apophyllite, Kyanite, Lapis Lazuli, Star Sapphire, Diamond

ASSOCIATED BEINGS, GODS, GODDESSES & ARCHETYPES ★ All Beings and Entities in the Universe, Earth Mother, Nimba, Tenga, Atlantia, Clinia, Flora,

Sucellus, Anu, Lakshmi, Hestia, Opshun, Bast/Bastet, Isis, Min, Geb, the Dagda, Venus, Ganesha, Ptah, Nike, Gaia, the Earth Gods and Goddesses, all Alchemical and Metaphysical Beings and Entities, the Universal Spirit that Permeates All, All That Is, the Eternal Circle Spiral.

ARCHETYPES ★ The World depicts the never-ending, ever-evolving spiral dance of life and the Absolute. It is a card of completion and success – as well as a new dawn rising. It is the Anima and Animus, the Destroyer and the Creator, the Divine Child, the Shaman, the Fates, the Self, the God and Goddess.

CHAKRAS ★ Use this card to balance and meditate upon the Solar Plexus and Crown chakras.

Solar Plexus ★ Behind the Navel ★ Yellow ★ Fire ★ Personal Power, Confidence & Control

Crown ★ Top of Head ★ Purple ★ Thought/Knowing ★ Spiritual Wisdom & Enlightenment

TREE OF LIFE ★ In western magic, which combines the Tarot paths of the Major Arcana with the ten sephiroth on the Tree of Life, The World is regarded as a major initiatory path linking Malkuth and Yesod and also representing Kether on a lower plane: "As above, so below."

> We either fear that human culture is falling apart, or we can hold the Vision that we are awakening. Either way, our expectation is a prayer that goes out as a force that tends to bring about the end we envision. Each of us must consciously choose between these two futures.
>
> **James Redfield, *The Tenth Insight***

THE FOOL'S JOURNEY ★ At the end of his journey, The Fool has achieved wholeness and understands his place in the world. The World card is the card of achievement and success, where The Fool understands that life encompasses much more than himself and his own journey. He is ready to begin again on a new cycle of learning; the process of reincarnation from the world of experience to the innocence once again of The Fool.

> Tell me, what is it you plan to do with your one wild and precious life?
>
> **Mary Oliver**

THE STORY ★ A statue of a woman has come to life and is dancing, looking back at a leaf she holds in her outstretched hand. Just as the Earth, Divine Mother of us all, evolved from the stars and materialised into reality, so have our physical selves been created out of the same essence so that we may dance the dance of life just as She dances through the cosmos. This dream-like journey is one of going deep within and finding our essential harmony with All There Is. When we arrive at the knowledge of who we really are we gain The World.

Life itself is the most wonderful fairytale.

Hans Christian Andersen

THE MESSAGE ★ You have arrived at the beginning of the Path to Enlightenment or could be considerably advanced along it by now. The World card suggests a job well done - you have happily completed something of great significance. Enjoy these feelings of wholeness and completion as your amazing accomplishments have been well-earned. You're now ready to move onto something new. You have grown spiritually and have evolved to a whole new level in your understanding of the Universe and your place in it. As well as this, you have attained complete clarity, cosmic awareness, significant enlightenment, an expanded consciousness and above all, the true freedom that accompanies all this.

Live as if you were to die tomorrow. Learn as if you were to live forever.

Mahatma Gandhi

THE AWAKENING ★ The World is a symbol of accomplishment, of an end which is also a beginning. The journey is completed! Upon reaching The World your goal is attained and you are suffused with joy and fulfilment. Life is fully and rapturously embraced, and you are free to experience all that it offers. You realise that the end of a journey merely leads to the first step on a new one. By uniting and balancing your long-sought after inner harmony with the skills you have learned in this lifetime so far, you have achieved true success and The World can indeed be yours! Although hard work has been required to attain this, material rewards and inner peace are promised. But overall, you must view your life in the context of the whole of life and All There Is, before you can gain the wisdom you seek.

The key to immortality is first living a life worth remembering.

Bruce Lee

THE LESSON ★ The World imparts the message that each one of us carries a world inside of us, which is neither unattainable nor illusory nor utopian. It is simply what we are. All the elements are gathered here so that our conscience may awaken and our future will unfold as it is meant to before us. Form a circle with a group of friends, imaginary or real. Slowly move around it, dancing and swaying and chanting. Complete the circle twenty-two times. As you do so, close your eyes and visualise the Earth in the centre of your circle, bathed in white light, receiving the love, wisdom and healing energy from your group. Know that we are all blessed with the sacred duty of being the caretakers of our Mother Earth - and of finding our own place within it.

The Universe is full of magical things, patiently waiting for our wits to grow sharper.

Eden Phillpotts

SYMBOLISM ★ The World card symbolises completion and renewal. It incorporates the wisdom gathered throughout the journey of the previous 21 cards. The World embodies the essence of success, arrival, fulfilment and happiness. It shows a willingness to embrace life fully and to welcome in the new.

The central figure in The World card, hermaphroditic in appearance, symbolises the integration of the masculine and feminine principles to form a complete, unified entity. The wreath is a symbol of triumph, success, rebirth and renewal, while the surrounding creatures embody different aspects of human nature. It reinforces the sense of cosmic harmony because it is unbroken.

This female figure, entwined with a purple sash and holding two wands, and the four spiritual creatures in the corners, signify harmony between the ethereal realm and the world. The lady dancing in the centre is the feminine sign for wisdom. In ancient times, it was common to characterise wisdom as being female in form. To the Greeks she was known as Sophia, and indeed the word 'philosophy', is derived from the Latin/Greek word *philosophia*, meaning 'love of wisdom'. Her purple-coloured sash symbolises the pinnacle of spirituality, purple being the colour of both occult and biblical associations.

One of the most ancient symbols of alchemy is that of Ouroboros ^, the dragon or serpent which lies in a circle with its tail in its mouth. This sleeping creature must be awoken for its potential to be realised, and its energies released, for us to begin - and achieve - the process of self-transformation. The circle around the dragon, a symbol without end and without beginning, symbolises the fact that one's beginning can also be found in its end, and vice versa. And so, the symbol for Ouroboros never loses its meaning, for its meaning is eternity and in a sense the journey is never really completed; each ending is followed by a new beginning. Even if we eventually arrive back at the place where we first began our journey, nothing will be the same; all is transformed.

> If we are using ourselves as the alchemical vessel, and our life as the laboratory, then we must search for our 'prime substance' among our own experiences. Some people believe that they must go off to the Far East to find wisdom, or leave their jobs and families to begin their true quest. Alchemy says the opposite: begin with what you have, and work with it skilfully, consciously and imaginatively. This will produce pure transformation. The Ouroboros, the sleeping serpent or dragon with its tail in its mouth, is the symbol of this unconscious potential. We have to wake it up.
>
> **Cherry Gilchrist**

The World or Universe card brings us to the culmination of our Tarot journey. The final card of the Major Arcana, it is the supreme symbol of unity and wholeness. It commonly depicts a dancing figure holding The Magician's wand and encircled by a laurel wreath. The wand is symbolic of the magic of self-transformation, while the laurel is the plant of success, victory and high achievement. The circle represents the Ouroboros (a serpent or dragon eating its own tail), a symbol of eternity. In each corner are the four Fixed signs of the zodiac: Taurus the Bull, Leo the Lion, Scorpio the Eagle and Aquarius the Man, which correspond to the four seasons of spring, summer, autumn and winter respectively, the four evangelical qualities of Man: humanity, spirituality, courage and strength, and also the four elements, which the alchemists combined to create a perfect fifth - the 'quintessence', or fifth element.

This fifth element is symbolised by the central figure in the card, a genderless hermaphrodite, an image of the reconciliation of opposites, and also of balance. The card's number is twenty-one, the number of completion (three times seven, the two most magically significant numbers). The wreath may also represent zero, the symbol of infinity, with which you started the journey; therefore, the end of one journey is marking the beginning of another.

Astrologically, The World seems to be the most strongly related to the Midheaven, which is the highest point in the sky at the moment of birth. The World's divinatory meanings are completion, perfection, the rewards of labour, inner satisfaction, the end result of all your efforts, success, synthesis, fulfilment, capability, eternal life, admiration from others, ultimate change, and triumph in all your undertakings. The World is congratulating you. As a symbol of completion, attainment, success and self-knowledge, she suggests that you remind yourself of what you have already achieved, and know that others are aware of you, appreciate and truly admire your past efforts. She tells you that you are now entering an extremely rewarding phase of your life when you will enjoy the benefits of all your hard work. Enjoying your time to the fullest in any way that you know will bring you further pleasure and sheer joy.

OVERALL ★ CONNECTING IT ALL UP ★

To be free is to have achieved your life.

Tennessee Williams

The World is a superb card, with enchanting meanings and symbolism. Without attachment, the figure in The World image releases the past and dances ecstatically into the future, in an open space and to his or her own rhythm, within a circle of support. The Tarot traveller, at the end of the journey, realises that the individual is the symbol of the whole world, embracing all things within the enlightened self.

This is considered the most auspicious card in the pack, indicating great success, and showing that battles have been fought and won, challenges have been faced, and victory is yours. When The World appears in a reading, it means you have in some sense mastered the three planes of mind, body and emotions, having come to know yourself in a way that makes you feel at home with yourself. You have reached a great balance and integration and are in a place of knowing all parts of yourself and using them for the expression of your real self in the world. As well as triumph, this card also signifies transcendence, and your experience of it may be hard to define or put into rational words. You may just sense and feel that you are elated, spirited and aware, with the new wisdom and insights you've gathered along the way to carry into your next phase.

The World card officially ends your Tarot journey - or is this merely back to the beginning? All the best in your circular travelling, whichever way the Tarot's Wheel of Fortune is turning for you or stopped for you at any given time. Sometimes it is fate which dictates the flow, at other times it is your own free will. Whatever you believe to be true, enjoy the journey and remember - sometimes you're at the top, sometimes the bottom, sometimes the end, sometimes the beginning. And 'round and 'round we go! Enjoy your travels and take care out there, for life is always imitating *art*.

^ The ouroboros symbol can be drawn on candles, petitions, or other magical items to draw forth the power of the circle and the unity of all beings. It is also an excellent protective device. Magical themes for the ouroboros include wisdom, self-sufficiency, Divine parents, time, order from chaos, alpha and omega symbolism, potential of birth, immortality, infinity, and the cycle of life, death and rebirth.

★ HOW THIS CARD RELATES TO SATURN & THE ELEMENT OF EARTH ★

The initiatory ordeal is by definition a solitary experience that leads us to self-reflection. Solitude, Saturn's sacramental activity, is the portal to the magic realm where power larger than us resides. Very often when we are alone we feel most connected to everything. Time spent alone allows us to 'consider' our lives, to align the inner gods with the outer gods of the cosmos, to disentangle ourselves from the phantasmagoria of seductive distractions.

Caroline W. Casey

If you are of the belief that we come from the Earth at our supposed conception, and we return again to it upon our death, and that nothing in the entire Universe has an end *or* a beginning, you will have grasped the concept and essence that the Universe/World card embodies. The World is a symbol of accomplishment, of an end which is also a beginning, for its meaning is eternity and in a sense the journey is never really completed, for each ending is followed by a new beginning. We are born of the Earth, and we re-enter it at the time of our physical death, only to be born anew in a new cycle when our next 'time' has arrived and the Divine calls us once again into form. But this next time around, nothing will be the same; all is transformed. Most versions of The World feature a triumphant figure dancing and spinning endlessly within the 'confines' of a laurel wreath. The circular wreath, a symbol of eternal life, appears to form a protective enclosure that frames her movements, and represents the simple law of physics: that is, that we are made of energy, and energy cannot be created or destroyed, it is just transformed. But while The World card hints at an entire Universe of infinite possibilities, it also contains the sense, through its Saturnian connections, that one also recognises one's Earthly limits, thereby making wise and sound decisions within the time and space one is given. This is not to say that one can't rebel against the boundaries that Saturn imposes; indeed, most people like to feel free and unencumbered, and The World certainly offers this hope. But it also acknowledges that we have never truly reached the destiny, for we are on a ceaseless, unending adventure, and what is seen as a triumphant ending is in fact the attainment of one thing which ultimately marks the beginning of another, new thing or cycle.

The Earth relates to The World as the source of our apparent origins and our apparent endings, but it stands as a solid symbol that it sustains, grows and maintains us throughout each cycle of life and death, and starts and finishes. The astrological glyph of Saturn combines the crescent of consciousness with the cross of the Earth, or matter; in other words, the mastery of the conscious mind in relation to its position and experience of the physical environment. Although associated with doom, gloom, boundaries and restrictions, in astrological tradition Saturn's benefits may be greater - or at least more substantial - than those of all the other planets. His lessons may be tough, but they are what we need to learn in order to grow, materialise and manifest through what is learned and applied from these tests. Throughout the Tarot journey, we are tempted by the illusions of material gain, our shadow selves, false love, self-delusions and even physical immortality, but no matter how much influence, affluence or abundance one possesses in one's lifetime, one will inevitably lose out to Saturn, Satan's ally, for we are mortal and Saturn is Father Time, the Old Man, and the Grim Reaper who deals in forces of Light and Dark. Although Saturn can be cruel to mere mortals, he can also play the role of bestower of gifts to the well-behaved and worthy - and the withholder of rewards from the undeserving. And one who passes Saturn's many tests is blessed by being helped along the Path to greater illumination and that quality which eludes many - *wisdom*. Once we reach the stage of the journey that The World represents, it is usually a sign that we have learned our Earthly lessons and Saturn's inherent wisdom, and are overcome by a profound sense we have arrived at the pinnacle of success. And we instinctively know that the only way from here is back to the beginning for another beautiful trip around the never-ending circle that symbolises the Tarot experience and Eternity. Although unseen by the physical eyes, The Fool is indeed in The World card, and is still holding your hand, as he whistles his sweet tune and lures you back to the start of the Great Circle. And you both know on a profound level that this time around, you are a little wiser and changed for the better. Happy travelling! You are within the Universe but more importantly, the Universe is within *You*.

★ DIVINE MANIFESTATION USING THE WORLD ★

You can Divinely manifest things in your experience through tapping into your inner Universe.

The World, like The Fool that began our Tarot journey, is a paradox and inherently dual-natured, in that it is the end *and* the beginning. The World, at the surface level at least, marks the end of a period of time, the completion of a task, which has its new beginnings as a seed within. It denotes a time of celebration and the wonderful feelings that accompany any occasion during which something is finished, or made whole. It represents a deeply satisfying sense of achievement and fulfilment, suggestive of a peak experience - and expanded horizons ahead. On another level, however, any accomplishment or completion may be followed afterwards by a feeling of emptiness or deflation, as the goal has been realised and the dream made a reality. But never despair, for as the Death Tarot card teaches us, the ending, loss or death of something only means that a new beginning can emerge to fill the space that has been left behind. At this point of the Tarot journey, the crowned dancing figure in The World card who celebrates reaching the finishing mark, suddenly morphs again to embody a foetal-like being, waiting to re-evolve and rebirth itself as The Fool in the never-ending circular journey; in this way, The World symbolises the ending of one cycle and the commencement of another, and indeed The World represents a course that has now come full circle, and suggests you can rest on your laurels for a time before moving onto this next phase, as you have rightly earned it. You now understand your place within the system, and will soon be ready to begin a new phase from the beginning, but next time around, your journey will be informed from an elevated place of better knowledge, profound experience, acquired wisdom, greater self-awareness, spiritual truths, and a special kind of inner knowing.

★ EXERCISE TO TAP INTO YOUR INNER WORLD ★

★ You have reached the end and the beginning all at once. Metaphysical experts claim that we never really reach a destination, that we never really 'get there', and the reason for this is that we are in a continual and eternal state of unfoldment, alternating between closing up and unfurling ourselves again, in a neverending swirl of ever-circulating energy. Has someone you loved ever died? Did you ever think about this death from the perspective that because energy cannot ever be created or destroyed, that we all carry on in some form or another, even if our physical forms no longer exist? If you did, did this perspective comfort you, or create more curiosity and questions than you had ever dared ask before? The questions you need to ask yourself from the unique vantage point of having just journeyed through the whole Tarot experience, are these: You have come to the end. But is it really an ending? And if it is not an ending, but the supreme catalyst for a brand-new beginning, do you dare go back to being The Fool, innocent, pure, and born again? Do you have the courage to start over, this time different, stronger, and wiser? Skip along now, for The Fool is calling you back into the swirling vortex of endless and boundless creation. Enjoy the journey!

We shall not cease from exploration
And the end of all our exploring
Will be to arrive where we started
And to know the place for the first time.

T.S. Eliot

★   ★   ★

GLOSSARY

Allegorical cards ★ The 22 Major Arcana cards from the Tarot deck which bear pictorial and symbolic representations.

Arcana ★ Taken from the Italian *arcano* and Latin *arcantum*, meaning secret or esoteric knowledge.

Cartomancy ★ The art of using cards for any means of divination or fortune-telling.

Court cards ★ The King, Queen, Knight and Page in each of the four suits of the Tarot deck.

Divination ★ Fortune-telling or prophesising by various means including but not limited to Tarot cards.

Diviner ★ A person who reads and interprets the card spread (or other materials) for the purpose of reading the future.

Greater Arcana ★ Another name for Major Arcana.

Kabbalah ★ Ancient occult theosophy widely transmitted in medieval Europe and based upon esoteric interpretations of the Hebrew Scriptures. The word 'Kabbalah', sometimes spelt with a C or Q, is derived from the Hebrew Qblh, the literal interpretation of which is 'an unwritten or oral tradition'. Other interpretations of its meaning are "to receive," or "that which is received." Broadly speaking, the idea of emanation and manifestation is central to Kabbalistic thought, and it combines both philosophical and magical concepts and principles.

Lesser Arcana ★ Another name for Minor Arcana.

Major Arcana ★ The 22 emblematic and symbolic picture cards in the Tarot deck.

Minor Arcana ★ The 56 cards comprising 14 cards in each of the four suits from King to Ace.

Mysteries ★ Another name for Tarot cards.

Numeral cards ★ The 40 cards in the Minor Arcana which are numbered from 10 through Ace in each of the four suits.

Pip cards ★ Cards numbered 10 through Ace in each of the four suits.

Querent ★ Person seeking guidance or an answer to a question through means of cartomancy. Also known as questioner.

Rider-Waite deck ★ Famous 78-card Tarot deck designed by Pamela Colman Smith under the direction of Arthur Edward Waite.

Spread ★ The manner in which the Tarot cards are laid out for the purpose of reading the cards.

Suits ★ The four suits comprising the Minor Arcana cards, usually known as Wands (Clubs), Pentacles (Diamonds), Swords (Spades) and Cups (Hearts).

Tarot deck ★ The complete 78-card fortune-telling deck comprising of 22 Major Arcana and 56 Minor Arcana cards.

OTHER BOOKS BY LANI SHARP:

~ *12 Lucky Astrology Book Series*

~ *Crystal Alchemy: Manifesting Love, Magic, Spirit & Abundance Using the Powers of Gemstones*

~ *Divine Zodiac Messages: Guidance from Angels, Tarot, Genies, Animals, Runes, Devas, Crystals, Numbers, Chakras, Gods & Goddesses for Each Star Sign*

CONTRIBUTING AUTHOR TO:

~ *Writing: The Powerful Healer*

~ *Journey of a Lightworker*

~ *The Book of Inspiration For Women by Women*

White light
PUBLISHING

www.ingramcontent.com/pod-product-compliance
Lightning Source LLC
Chambersburg PA
CBHW071909290426
44110CB00013B/1331